A HISTORY
OF THE WORLD IN
500
WALKS

Quarto is the authority on a wide range of topics.

Quarto educates, entertains and enriches the lives of our readers – enthusiasts and lovers of hands-on living.

www.QuartoKnows.com

First published in Great Britain 2016 by
Aurum Press
74–77 White Lion Street
London, N1 9PF

All correspondence concerning the content of this book should be addressed to the Editorial Department, Quintet Publishing, at the address below.

This book was conceived, designed, and produced by
Quintet Publishing Limited
114–116 Western Road
Hove, East Sussex BN3 1DD

QTT.HWW

A catalogue record for this book is available from the British Library.

ISBN 978 1 78131 600 9

2020 2019 2018 2017 2016

10 9 8 7 6 5 4 3 2 1

Printed and bound in Hong Kong by
Printplus Limited

Quintet Publishing Team:
Editor: Sonya Patel Ellis
Project Editor: Caroline Elliker
Designer: Tania Gomes
Illustrators: Lynn Hatzius, Paula Lewis
Art Director: Michael Charles
Publisher: Mark Searle

Image Credits:

Alamy: Eric Nathan 22; Larry Geddis 26; Prisma Bildagentur AG 43; Travelscape Images 63; Keith Douglas 101; Al Argueta 123; Ivan Vdovin 133; Tongro Images 195; Toni Spagone 151; Look Studio 231; Pep Roig 267; Jon Sparks 297; Juhani Viitanen 319; Middle East; Robert Mora 381; incamerastock 394

Corbis: Angelo Cavalli 33; Krista Rossow 67; Christian Kober 117; Thierry Tronnel 171; René Mattes 177; BODY Philippe/Hemis 178; John Heseltine 189; Blaine Harrington III 277

Getty Images: www.sergiodiaz.net 74–5; Boy_Anupong 121; shan.shihan 136–7; John S Lander 145; Churrito 147; Pall Gudonsson 200–1; Bob Wickham 211; ullstein bild 217; narvikk 223; Humberto Olarte Cupas 242; images say more about me than words 247; Judy Bellah 249; Matteo Colombo 262–3; Jared Alden 271; Odd Katya/EyeEm 280; Jung-Pang Wu 282; Tan Yilmaz 328–9; Danita Delimont 344; Andrew Peacock 349; Philip Game 357; Colin Monteath/Hedgehog House 361; Juergen Ritterbach 375; David Ramos 390; mbbirdy 392

iStock: r.m.nunes 4; oversnap 6; FedevPhoto 10; rmnunes 29; Sjoerd van der Wal 48; Guenter Guni 53; GibasDigiPhoto 57; Benny Marty 61; Nick Webley 69; gunarts 79; Hung Chung Chih 93; whammer121736 192; gregobagel 215; Piet Veltman 310; Paul Tessier 332; Bartosz Hadyniak 339; lechatnoir 341; Tomas Sereda 353; Daniel Kay 363; huad262 367

National Geographic Creative: Joe Riis 15; Jason Edwards 19; Nigel Hicks 21; Anne Keiser 37; Frans Lanting 40; Beverly Joubert 47; Paul Chesley 73; Matt Moyer 83; Annie Griffiths 88; Martin Gray 95; Design Pics Inc 105; Sergio Pitamitz 108; O. Louis Mazzatenta 127; Babak Tafreshi 129; Sean Gallagher 141; Michael Melford 155; Michael Poliza 165; Dan Westergren 169; Shaun Barnett/Hedgehog House/M 173; Jad Davenport 185; Bill Hatcher 208; Lynn Johnson 219; Melissa Farlow 224; Christian Ziegler 243; Design Pics Inc 253; Jad Davenport 257; James P. Blair 285; Mauricio Handler 291; Tim Laman 293; Jill Schneider 315; Matthieu Paley 323; Design Pics Inc 337; Michael Nichols 371; Andy Bardon 376

Shutterstock: Helen Hotson 9; Dave Allen Photography 32; lkpro 87, 99; Nila Newsom 112; hecke61 159; ckchiu 182; orangecrush 205; KAppleyard 235; Olimpiu Pop 238; Pecold 261; Milosz_M 273; Patrick Poendl 287; Ondrej Prosicky 295; Paul Daniels 302; Helen Hotson 308; Baciu 325; Baciu 387

While every effort has been made to credit photographers, Quintet Publishing would like to apologise should there have been any omissions or errors, and would be pleased to make the appropriate correction for future editions of the book.

A HISTORY

OF THE WORLD IN

500
WALKS

Sarah Baxter

Aurum
Press

CONTENTS

The 'lost city' of Machu Picchu is the finale of the Inca Trail (pp. 181–183).

INTRODUCTION

Ask anyone what superpower they would most like to have, and I'd wager that time travel would be in most people's top three. It's such a tantalising prospect: the chance to sneak a glimpse at an era long gone, and to understand our modern world by bearing witness to the moments that delivered us to it. How illuminating would it be, to see Allied troops fighting in First World War trenches, or the rise and fall of the Roman Empire? Imagine travelling back to the time when Africa's early hominids first stood erect, or when the dinosaurs roamed the world.

Yet, you *can* travel back in time by choosing the right mode of transport – namely walking – and using a little imagination. Walking is as ancient as those early hominids. Eschewing cars, planes, and trains puts us on a level playing field with our forebears, and allows us to see the world through their eyes. Even if elements of the view have changed over the millennia, treading on ground stomped by the soldiers, kings, pioneers, and pilgrims of the past provides a connection back to them.

So let this book be your time-travel guide. *A History of the World in 500 Walks* is a compendium of trails – of varying distances and difficulties, spanning the globe – designed to help you connect with the past. Arranged chronologically, in six chapters, the book moves along the timeline of our planet. It starts at the very beginning – prehistory – a mysterious era before written records, when the world was busy making itself: tectonic plates were shifting, volcanoes were spewing, mountain ranges were inching up and weathering down, and man was making his first forays into the world.

From these geological glory days, we reach the dawn of civilisation, and – via indigenous Australian peoples, San Bushmen, ancient Greeks, Roman emperors, Buddha, and Jesus – we eventually plunge into the centuries Anno Domini (AD). These past 2,000 years are liberally woven with pilgrimages, trade routes, military marches, and the adventures of great explorers. We follow famous expeditions, chart revolutions and the Renaissance, witness the beginnings of leisure tourism (that is, walking for walking's sake), and even amble with astronauts. Each trail, be it one mile or one thousand, has something to say about the origins of the planet.

So where to begin? There are 500 individual walks here, accompanied by inspirational maps and photography. In the main they are measurable, definable trails: routes with a known start, end, and distance, and perhaps an evocative name – South Africa's Fugitive's Trail (pp. 279–281), Japan's Philosopher's Path (p. 382), or Italy's Cammino dei Dinosauri (p. 19), for example. Some walks are covered in greater detail, to give you a good idea of what awaits. Others are intriguing snippets to make your feet itch and your imagination fire. All are firmly rooted in history, and all unravel as if they are the very best textbook brought to life in full colour, surround sound, Smell-O-Vision, and 3-D. Simply, in these walks, the history of the world comes to life.

As I was compiling a list of walks for this book, some walks immediately stood out. For instance, the Inca Trail (pp. 181–183), a four-day hike through the Peruvian Andes that traces precision-laid, fifteenth-century pavements to reach the hill-teetering city of Machu Picchu, never found by the Spanish conquistadores. What better way to comprehend the engineering genius, societal structures, and spiritual beliefs of this once-dominant South American civilisation than by walking amid the mist-swirled mountains – little changed in the past 500 years – that they called home?

Likewise, the rim-to-rim trails across the Grand Canyon (pp. 25–27) seemed a must. To descend from one lip of this ravishing ravine and climb back up the other is to observe millions of years of rock formation and erosion in extreme close-up. It is more vivid and accessible than any geography lesson.

Then there's the Berlin Wall Trail (pp. 340–342), which tells a more contemporary tale. Following the footprint of the

The mining heritage of
St Agnes in northern
Cornwall is just one of the
treasures of the United
Kingdom's South West
Coast Path (pp. 307–309).

barrier that once encircled West Berlin, and which only came down in 1989, this circuit reveals history at its most raw and freshly formed. To stand at Checkpoint Charlie, or beside hunks of graffitied concrete amid the now-thriving city, will make your spine tingle.

There are so many enticing trails packed into these pages, with something to suit every interest and mood. A few favourites? How about Greenland's awesome Arctic Circle Trail (pp. 56–58), which encompasses both centuries of steady sculpting by Mother Nature and the modern issue of climate change? Or Jordan's Dana–Petra trek (pp. 88–89), which crosses the desert via Bedouin pathways to reach the 2,000-year-old rock-hewn city via a little-known passage? Then there's England's spectacularly squiggling South West Coast Path (pp. 307–309), a shore-hugging ramble with nineteenth-century smugglers, plus shanty singers, basking sharks, and Cornish pasties. And the new Hillary Trail (pp. 380–381), which cuts through New Zealand landscapes beloved of Sir Edmund Hillary, one of the first men to conquer Mount Everest.

Hike up a mountainside and you might appreciate its grassy meadows or snow-cloaked drama. But know that a whole legion once marched here, or that these slopes inspired a composer to pen a masterpiece, and the whole scene changes. The mountain remains dramatic, but it now also becomes a strategic obstacle or a musical muse.

The main lesson I've learned from writing this book is that there is history to be found everywhere. Whenever and wherever you walk – and it's great to walk, widely and often – someone or something has almost definitely gone before. And that is not a bad thing. It enriches every ramble. It means we can stride out amid landscapes made wonderfully weird by geothermal activity. We can stroll via crumbling castles, walls that kept people in, walls that kept people out, furrows made by slaves and escapees, streets lined with epoch-defining architecture, or really, really old trees.

If only the earth could talk. Though if you look closely – at the grooves and the hummocks, at the scattered ruins and the well-preserved remains – you'll find it actually does . . .

LEFT: Trek through the desert to Jordan's famed rose-red city of Petra (pp. 88–89).

CHAPTER ONE
PREHISTORY

{ Walk amid ancient mountains, fiery volcanoes, glorious geology, and Neolithic remains for an education in the earth's formation. }

1
MOUNT RORAIMA

Canaima National Park, Venezuela

{ Scale Venezuela's prehistoric tabletop mountain – via tangled jungle, slippery slopes, and strange endemic species – to discover a unique lost world. }

Need to know
- *Point in time: 2 billion years ago (mountain rock first formed)*
- *Length: 5–6 days*
- *Difficulty: Moderate/ strenuous – steep; humid and rainy; biting flies*
- *Best months: Nov–Apr*
- *Top tip: Independent climbs not permitted – you must hire a guide*

If only Mount Roraima could talk. One of 115 *tepuis* (flat-topped mountains) rearing up from the Gran Sabana (Great Savanna) at the meeting point of Venezuela, Guyana, and Brazil, it is one of the oldest geological formations on the planet. The granite core of Roraima and these other mighty mesas was created around 2 billion years ago, when South America, Australia, and Africa were still joined as the supercontinent Gondwana. Subsequent millennia have seen the softer surrounding sandstone eroded away, leaving these lone lumps of rock standing isolated and aloof over the tropical jungle of Canaima National Park.

According to the indigenous Pemón people, a tribe unknown to the Western world until the mid-eighteenth century, these mountains are home to *mawari* (ancestor spirits). Legend goes that the huge Wazacá tree (tree of life) once thrived here, and on it grew all the world's fruits and vegetables. One day, one of the *mawari* cut down the tree. Mount Roraima is the remaining stump.

By the late nineteenth century, Roraima was still considered utterly inaccessible. Tempting though this strange 2,810m (9,220ft) summit was to the era's adventurers, it was deemed too remote, too steep, and too tough. That is, until 1884, when author, botanist, and photographer Everard im Thurn and his assistant Harry Perkins proved everyone wrong, and made the first successful ascent. Actually, it wasn't as tricky as everyone had believed. A natural sloping ledge on Roraima's southern flank makes it the simplest of the Gran Sabana's

tepui to top, and today's hikers still follow im Thurn's historic route.

The trek in question starts in the remote Pemón village of Paraitepui, a bumpy 17-mile (27km) drive off the Trans-Amazonian Highway at San Francisco de Yuruaní. From Paraitepui, it takes two or three days to tackle Roraima. Most hikers spend a day and a night on the summit, and then take two days to trek back down to Paraitepui.

Although the way is now well worn, the challenge remains gruelling. As you hike, the leafy roots and fingers of the forest pull you back. Squelchy red clay sucks at your feet, and the numerous and hungry sandflies bite your flesh. The summit of Roraima also sees rain almost every day, even in the dry season.

So why bother? Because, having evolved in splendid isolation from everything around it, the summit plateau of Mount Roraima is utterly unique. Highlights of the climb include numerous endemic species, from bromeliads and bellflowers to carnivorous Heliamphoras (South American pitcher plants). There's also a chance of seeing the curious *Oreophrynella quelchii*, a tiny black toad that, when faced with danger, rolls itself into a little ball. Thankfully, the pterodactyls and tyrannosaurs of Sir Arthur Conan Doyle's tale *The Lost World* – inspired by this strange landscape – are nowhere to be found.

Exploring Mount Roraima's extraordinary tabletop summit is a must. You'll discover canyons of crystals and freezing quartz-lined pools. There are stark rocks, hanging gardens, and streamlets. And you can stay in one of the 'hotels', the somewhat misleading name for the rocky overhangs that can help protect tents from the elements. The ultimate view, though, is from La Ventana – 'The Window'. Crawl on your belly to the edge of this ledge to look out over the timeless land: a sweep of cloud-swirled mesas poking out of the pristine, prehistoric green.

2
Arkaba Walk

South Australia

Trace 600 million years of history in the ancient strata of Wilpena Pound and the Elder Range via a luxurious, guided 28-mile (45km) bush walk. This is Outback hiking in style.

3
Fundy Footpath

Nova Scotia, Canada

Hike for 25 miles (40km) amid the ancient Acadian forests and geological cracks and fissures of Fundy National Park's highlands. These are the foothills of the billion-year-old Appalachian Range.

4
LARAPINTA TRAIL

Northern Territory, Australia

It was the Alice Springs Orogeny, an odd geological occurrence 300–400 million years ago, that made the Outback landscape of Australia's Red Centre so wonderfully weird. Unusually, these ranges are the result of forces from the continent's edges slowly transferring to its empty middle. What this means for walkers is a remote playground of bizarre, puckered, and ruptured quartzite, shrouded in the legends of Australia's Aboriginal peoples. Starting from Alice Springs, the 139-mile (224km), 11–16-day Larapinta Trail follows the spine of the West MacDonnell Ranges, passing red desert, plummeting gorges, cool creeks, termite mounds, and starry skies. The climax is a climb of 1,381m (4,530ft) Mount Sonder, perfect for a panoramic overview.

5
IMARIVOLANITRA TRAIL

Andringitra National Park, Madagascar

Madagascar, the wildlife-abundant speckle of land off the eastern coast of southern Africa, is the world's oldest island. It splintered away from other land masses some 80–100 million years ago, subsequently developing in splendid isolation. More than 75 per cent of the plant and animal species here are endemic, making a trek on this island truly unlike any other. Pic d'Imarivolanitra (2,658m / 8,720ft) is Madagascar's second-highest summit, and climbable in two or three days (9 miles / 14km one way). Better still, the climb takes you through Andringitra National Park, a preserve of granite peaks and gorges, great gneiss (a layered, metamorphic rock), unusual formations, and profuse plants. Look out for ring-tailed lemurs too.

6
ULURU BASE WALK

Northern Territory, Australia

{ Roam around Australia's great red rock, immersed in Aboriginal Dreaming stories. }

Need to know
- *Point in time: Around 600 million years ago (rock formation began)*
- *Length: 6.5 miles (10.5km); 3.5 hours*
- *Difficulty: Easy – flat; short; hot*
- *Best months: Apr–May; Aug–Sept*
- *Top tip: Start early to avoid the heat*

Around 290 miles (467km) west of Alice Springs, Uluru is like a hot-orange iceberg in the Australian Outback. It rises 347m (1,140ft) from the surrounding desert, measuring more than 1 mile (1.6km) wide and almost 2.5 miles (4km) long – yet the majority of its mass remains hidden underground. Its formation began around 600 million years ago, the result of sandy deposits compressed into rock at the bottom of an ancient sea (now long gone), and then tilted ninety degrees, and eventually smoothed into the magnificent monolith that exists today.

Australian Aborigines, who have lived in Uluru's shadow for more than 10,000 years, have different ideas. To them, Uluru is sacred, and central to their Dreaming stories. They believe the rock was created at the dawn of time by ten spirit people, and that its various cracks and fissures are scars left by the mythical figures' births, battles, and bloodshed.

The 6.5-mile (10.5km) walk around the base of the rock will introduce you to these geological features and the cast of characters behind them: the ancestor snakes Liru and Kuniya; the Mala hare wallabies; Kurpannga the spirit dingo. Pick up the flat dirt trail from the Mala car park and walk clockwise (keeping Uluru on your right) amid acacias, bloodwoods, rock art, and Aboriginal legends. This is the best way to appreciate the rock; it's legally possible to climb it, but the Anangu people (traditional owners of Uluru-Kata Tjuta National Park and the surrounding land) ask you not to, as they consider it a most sacred site.

RIGHT: Discover the vibrant sandstone landscapes and creation stories of Uluru.

8

GOLD COAST HINTERLAND GREAT WALK

Queensland, Australia

This Great Walk is a lush, 34-mile (55km) rainforest traverse, connecting the Lamington and Springbrook plateaus on Australia's east coast. It travels through the World Heritage–listed Gondwana Rainforests of Australia, which boast primitive species harking back to the birth and spread of flowering plants over 100 million years ago. Start your walk in Lamington National Park, a two-hour drive south of Brisbane. Then head into Springbrook National Park, via the rim of the ancient Tweed Volcano, which erupted around 25 million years ago. Walk past vivid rhyolite cliffs, through cool beech woods, and along the banks of crystal-clear rivers. This is also a great way to learn about the Woonoongoora creation stories of the Yugambeh people, who first walked this landscape millennia ago.

7
Cammino dei Dinosauri

Trentino, Italy

Take a walk in the footsteps of dinosaurs, in Italy's Vallagarina Valley. This 5-mile (8km) trail follows a set of fossilised, 200-million-year-old dinosaur footprints, with information about each imprint.

9
JURASSIC COAST

Devon and Dorset, United Kingdom

{
Stretch your legs alongside layers
of fascinating rocks and fossils that
date back to dinosaur days.
}

Need to know
- *Point in time: 185 million years ago (age of oldest rock)*
- *Length: 95 miles (153km); 7–8 days*
- *Difficulty: Moderate – undulating; steep sections*
- *Best months: Mar– June; Sept–Oct*
- *Top tip: Part of the walk (near Lulworth) bisects a military range; check times of public access*

Travellers of a curious disposition have been visiting the coast of Dorset and east Devon since the late eighteenth century. Back then, many left with strange souvenirs called 'snake stones' and 'devil's fingers' – ammonites and belemnites, as we know them today. But this shoreline isn't just special for its abundance of fossils. Thanks to some colossal planetary ructions around 100 million years ago, the layers of Triassic, Jurassic, and Cretaceous rocks were tilted, and left unusually exposed. This means that the footpath hugging the length of this World Heritage–listed coast, which runs from Orcombe Point near Exmouth in east Devon to Old Harry Rocks near Swanage in east Dorset, is a true walk through time.

Walking west to east, keeping the English Channel to your right, you'll pass the quaint seaside town of Beer and the wildlife-rich Undercliff, created by eighteenth-century landslides. You can search for fossils and walk the Cobb (harbour wall) at Lyme Regis. Next is Golden Cap – at 191m (627ft), the hike's highest point. There's also the chance to marvel at some seriously majestic rock formations, from the chalky headland of White Nothe to the arch of Durdle Door. Most dramatic of all is the stretch from near perfectly circular Lulworth Cove to the dramatic sea stacks of the Pinnacles at Foreland Point. En route lie the petrified remains of an ancient cypress forest, where dinosaurs once roamed. There's also a ghost village, Iron Age hill forts, and a lot of crazily crumpled stone.

RIGHT: The Jurassic Coast is a treasure trove of fossils and rock formations.

10
Bruce Trail

Ontario, Canada

The Niagara Escarpment began to form 443 million years ago, following the retreat of a tropical sea. The Bruce Trail traces the entire ridge for 560 miles (901km).

11
BURREN WAY

County Clare, Ireland

The area known as the Burren takes its name from the Irish word *boireann*, meaning 'stony district'. It's a good description of the vast clump of fractured and terraced carboniferous limestone on Ireland's west coast. The rock was laid down around 350 million years ago, the sediment of a tropical sea. Today, it's above water, a sweeping pavement of grikes (cracks), clints (rocks), hillocks, valleys, and fossilised urchins and corals. The 71-mile (114km) Burren Way, from Lahinch to Corofin, crosses the ancient karst via *boreens* (country roads), drovers' paths, and forest tracks. Most hikers finish it in five days, taking in Slieve Elva (344m / 1,129ft), Neolithic sites, early Christian ruins, and the traditional music hub of Doolin en route.

12
Traversée de Charlevoix

Québec, Canada

Some 350 million years ago, a meteorite crash rocked this region. This 65-mile (105km) traverse hikes right through the resultant crater, now a biosphere reserve.

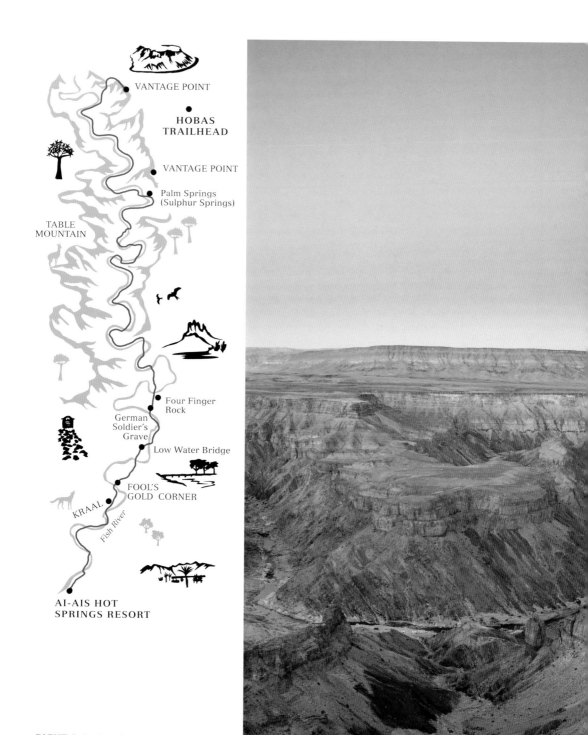

VANTAGE POINT

HOBAS TRAILHEAD

VANTAGE POINT

Palm Springs
(Sulphur Springs)

TABLE
MOUNTAIN

Four Finger
Rock

German
Soldier's
Grave

Low Water Bridge

FOOL'S
GOLD CORNER

KRAAL

Fish River

**AI-AIS HOT
SPRINGS RESORT**

RIGHT: Delve into the snaking depths of Fish
River Canyon in Namibia.

13
FISH RIVER CANYON TRAIL

Southern Namibia

{ Follow this sinuous gorge – reputedly Africa's biggest – for a wild walk amid millennia of ravishing rock. }

According to the indigenous Nama people, the serpentine Fish River Canyon was created by the agonised writhing of Koutein Kooru, an injured giant snake. However, science explains that this 100-mile-long (161km) gorge is hewn from 1.8-billion-year-old rock. Its layers of gneiss (metamorphic rock) formed when Gondwana – the supercontinent that broke up to form South America, Africa, Antarctica, Australia, and parts of Arabia – was torn in three. Eons of subsequent superheating, earthquakes, erosion, and the eventual flow of the Fish River itself have carved what you see today. It's reputedly the world's second-biggest canyon, after Arizona's Grand Canyon, although Ethiopia's Blue Nile Gorge begs to differ. In any case, its scorched labyrinth of flying buttresses, flat-topped buttes, and sweeping horseshoe turns is world-class.

Hiking here is a hot and dusty challenge. Only around 3,000 intrepid visitors attempt it each year, starting with the knee-rattling descent from the canyon rim at Hobas. The route follows the sandy, boulder-strewn bottom for 53 miles (85km) to Ai-Ais Hot Springs Resort. Here, the sudden civilisation is both a bit of a shock and a welcome finale after days of splendidly isolated self-sufficiency.

Rewards en route are manifold, however: fleeting sunsets, when the canyon walls are suddenly set ablaze; cooling dips in the river, which (season dependent) can be a torrent or a trickle; glimpses of rock hyrax; and the call of a jackal as you gaze at a ceiling of countless stars.

Need to know
- *Point in time: 650 million years ago (canyon first formed)*
- *Length: 53 miles (85km); 4–5 days*
- *Difficulty: Strenuous – rugged terrain; isolated; no facilities; potentially hot*
- *Best months: May; Sept*
- *Top tip: Trail is open May to mid-Sept*

14
Dinosaur Provincial Park

Alberta, Canada

A series of short, self-guided trails show you where dinosaurs once roamed some 75 million years ago, and where fossil hunters discovered their remains.

15
CONTINENTAL DIVIDE TRAIL

United States

Simply, the Continental Divide Trail (CDT) is huge. Weaving across the United States, it's an epic, 3,100-mile (4,989km) hike from Glacier National Park, on the border with Canada, to Big Hatchets Wilderness, on the Mexican frontier. The trail traces the spine of the Rocky Mountains, a range that first began to rise 80 million years ago. The mountains now form the divide between the United States' Atlantic and Pacific watersheds. The CDT is also a self-claimed 'living museum of the American West', taking you through five states, showcasing the indigenous culture, pioneer past, and almost endless natural splendour of each.

16
Ol Njorowa Gorge

Hell's Gate National Park, Kenya

Day hikes probe into this volcanic cleft, where the waters from Lake Naivasha once flowed. See vivid rock, hot springs, and gorgeous waterfalls.

17
TIGER LEAPING GORGE HIGH TRAIL

Lijiang, Southwest China

Tiger Leaping Gorge is so very narrow – 30m (99ft) at its thinnest – that a tiger once leapt across it. Or so the legend goes. At around 10 miles (16km) long, this isn't the world's longest gorge either. It is, however, one of its most fathomless, a 3,900m (12,795ft) deep cleft through the Haba Snow Mountain range. It was carved by the Jinsha River (the Chinese name for the Upper Yangtze) some 10 million years ago. Buses from Lijiang run to Qiaotou, the starting point for the High Trail. It's then a two-day squeeze along skinny footpaths, via rice terraces, flower-cloaked slopes, and sheer drops, with the river churning way down below.

18

BRIGHT ANGEL AND NORTH KAIBAB TRAILS

Grand Canyon, Arizona, United States

{ Walk rim to rim across the world's most gorgeous gorge – a geological widescreen epic spanning 1.75 billion years of earth in the making. }

Need to know
- *Point in time: 1.75 billion years (age of canyon's oldest rock)*
- *Length: 21 miles (34km); 2–3 days*
- *Difficulty: Strenuous – steep descent and ascent; hot*
- *Best months: May; Sept–Oct*
- *Top tip: Backcountry permits required to overnight in the canyon*

First, some numbers. The Grand Canyon, which cuts an almighty dash through the Colorado Plateau, is 277 river miles (446km) long. At its broadest, it is 18 miles (29km) wide. At its most plunging, it is more than 1 mile (2km) deep. The schist at its bottom is just shy of 2 billion years old. Striking statistics, but nothing compared to your first sight of one of the Seven Natural Wonders of the World.

It's a vision in red-orange, a rapture of rock spreading as far as the eye can see, and farther. To those in the know, it's a textbook made three-dimensional. A geologist can read the striped strata of stone and sediment here like a calendar, one that charts millions of years of earth-shifting and creation. To the amateur observer, it is simply spectacular.

However, while most of the 5 million people who visit each year stick to its rims, to really know the Grand Canyon you need to hike into it. Up at the top, the views across to the multifarious terraces, buttes, and buttresses are magnificent, but somehow disengaged. The scene is too vast, the spectacle is too remote. By taking a trail to the bottom and hiking back up the other side, you can immerse yourself in its millions of years of history.

The Bright Angel Trail wends down from the canyon's South Rim, while the North Kaibab Trail leads down from the North Rim. The two trails meet by the river, on the baking valley floor. Combining them in a cross-canyon hike makes for the ultimate traverse.

The Bright Angel Trail was used by Ancestral Puebloan people 1,000 years ago, although its origins date even further back in time. Starting from the canyon's Kaibab Limestone cap (the 'youngest' layer, at 270 million years old, yet still too ancient to contain dinosaur remains), the rock soon transitions to Coconino Sandstone. Quartzite-rich, this stratum sometimes appears to sparkle. Dropping further down into the canyon, you pass the deep-red Supai Group (up to 315 million years old), where the keen-eyed may spot Ancestral Puebloan pictographs etched into the rosy walls. The route follows the sheer cliffs of Redwall Limestone, negotiated at this point via Jacob's Ladder – some forty switchbacks of solid rock steps. It then leads to the unexpected lushness of Indian Garden. The indigenous Havasupai people grew crops and made settlements here, until most were evicted in the 1920s.

More strata and jaw-dropping views follow: 525-million-year-old Muav Limestone; Bright Angel Shale; and Tapeats Sandstone. The latter has been eroded into Tapeats Narrows, an idyllic side canyon that's tickled by a tiny and shallow stream. Finally you hit rock bottom – the Grand Canyon's great granite bowels of Vishnu Schist, which date back 1.75 billion years. Down here, the rim tops are invisible, and the Colorado River, gnawing architect of all this splendour, flows by. To overnight amid the cottonwood and willow trees, either in a tent or a proper bed at Phantom Ranch (both of which must be booked well in advance), is to feel not quite of this world.

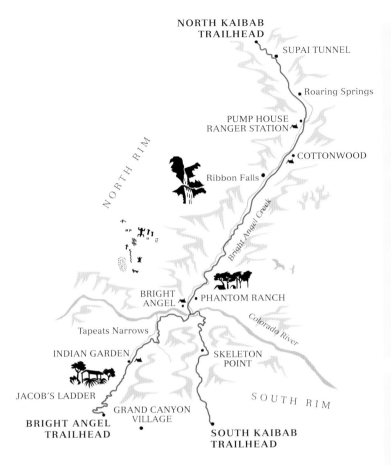

NORTH KAIBAB
TRAILHEAD

SUPAI TUNNEL

Roaring Springs

PUMP HOUSE
RANGER STATION

COTTONWOOD

NORTH RIM

Ribbon Falls

Bright Angel Creek

BRIGHT
ANGEL

PHANTOM RANCH

Colorado River

Tapeats Narrows

INDIAN GARDEN

SKELETON
POINT

JACOB'S LADDER

SOUTH RIM

GRAND CANYON
VILLAGE

BRIGHT ANGEL
TRAILHEAD

SOUTH KAIBAB
TRAILHEAD

19
Blyderivierspoort
Hiking Trail

*Mpumalanga,
South Africa*

This 20-mile (32km) hike slices through the vast Blyde River Canyon, crafted an estimated 60 million years ago. It starts from the 'God's Window' lookout on the Drakensberg escarpment, then runs via soaring red cliffs, tumbling cascades, and Afromontane forest.

20
Colca Canyon Trek

Southern Peru

The 35-mile (56km) hike from Cabanaconde to Andagua takes you through one of the world's deepest canyons. This wild terrain is circled by condors and dotted with traditional village settlements, topping out at the 5,090m (16,700ft) Cerani Pass.

Ascending the North Kaibab Trail to reach the Grand Canyon's less-visited North Rim is the same history lesson but in reverse, old to young. Thankfully, it is a gentler, shadier ascent than the precipitous way down. This is one reason why it's recommended that you hike south to north. The North Rim is higher than the South Rim, however, so you'll end up doing more climbing overall.

Highlights on the way up include admiring the double cascade of Ribbon Falls, cooling off in Roaring Springs, and traversing a dramatic ledge of Redwall Limestone, with a giddying drop-off to your side. Attaining the top of the North Rim, some 2,438m (8,000ft) up, you'll be sweaty, dusty, and exhausted – but elated to have mastered one of Mother Nature's most awesome obstacles.

21
GREAT HIMALAYA TRAIL

Nepal

{ Tackle an epic hike across the entire Nepalese Himalayas, mixing mountain glory and high-altitude hospitality. }

Need to know
- *Point in time: Around 55 million years ago (mountains formed)*
- *Length: 1,060 miles (1,706km); average 150 days*
- *Difficulty: Very strenuous – long; high altitudes*
- *Best months: Feb–July*
- *Top tip: High levels of fitness, mountain skills, and permits required*

It's the most tantalising trekking notion – to traverse the length of the world's highest mountain range, ticking off glimpses of towering summits as you go. Indeed, the Himalayas are home to nine of earth's ten highest peaks, including Mount Everest – at 8,848m (29,029ft), the most towering peak of all.

The Himalayas – Sanskrit for 'Abode of Snow' – arc across South Asia for around 1,500 miles (2,400km), from Nanga Parbat, Pakistan, in the west, to Namcha Barwa, Tibet, in the east. They also pass through India, Nepal, and Bhutan en route. As far as mountain ranges go, the Himalayas are youngsters, formed after the collision of the Indian and Eurasian tectonic plates around 20 to 50 million years ago. As the Indian plate continues to push northward (at a speed of 6cm / 2.5in a year), the range continues to rise about 1cm (0.4in) annually. Some Himalayan peaks also 'shrank' after 2015's deadly 7.8-magnitude earthquake, an estimated 2.5cm (1in) in the case of Everest.

There are many fine treks amid these mountains, but the Great Himalaya Trail (GHT) is the most impressive of all, and the only one that tackles the range in its entirety. The idea of such a traverse has long existed, as have many other routes through the Himalayas. However, it wasn't until 2011 that the 1,060-mile (1,706km) Nepalese section was launched in any sort of official manner, as the Great Himalaya Trail.

Australian trekker Robin Boustead mapped a route across the country, noting key facts such as water sources and camping areas. He also broke the gargantuan GHT High

Route (the route's full traverse) into nine shorter and more manageable trail sections, for those who don't have 150 days to spare. One day it's hoped that the GHT will form a cohesive route from Pakistan to Tibet.

Travelling from east to west (the direction to walk if you want the sun on your back), the GHT High Route starts in the Kanchenjunga region, in the shadow of Mount Kanchenjunga, the world's third-highest peak. It finishes at Hilsa, on the Tibetan border. Along the way lie views of all Nepal's highest mountains, including Everest, Annapurna I, and Dhaulagiri I. The trail crosses twenty-one passes above 5,000m (16,400ft), reaching a breathtaking maximum altitude of 6,500m (21,325ft). It negotiates high plateaus, glittering lakes, creaking glaciers, and forested valleys. In total, it notches up 150,000m (492,125ft) of ascent and descent. Sturdy knees are required, and mountaineering experience is highly recommended.

Although this sounds like a wilderness expedition, there's a major human element too. One of the GHT High Route's main aims is to ensure that tourist dollars reach the remote communities that really need them. And on this trail, trekkers

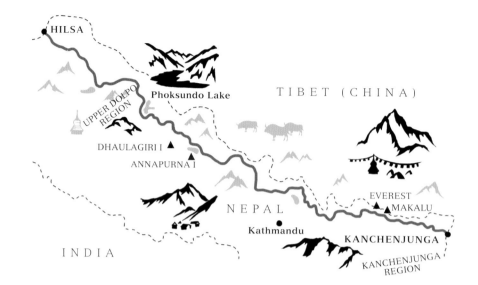

depend on those remote communities, which provide plentiful *dal bhat* (lentils and rice), big smiles, and insight into mountain culture. You'll encounter many Buddhist *gompas* (monasteries or temples), yak herds, fluttering prayer flags, and welcoming teahouses en route.

Hiking the GHT end to end in one go is a logistical challenge. Despite the scattered villages, you'll need to arrange regular supply drops, plus porters and pack animals to cart the gear. You'll also need to plan around the weather. Starting the trail in February is recommended, to ensure high passes are traversable. This does mean that you'll encounter the monsoon rains that fall between June and September, however.

But even if you can't walk the whole GHT, you can tackle a section. If time is limited, consider focusing on the mysterious Upper Dolpo region, one of the last bastions of semi-nomadic Tibetan culture, home to sapphire-blue Phoksundo Lake. Or trek via vertiginous cliffs and hanging glaciers to the base camp of 8,473m (27,800ft) Mount Makalu, the world's fifth-highest peak. Whichever stretch of the GHT you pick, peerless mountain trekking and legendary scenery are guaranteed.

22
Chimborazo
Ascent

Ecuador

Mount Chimborazo is a 6,268m (20,565ft) stratovolcano near the equator. Follow the tough two-day trail to its summit and you're at the furthest point from earth's centre, due to the planet's not-quite-round shape.

23
Bandera Trail

Chiapas, Mexico

El Triunfo Biosphere Reserve is a primary refuge of ice age animals and plants. Explore it via the Bandera Trail, which climbs 305m (1,000ft) up to Cerro Bandera for views over the cloud forest.

24
Mount Meru

Tanzania

It takes three or four days to summit this 20-million-year-old Rift Valley volcano. At 4,556m (14,947ft), it's a good acclimatisation hike before climbing neighboring Kilimanjaro.

25
Fairy Meadows

Gilgit-Baltistan, Pakistan

This four-hour hike off the Karakoram Highway in Pakistan leads to a magical dell at 3,292m (10,800ft). This lush, green plateau gives amazing views of Nanga Parbat, or 'Killer Mountain', at the western end of the 55-million-year-old Himalayas.

26
Wave Trail

Utah and Arizona, United States

The 3-mile (5km) Wave Trail is a short but spectacular hike through the 200-million-year-old sandstone swirls of Coyote Buttes. Find the 'Wave', a naturally formed curved rock, on the northwest edge of Top Rock. Permits are required.

27
SON DOONG CAVE TREK

Phong Nha–Ke Bang National Park, Vietnam

Hang Son Doong, meaning 'Mountain River Cave', is about 3 million years old – but until 1991, no one knew it existed. It's the world's largest cave, at 198m (650ft) high, 149m (490ft) wide, and over 5.5 miles (9km) long. It is so big, in fact, that it has its own river, jungle, and microclimate inside. Exploring this yawning cavern is a tough five-day, 30-mile (48km) expedition from near Dong Hoi, and includes a 79m (260ft) rappel. This is the only way in. Only a few hundred people are allowed to hike here each year. Those who do will descend to a secret realm of oxbow lakes, rock spikes, coral fossils, and bizarrely thriving trees that make the cave feel both under and out of this world.

APPALACHIAN TRAIL

Eastern United States

> Trace arguably the world's oldest mountains – the Appalachians – across the United States' Eastern Seaboard.

Need to know

- *Point in time: From about 480 million years ago (mountain formation)*
- *Length: 2,190 miles (3,524km); 6 months*
- *Difficulty: Moderate/ strenuous – tough in places; very long*
- *Best months: Start Mar–Apr*
- *Top tip: Hike northbound – a southbound thru-hike is significantly harder*

Formed around 480 million years ago, the Appalachians are the oldest mountains in North America. However, they are not especially high, having been exposed to the eroding forces of Mother Nature for so many years. Where the Appalachians once towered as tall as the Rocky Mountains (high point: 4,401m / 14,440ft Mount Elbert), they now average a more lowly 914m (3,000ft). Indeed, today the highest point of the Appalachians is 2,037m (6,683ft) Mount Mitchell in North Carolina.

But height isn't everything, as the Appalachian Trail (AT) reveals. A 2,190-mile (3,524km) epic from Springer Mountain in Georgia to Mount Katahdin in Maine, the hike cuts through fourteen states. It wends through one of the most vital temperate zones on the planet, home to sugar maples, mountain laurels, moose, beavers, and bald eagles. It rolls from the Great Smoky Mountains to the

MOUNT KATAHDIN

MAINE

VT.

CANADA

White Mountains
N.H.

MASS.

NEW YORK

CONN. R.I.

Hudson River

NEW YORK
CITY

Hawk Mountain

PENNSYLVANIA

N.J.

UNITED
STATES

MD.

DEL.

OHIO

Shenandoah Valley

WEST
VIRGINIA

KENTUCKY

ATLANTIC
OCEAN

VIRGINIA

Great Smoky
Mountains

NORTH CAROLINA

TENN.

Mount Mitchell
Chattahoochee National Forest

SPRINGER
MOUNTAIN

SOUTH
CAROLINA

GA.

APPALACHIAN MOUNTAINS

29
Piatra Craiului Ridge

Carpathians, Romania

Scramble along this dramatic 15.5-mile (25km) rib of Jurassic limestone in the wild Carpathian Mountains, which tops out at over 2,195m (7,200ft).

30
Volcano Concepción

Ometepe Island, Nicaragua

This active 1,610m (5,282ft) volcano rises from Lake Nicaragua. The strenuous ten-hour hike to its summit and back reveals an agitated crater, liable to spew ash at any second.

Shenandoah Valley, from Pennsylvania's Hawk Mountain to the Hudson River. The trail also connects the majestic White Mountains of New Hampshire with Maine's 100 Mile Wilderness – the longest section of the AT not to cross a paved road. En route are 250 rustic, three-sided shelters and a gauntlet of black bears and rattlesnakes. The total elevation gain and loss of 141,569m (464,464ft) is the equivalent of climbing Mount Everest sixteen times. Only one in four walkers who attempt a continuous thru-hike successfully complete the AT, gaining lauded '2,000-miler' status. Section-hiking it is a more manageable, yet still rewarding, option.

LEFT: Rhododendrons bloom on the North Carolina section of the Appalachian Trail.

VIA ALPINA RED TRAIL

Alps, Europe

{ Traverse the entire Alps, exploring eight different countries as you go. }

Need to know
- *Point in time: 25–35 million years ago (when the Alps rose above sea level)*
- *Length: 1,550 miles (2,495km); 4 months*
- *Difficulty: Strenuous – some steep, vertiginous hiking*
- *Best months: June–Sept*
- *Top tip: Non-EU nationals will need a Schengen visa (valid for 90 days)*

Tens of millions of years of geological activity have gone into shaping the Alps. Now, following the prehistoric crash of European and African tectonic plates, numerous ice ages, and the wanderings of early man, the range is looking simply splendid. It arcs for around 750 miles (1,207km), from Monaco into France, Italy, Switzerland, Germany, Liechtenstein, Austria, and Slovenia. It is absolutely riddled with hiking trails, but the Via Alpina Red Trail is the king of them all – a comprehensive 1,550-mile (2,494km) meander from Monaco to Trieste, through all eight countries and millennia of mountain-making.

The scenery is a joy, with views of A-list peaks such as the Matterhorn and range-topping 4,810-m (15,781ft)

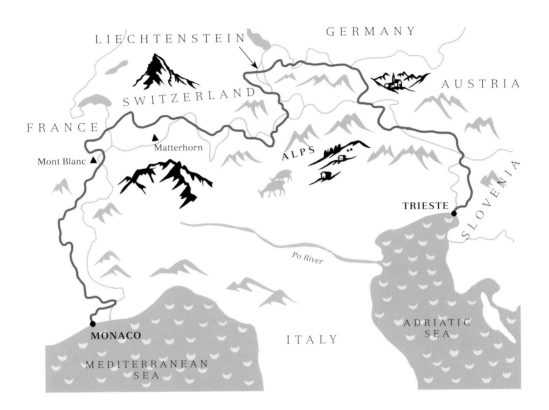

LEFT: The Matterhorn lords over parts of the Via Alpina.

Mont Blanc. There are also innumerable lakes, glaciers, valleys, and plateaus. But the main draw is the human touch. These mountains are lived in by millions of people, going about their everyday lives. As such, the wildflower meadows, snowy peaks, and rugged granite crags give way to remote farmsteads, rustic vineyards, and lively towns.

There's also an excellent network of mountain huts, which allows you to enjoy a comfortable dormitory bed and a hot meat stew or potato *rösti*, even when you're high up amid the peaks. As the trail criss-crosses international borders forty-four times, the culture, customs, cuisine, and dialects of this rich and varied Alpine walk are in constant flux. Thankfully, as all eight nations are in the EU, passport control isn't usually a problem, though non-EU members may require a Schengen visa.

32
CIRCUIT TRAIL

Torres del Paine National Park, Chile

{ Plunge into Patagonia, following the wildest hike around the spikiest range. }

Need to know
- *Point in time: 12 million years ago (origins of Paine Massif)*
- *Length: 93 miles (150km); 7–10 days*
- *Difficulty: Moderate – some steep sections; potentially wild weather*
- *Best months: Nov–Mar*
- *Top tip: A tent, camping equipment, and food supplies are required for a full circuit*

A hike around the Paine Massif shows the slow grind of glacial sculpting at its most striking. This Patagonian range, in Chile's deep south, dates back around 12 million years, when creeping ice wore away the layers of sedimentary rock to leave only hardy horns – or *cuernos* – of granite behind.

The 'El Circuito' or 'O' trek gets right in among all this stony spikiness, making a loop around the massif from the trailhead at Laguna Amarga in Torres del Paine National Park. The trekking itself isn't too arduous. The highest point is a modest 1,201m (3,940ft). However, the weather can be wild: freezing cold, sopping wet, and very windy. El Circuito, though, is worth the effort.

Head off on this circular trail anticlockwise, hiking along the Rio Paine and into lenga forest (a type of southern beech, which is fiery in fall), for close-ups with hanging glaciers. Admire the views from the glacially fed Lago Dickson. Top John Garner Pass to gaze over to Grey Glacier and descend to Lago Grey. Spot birds and flowers alongside luminous Lago Pehoe. Inch up the dramatic French and Ascensio Valleys. Then finish off with the ultimate view of the Cuernos del Paine (Horns of Paine), which soar up to 3,248m (10,656ft).

If you're pressed for time, the six-day 'W' trek is a shorter option, with *refugios* (cabins) along the whole route. It does cover El Circuito's most dramatic stretches but without getting behind the mountains – far from civilisation – so you miss out on that extra dose of wild.

RIGHT: The 'horns' of the Paine Massif give way to lush green valleys.

PYRENEAN HAUTE ROUTE

France and Spain

Linking the Atlantic and the Mediterranean, zigzagging across the French-Spanish border, and sticking almost unfailingly to the lofty main ridge, the Pyrenean Haute Route is a wild and wonderful but demanding walk. It traces the Pyrenees mountain range, a fine granite-and-gneiss fold created by 500 million years of rock formation and a 50-million-year-old tectonic collision. Starting in Atlantic-lapped Hendaye, the route covers 497 miles (800km) to reach Banyuls-sur-Mer. In between these two points sit big, fat summits – 3,298m (10,820ft) Vignemale is the highest – plus the hollows of glacially gouged cirques and canyons, pine forests, and national parks. Hikers need experience: storms, snow, steep scree, and scant waymarking are all dangers. But there is no better way to access the most pristine parts of these mountains.

34
MOUNT KINABALU

Sabah, Borneo

It takes only two days to conquer the massive, 15-million-year-old igneous pluton that is Mount Kinabalu. Which is good going because if you get to Kinabalu's summit, you'll be standing at the highest point between the Himalayas and New Guinea. Sitting in its namesake national park, 4,095m (13,435ft) Kinabalu is a granite intrusion thrusting up through the lush biodiversity of Malaysian Borneo. Indeed, the lower realms of this climb, which starts from Timpohon Gate, offer glimpses of exotic flora, chestnut forest, alpine meadow, and up to 300 species of birds. Split the trek with an overnight stop at Laban Rata rest house at 3,270m (10,728ft). You can then set your alarm for 2:00 a.m., to trek up to the summit in time for sunrise.

35
ENNEDI ETERNEL

Ennedi Plateau, Chad

Trekking across the landlocked, weird-rocked Ennedi Plateau is as close as most people will get to trekking on another planet. This is one of the oddest tracts of the Sahara desert, transformed into its current arid state by a dramatic climatic shift 5,000–10,000 years ago. In the Ennedi, sandstone is sculpted into a labyrinth of pinnacles, arches, 'castles', and canyons, while *wadis* (seasonally dry riverbeds) add flushes of green. The only signs of human life are camel-herding nomads and ancient rock art. The Ennedi Eternel trail – for which guides are essential – is a good introduction to the region. It begins near Fada, a five-hour drive from regional hub Faya-Largeau, and ploughs 88 miles (142km) into the Ennedi's alien sandstone terrain.

NAUKLUFT TRAIL

Namib–Naukluft National Park, Namibia

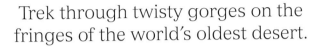

{ Trek through twisty gorges on the fringes of the world's oldest desert. }

- *Point in time: 45–80 million years ago (age of desert)*
- *Length: 75 miles (120km); 8 days*
- *Difficulty: Moderate/ strenuous – steep sections; hot*
- *Best months: Mar–Oct*
- *Top tip: Must be booked in advance; trekking groups must be 3–12 people*

Hiking the Naukluft Trail can be hot and thirsty work. But then again, this is a hot and thirsty place. The Namib is considered the world's oldest desert. Arid conditions have prevailed here for at least 45 million years, which is a long time to go without a drink. These days, the region receives no more than 13mm (0.5in) of rain each year.

The Namib is also enormous, sweeping along Namibia's Atlantic coast for around 1,200 miles (1,931km). It then sneaks inland for around 120 miles (193km) to meet the Great Escarpment, the plateau edge of southern Africa. The Naukluft Mountains form part of this escarpment, a barrier even older than the desert at its feet. Its granitic and volcanic base, dating back some 2 billion years, is topped with 500-million-year-old sheets of sedimentary rock, subsequently puckered into distinctive creases. In Namibia, parts of this desert and these mountains are embraced within the vast, unremittingly wild Namib-Naukluft National Park. Here, a rugged, mountainous expanse – riddled with deep *kloofs* (ravines), twisting gorges, deliciously cool pools, and surprisingly prolific wildlife – contrasts with the starkness of the surrounding sands.

Virtually no one lives in the enormous Namib-Naukluft National Park – it's empty even by Namibia's sparsely populated standards. This is a place dominated by folded and eroded inselbergs, isolated mountains that rise abruptly from level plains. It is dotted with cartoonish quiver trees somehow surviving the drought, squeaking rock dassies (fluffy rodents), and the black eagles that prey on them. It is also a landscape transformed by the hour: flushed purple-pink at sunrise,

blazed yellow by the cloudless sky at noon, warmed to
crimson at sunset. At night, far from any light pollution, it is
twinkled over by the most astonishing ceiling of stars.

The tough, circular, 75-mile (120km) Naukluft Trail is the
premier hike amid all this untainted nature. Places are limited
and the trek is popular, so lodgings must be booked in
advance. These range from simple huts to stone shelters,
which have water and toilets but little else. Also, treks are
permitted only between March and October, as Southern
Hemisphere summers (November to February) are just too
hot. Temperatures above 38°C (100°F) are not unusual.

To get to the start, it's a three-hour drive from the capital
of Windhoek to the park entrance and the Hiker's Haven
bunkhouse. Many a Naukluft Trail completer has stayed here
after their hike, and been moved to graffiti their thoughts
onto the walls. For those about to set off on the walk, this can
make for inspirational – or terrifying – reading.

The first day of the Naukluft Trail is relatively easy,
following a zebra path along a dry riverbed before rearing up
the side of a somewhat abrupt mountain. Days two and three
get tougher still, traversing a rippling plateau, descending
into Ubusis Kloof, and then climbing back up again. The
views are worth it, however, including a chance to spot kudu
antelope en route. Day four combines some level strolling
with spectacular Tsams River Gorge and several springs. Day
five is steep again, and dotted with clusters of quiver and

Tufa
Shelter

Δ
To
Windhoek

ARBEIT ADELT VALLEY

Day 6   Day 7

Die Valle Waterfall

N A M I B - N A U K L U F T   N A T I O N A L   P A R K

NAUKLUFT
MOUNTAINS

Day 5   Day 8

NAMIB DESERT

Day 4

Tsams-Ost Shelter

TSAMS RIVER GORGE

HIKER'S
HAVEN

Day 1

Day 3

Day 2   Putte Shelter

Ubusis Hut

UBUSIS KLOOF

37
White Desert Trek

Western Desert, Egypt

Hike amid the White Desert's surreal 'sculptures', made of eroded chalk and limestone. These rocks were formed from corals and sea creatures that lived here 80 million years ago.

38
Curonian Spit

Lithuania

The narrow, 61-mile (98km) tendril of shifting sand on the Baltic coast, known as the Curonian Spit, was formed 5,000 years ago. Today, short trails lead through its dunes, meadows, and nature reserves.

moringa trees. Day six passes the (usually dry) Die Valle Waterfall and heads down the Arbeit Adelt Valley. Day seven starts vertically – with chains to help you clamber up a waterfall – but the plateau at the top offers jaw-dropping valley views. Day eight comes all too soon. After following a jeep track to the Naukluft River (where you can cool off), you loop back to Hiker's Haven, where you can write your own celebratory sentiments on the bunkhouse walls.

39
KALALAU TRAIL

Kauai, Hawaii, United States

Skirt the dramatic cliffs of the ancient
Na Pali Coast, walking in the footsteps
of Polynesian pioneers.

Need to know
- *Point in time: 5.1 million years ago (Kauai formed)*
- *Length: 11 miles (18km) one way; 1–2 days*
- *Difficulty: Moderate – short but tough; no facilities*
- *Best months: May–Oct*
- *Top tip: Permits are required to hike beyond Hanakapiʻai*

Kauai is the oldest of the Hawaiian islands. The Pacific plate on which the archipelago sits is slowly inching northwestward over a fixed volcanic hot spot. Every now and then that hot spot burps out another mass of magma, which rises up from the seafloor and creates another Hawaiian isle. Indeed, the tropical chain is like a series of diminishing smoke rings. Kauai was puffed first, some 5.1 million years ago. Volatile Hawaiʻi, or Big Island, at the southeasterly end, was exhaled most recently, less than 500,000 years ago.

Each Hawaiian island has its fascinations, but time and tides have had longer to sculpt the landscapes of Kauai, and to dramatic effect. Nowhere on the island is quite as dramatic as the north shore's Na Pali Coast (*na pali* meaning simply 'the cliffs'). This 17-mile (27km) stretch of seemingly impenetrable rock is Mother Nature's answer to the Great Wall of China – a barricade impenetrable by any but the birds and the brave.

Polynesians were the first humans to arrive here, in around AD 1200, following long ocean crossings in their double-hulled outrigger canoes. They navigated the coast, blazed foot trails, and laid down roots in Na Pali's otherwise inaccessible valleys. The extreme topography provided the early settlers with a natural fortress, while the sea and rivers supplied plentiful fish. By irrigating the hanging valleys, they could also grow crops such as taro and breadfruit. When English seafarer Captain James Cook 'discovered' Kauai in 1778, there was already a healthy community living in this unlikely place.

Those early pioneers are now long gone, replaced by hikers. Helicopters fly over Na Pali and boats sail by, but to really get in among these towering precipices – in places, up to 1,219m (4,000ft) high – you have to hit the Kalalau Trail. This 11-mile (18km) route utilises original paths to traverse five valleys, skirt the pounding Pacific, hack through bush, disclose beautiful beaches, and offer extreme close-ups of the fluted cliffs. It is a hike that many have made, but which remains utterly untamed. Trekkers here might face landslides, falling rocks, flash floods, and rogue waves. But for the fit, this is the ultimate Kauai adventure.

The Kalalau trailhead is at Ke'e Beach, at the end of the Kuhio Highway. The first two miles are a scenic start, wending over slippery rocks and via ohia lehua and candlenut trees to reach Hanakapi'ai Valley. Permits aren't required to hike to Hanakapi'ai, so this section can get busy. But with your permit secured, and the right gear packed, you can escape the crowds to reach Kalalau's most impressive parts.

The route beyond Hanakapi'ai Valley gets more lung-gasping over the next 4 miles (7km), switchbacking

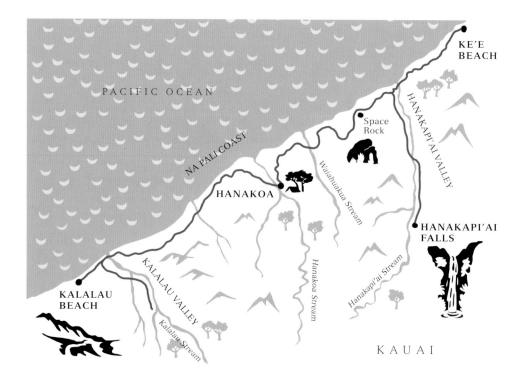

up 244m (800ft) of rocky splendour to the high point at Space Rock. It then hops over waterfalls and mini hanging valleys to reach Hanakoa. There's a campsite here, although you're encouraged not to use it. Rather, push on, hitting the most strenuous but most spectacular section. For the next 5 miles (8km), the Kalalau Trail is at its skinniest and steepest, climbing via coffee and ti plants (used to fashion Hawaiian skirts) and affording the most mesmerising views of the Na Pali cliffs. Rocks soar like spires, cloaked in a fuzz of green, tinkled by waterfalls, and sloping down to the turquoise sea.

Kalalau Beach, a mile (1.6km) of secluded sand, is the official end, although an extra trail leads inland down the Kalalau Valley, past old agricultural terraces now overgrown with guava and plum. There's a campsite at Kalalau, behind the beach. The maximum number of consecutive nights you're allowed to spend here is five, but with the waves lapping, the cliffs rearing, and the wilderness calling, you can understand why those original settlers chose to stay for the long term.

40
Mount Washburn

*Wyoming,
United States*

Hike the 3.2 miles (5km) up to the summit of Mount Washburn for views across the huge Yellowstone Caldera, formed during this still-active supervolcano's last big blast, 2.1 million years ago.

41
GR R1

Réunion

The French have an extensive network of long-distance hiking trails, or Grande Randonnées (GR), but this one is unlike most. Far from the motherland, the GR R1 is on the overseas department of Réunion, a gloriously rugged, green island in the Indian Ocean. The 37-mile (60km) trail is a tour of the Piton des Neiges, a currently inactive 3,069m (10,070ft) shield volcano that burst out of the water around 2 million years ago. Today, it dominates Réunion. The route weaves a dramatic loop, taking in the cirques of Cilaos, Salazie, and Mafate – three dramatic amphitheatres of unruly nature that are riven with ravines, drenched in waterfalls, snaggle-toothed with peaks, and accessible only by foot.

42
MOUNT TEIDE

Tenerife, Spain

You can cheat your way to the top of Spain's highest mountain – a cable car runs 3,550m (11,647ft) up 3,718m (12,198ft) Mount Teide. But where's the satisfaction in that? Instead, start from the trailhead (near the lower cable car station) and make the five-hour haul up via adjacent Montaña Blanca. Hiking offers a more intimate encounter with this stratovolcano, formed inside a caldera that collapsed 160,000 years ago. The route appears alien, ascending via a mix of orange pumice, black lava, crumbly cinder, sulfurous vents, and lava boulders – strange rock formations known as Los Huevos del Teide, or 'Teide's Eggs'. Permits are required to hike the final 92m (300ft) to the top, in order to protect this strange yet delicate land.

43
KILIMANJARO

Northern Tanzania

{ Scale a gargantuan dormant
volcano to look out over
an entire continent. }

Need to know
- *Point in time: 750,000 years ago (Kilimanjaro started forming)*
- *Length: From 28 miles (45km); 6–10 days*
- *Difficulty: Strenuous – high altitude*
- *Best months: Jan–Mar and June–Oct*
- *Top tip: Independent climbing is not allowed*

Kilimanjaro, known as the 'Roof of Africa', is a relative youngster of a volcano, formed by a Rift Valley lava spew some 750,000 years ago. It is the highest point on the African continent, rising large and lonely from the plains of northern Tanzania. It is so lofty, in fact, that despite loitering just a few clicks south of the equator, its 5,895m (19,340ft) summit is capped with a sparkle of snow.

The first man to scale this dormant behemoth was German geologist Hans Meyer in 1889. Gradually, such exploits caught on, and now around 35,000 people attempt to conquer 'Kili' each year. A fair number do not succeed. It's not an overly tough or technical climb – it's just so very high. Trekkers today use one of five main routes: popular Marangu (the only route with huts); equally popular and arguably most scenic Machame; Rongai, the only approach from the Kenyan side; lengthier, plateau-crossing Shira/Lemosho; and tough Umbwe.

Whichever route you choose (and longer is better for altitude acclimatisation), you'll end up climbing from lush, monkey-swung cloud forest, to moorland, to the volcano's moonlike upper slopes. The final challenge is 'summit night', when hopeful hikers leave their base camps around midnight to snake *pole pole* (slowly, slowly) up the last breath-stealing slopes. The aim is to break the crater rim and reach the sign at Uhuru Peak – Kili's precise zenith – as the sun rises over Africa.

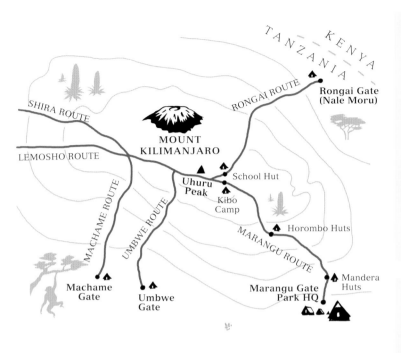

T A N Z A N I A · K E N Y A

SHIRA ROUTE

LEMOSHO ROUTE

MOUNT KILIMANJARO

RONGAI ROUTE

Rongai Gate (Nale Moru)

MACHAME ROUTE

UMBWE ROUTE

Uhuru Peak

School Hut

Kibo Camp

Horombo Huts

MARANGU ROUTE

Machame Gate

Umbwe Gate

Marangu Gate Park HQ

Mandera Huts

44
Route of the Volcanoes

La Palma, Spain

Take an 11-mile (18km) walk through the weird volcanic landscapes of this 1.9-million-year-old, geothermally glorious Canary island. Pass lava lakes and creepy craters en route.

45
Napau Trail

Big Island, Hawaii, United States

Cross lava rivers and cinder fields on this 14-mile (23km) hike to Napau Crater. See the blaze of volcanic cone Pu'u 'O'o, which has been continuously erupting since 1983.

LEFT: Trekking to the top of 5,895m (19,340ft) Kili is breathtaking in every sense.

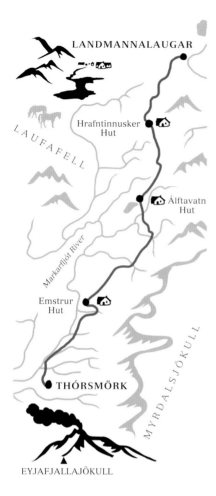

LANDMANNALAUGAR

L A U F A F E L L

Hrafntinnusker
Hut

Álftavatn
Hut

Markarfljót River

Emstrur
Hut

THÓRSMÖRK

M Y R D A L S J Ö K U L L

EYJAFJALLAJÖKULL

RIGHT: Wonder at the multicoloured rock
formations along Iceland's Laugavegur trail.

46
LAUGAVEGUR

Southern Iceland

{ Hit Iceland's most popular trail for an introduction to the country's most peculiar terrain. }

Iceland is odd. Here, on this 20-million-year-young island on the cusp of the Arctic Circle, geology is still very much – and very visibly – in action. Fumaroles (vents) smoke, geysers spew, fissures fizz, and a multitude of overactive volcanoes put on mighty pyrotechnic displays. The result is a landscape that's as inchoate, energetic, and pimpled as a pubescent boy.

The Laugavegur trail – Iceland's most iconic walk – is a good introduction to these geological growing pains, and can be walked independently or with a guide. Starting at the steaming hot springs, hot water streams, and lava fields of Landmannalaugar, the trail plunges south towards the lush, waterfall-flecked nature reserve of Thórsmörk (named after the Norse god of thunder, Thor). Over 34 miles (55km), the Laugavegur passes a technicolour treat of rhyolite mountains, streaked red, purple, yellow, and green. It slips past groaning glaciers and shimmering ice caves. It cuts through narrow ravines, black-sand deserts, and intense emerald pastures where Icelandic ponies might be seen. En route are well-spaced huts providing beds, showers, cooking facilities, and camaraderie. The season for this popular trail is short, so expect to meet plenty of other people.

Most hikers complete the trail in four days, although taking an extra day allows for a detour up troublesome Eyjafjallajökull – the volcano reponsible for the European air travel mayhem in 2010.

Need to know
- *Point in time: 20 million years ago (Iceland began forming)*
- *Length: 34 miles (55km); 4 days*
- *Difficulty: Easy/ moderate – inclement weather possible*
- *Best months: Late June–early Sept*
- *Top tip: Huts must be booked well in advance; take a sleeping bag*

47
GROS PITON

St Lucia

St Lucia's two iconic, pointy peaks – Gros Piton and Petit Piton – have existed for less than a million years. Indeed, they are relative newcomers on an island that first began to form 19 million years ago. Gros Piton (771m / 2,530ft) is the slightly taller summit, and is easier to ascend. It takes just four to six hours to reach the top. Hire a guide to locate the tangled trail that climbs up from Fond Gens Libre (Valley of the Free People). It will lead you through the lush, humid forest and up the steep, rocky steps. From the summit, gaze across to St Vincent, Martinique, and all that perfect, sparkly blue sea.

48
TONGARIRO ALPINE CROSSING

Tongariro National Park, North Island, New Zealand

This one-way, 12-mile (19km) tramp is allegedly the world's best day walk. It's a claim made long before this landscape body-doubled for Mount Doom in the *Lord of the Rings* films. The crossing starts in Mangatepopo Valley. From here it climbs the steep Devil's Staircase and across moonlike South Crater to Red Crater, the highest point. Here, views stretch to stinky sulphurous pools, vivid turquoise lakes, and Mounts Ngauruhoe and Tongariro. Then it's downhill to the finish at Ketetahi, via crimson-stained springs, large totara trees, and numerous Maori legends.

49
MOUNT ELGON

Kenya and Uganda

Mount Elgon is massive. Looming over the Kenya-Uganda border, this 4,321m (14,177ft) volcano – which first erupted around 24 million years ago – has the world's largest intact caldera. It also has slopes cloaked in cedars and giant lobelia, tickled by waterfalls, and riddled with lava tubes where elephants come to lick the salt. The tough, four-day Sasa Trail, on the Ugandan side, is the quickest route up. It starts in Budadiri, and passes BaMasaaba homesteads. It then enters bamboo forest before hitting the cooler upper moorland slopes. Wagagai Peak is the summit, but the real goal is dipping into that vast caldera to find the hot springs and secrets that lie within.

50
NORFOLK COAST PATH

Norfolk, United Kingdom

They call Norfolk's shoreline the 'Deep History Coast' – with good reason. In 2013, along the soft, crumbling cliffs of Happisburgh, the earliest human footprints outside Africa were discovered, fossilised in the mud more than 800,000 years ago. But Happisburgh is just one stop on this gentle 60-mile (97km) stride from Hunstanton to Sea Palling. You'll also pass grand, nineteenth-century Holkham Hall, Cromer's Victorian pier, plus the discovery sites of Seahenge (a Bronze Age timber circle) and the West Runton Elephant (a 600,000-year-old mammoth skeleton). In addition, there are bird reserves, seal sanctuaries, and rows of rainbow-coloured beach huts to enjoy.

51
TRANS-RIFT TRAIL

Great Rift Valley, Kenya

{ Traverse the birthplace of mankind, where early humans first walked – and modern man still does. }

Need to know
- *Point in time: 25–30 million years ago (Great Rift Valley began forming)*
- *Length: 87 miles (140km); 6–8 days*
- *Difficulty: Moderate – ups and downs; hot*
- *Best months: July–Sept*
- *Top tip: Malaria tablets are recommended*

Slowly but surely, the East African land mass is coming apart. Tectonic forces have been tearing at the continent for around 30 million years, resulting in a mighty fracture. In the late nineteenth century, the British geologist and explorer John Walter Gregory christened it the Great Rift Valley. The Rift is said to stretch for some 3,700 miles (5,955km), from the Middle East down to Mozambique. On average, it is 30–40 miles (48–64km) wide.

The most arresting section of this super-fissure is the eastern branch of the East African Rift, which gouges a north–south path right through Kenya and beyond. Here, millennia-old escarpments of basaltic and sedimentary rock rise up to around 914m (3,000ft) and frame a furrow of lush greenery, lakes, hot springs, and abundant wildlife.

The Great Rift Valley has also been called the 'Cradle of Mankind'. Some of the earliest hominid skeletons ever found (dating back over 5 million years) have been unearthed right here. Some scientists even believe that climate changes, brought about by the formation of this tectonic trough, may have been the evolutionary kick required for our early ancestors to stand on two feet and develop bigger brains.

Humanity continues to feature prominently in the Great Rift Valley, as a hike along the Trans-Rift Trail will reveal. The trail, which officially opened in 2011, runs for just under 90 miles (145km), weaving from Mochongoi, up on the eastern escarpment, to Chororget, up on the west. It follows the route used by some of the area's early

RIGHT: The Trans-Rift Trail leads through the very cradle of humanity.

explorers – such as Scottish geologist Joseph Thomson and Hungarian Count Sámuel Teleki de Szék – as they searched for the source of the Nile. And it utilises old trading and grazing routes still used by local people on a daily basis. This means that, far from being a pure wilderness hike, the Trans-Rift Trail is an insight into rural Kenya, in a region relatively untouched by tourism.

Hiking here is win-win: local communities directly benefit from your tourist pounds, while you benefit from the resulting cultural interactions. Indeed, on this route you'll find yourself swapping stories in simple straw-roofed homesteads, chatting to goatherders and farmers planting maize; sampling honey straight from log-hewn hives; and tucking into Kenyan chai tea and chapattis cooked up by locals. You might even spy people travelling much faster than you. This is the domain of the Kalenjin people, a tribe renowned for their distance-running prowess. Many of the world's great marathon runners train nearby. The stars of the future are hot on their heels.

The Trans-Rift Trail doesn't stint on natural splendour either. The starting point, up on the Laikipia Plateau (a six-hour, equator-crossing drive north of the Kenyan capital of Nairobi) is a case in point. From the first day's ridge walk, you'll gaze down on Lake Bogoria, a silvery World Heritage–listed shimmer on the landscape. It fizzes with geysers and hot springs, and is abuzz with birds, including black-necked grebes, African spoonbills, and yellow-billed storks. The Lake Bogoria National Reserve is also a vital habitat for lesser flamingos. Flocks numbering in the hundreds of thousands can sometimes be seen. Although this isn't classic safari territory, there are plenty of other animals to spot, from zebras and antelopes to boisterous baboons.

Down on the valley floor, in the Kerio Valley, you're plunged into Africa at its earliest: rippled rock, red dust, flat-topped acacias, and perishing heat. But the route also has its fair share of coolness, from the shady forests of the Tugen Hills, to moments watching the sun set over all that ancient rock – just as it has done for millions of years.

52
Chimp Trek

Gombe Stream, Tanzania

Trek in the north-shore forests of Lake Tanganyika, on the trail of chimpanzees. Scientists believe that humans and chimps descended from a single common ancestor species that lived six or seven million years ago.

53
Prehistoric Loop Hiking Trail

Les Eyzies, France

Take a 7.5-mile (12km) hike back 28,000 years in the archaeologically rich Dordogne. It was here, in a rock shelter, that the original Cro-Magnon man skeleton was found.

54
TE ARAROA

New Zealand

Appreciate the full span of New Zealand's 75-million-year-old geological history on the Te Araroa trail. 'The Long Pathway' traces the length of the country, snaking for 1,864 miles (3,000km) from Cape Reinga, at the top of the North Island, to Bluff, at the bottom of the South Island. It's a dramatic trail, not least because this is a rambunctious place. New Zealand now straddles the gap between the Pacific and Australian tectonic plates, resulting in a country of high mountains, deep lakes, volcanic outbursts, fizzing fumaroles, and burping pools. Te Araroa can be walked in either direction, but most people start at Cape Reinga in October or November. A tramp usually takes from fifty to eighty days per island.

55
SIMIEN MOUNTAINS TRAVERSE

Ethiopia

Hominids have hiked in Ethiopia's Simien Mountains for at least 3.2 million years. It was near this World Heritage–listed range that paleontologists discovered 'Lucy', an upright-walking *Australopithecus afarensis* – the oldest and most complete hominid ever found. It's certainly a fine place to be bipedal, with broad valleys, high plateaus, the pinnacles of ancient volcanoes, and centuries-old paths to explore. A classic route starts in Sankaber (near the market town of Debark) and involves five to nine days' trekking towards country high-point Ras Dashen (4,550m / 14,930ft). This takes you via the Geech Abyss, escarpment edges, wildlife-rich Chenek, and Imet Gogo, a lookout with jaw-dropping Simien views.

56
ARCTIC CIRCLE TRAIL

West Greenland

{ Trek across pristine wilderness, away from civilisation, on this icy isle that is on the front line of climate change. }

Need to know
- *Point in time: At least 110,000 years ago (age of ice sheet)*
- *Length: 100 miles (161km); 9–11 days*
- *Difficulty: Moderate/ strenuous – hikers must carry large packs; wild and remote*
- *Best months: Late June–Sept*
- *Top tip: All waste must be carried out with you*

The name 'Greenland' is a bit of a misnomer. That is because Greenland, the world's biggest island (with an area of 836,109 square miles / 2,165,512km²), appears largely white: 80 per cent of its land mass is covered in a permanent sheet of ice. (Ironically, nearby Iceland appears largely green.) However, things could have been so different.

The formation of Greenland began about 4 billion years ago. It actually started life down in the Southern Hemisphere, before plate tectonics and continental drift transported the island to its current polar position. Since an ice age 2 million years ago, most of Greenland has been buried under a constantly shifting frosty glaze. At its thickest, the ice cap measures 3,200m (10,500ft) deep. At its oldest, the ice dates back at least 110,000 years.

So that accounts for 80 per cent of Greenland. But what of the other 20 per cent, the island's fringes, to which the inland ice sheet doesn't extend? This bit truly is green, with steeply rising mountains, countless streams, and sweeping tundra of grass, lichens, and shrubland. There are also sparsely scattered settlements – the few humans that do live in Greenland stick to its more hospitable edges. The edges are also where you'll find the Arctic Circle Trail (ACT).

A trek through some of the planet's most pristine wilderness, the 100-mile (161km) ACT explores some of that narrow belt of greener land, in the country's southwest. The route runs westward to the coast from the fjord-head village of Kangerlussuaq (population 520) to the colourful old fishing town of Sisimiut (population 6,000),

which has been inhabited for at least 4,500 years.

In between these two bustling hubs (well, bustling by Greenlandic standards) there is . . . nothing. Nowhere to buy provisions, check in for a shower, or catch up on the news. The only signs of civilisation are eight basic hikers' huts, which offer free shelter, bunks, and sometimes stoves and toilets. With only around 300 people tackling the ACT each year, you could be out on your own.

But then that's the joy – following the skinny trail across the tundra, with not a trace of the twenty-first century in sight. It's especially uplifting from June to August, when temperatures are at their warmest (up to around 16°C / 60°F). Also, the skies are constantly bright, as the entire route lies above the Arctic Circle, which guarantees weeks of midnight sun.

Kangerlussuaq is a handy trailhead, as it's home to Greenland's international airport. If you're interested in viewing the edge of the ice sheet, it can be seen at Isunngua, 25 miles (40km) to the east of the town. However, the ACT itself wends west. It first follows an asphalt-and-dirt road via the harbour to the research station at Kellyville, before dwindling to a narrow trail

GREENLAND

Innajuattok

Kangerluarsuk
Tulleq

SISIMIUT

Nerumaq

Eqalugaarniarfik

KANGERLUSSUAQ
Kellyville
Hundesø

Ikkattook

Katiffik

Canoe Centre

DAVIS
STRAIT

Søndre Strømfjord

beyond. The huts – located at Hundesø, Katiffik, the Canoe Centre, Ikkattook, Eqalugaarniarfik, Innajuattok, Nerumaq, and Kangerluarsuk Tulleq – are quite evenly spaced, although many hikers choose to camp instead, for greater flexibility. Carrying water is never an issue, as crystal-clear lakes, streams, and rivers are in abundance. Consider packing a lightweight fishing rod so you can land a fresh supper.

Besides fish, you might spot other wildlife, including reindeer, Arctic fox, hare, musk oxen, and a range of birds. And then there are the flowers, hardy splashes of colour that enliven the tundra for a few short, spectacular months. Annoyingly, mosquitoes like high summer too, so consider hiking in August or September for fewer bugs.

The ACT isn't that tough in itself. It's largely low-lying (below 152m / 500ft) but occasionally ascends to over 396m (1,300ft). There are a few rivers to cross, but these become easier to ford later in the season. The real challenge is the self-sufficiency, and pitting your body and your mind against the planet at its most wild.

57
Trail 1 and Trail 2

*Plitvice Lakes
National Park,
Croatia*

Combine Croatia's Trail 1 and Trail 2 for the ideal four-hour hike through Plitvice's cool karst landscape. Over thousands of years it has dissolved into a fairy tale of lakes, caves, and cascades.

58
CAUSEWAY COAST WAY

Legend has it that the Irish giant Finn MacCool made the magnificent pavement known as the Giant's Causeway so that he could cross the North Channel to fight Scottish giant Benandonner. In reality, the 40,000-plus hexagonal basalt columns were volcanically constructed 50–60 million years ago, and only revealed at the end of the last ice age. Either way, the Giant's Causeway is the headline act of the 33-mile (53km) Causeway Coast Way, which links Portstewart and Ballycastle. The route also takes in Dunluce Castle, a Spanish Armada wreck, minuscule St Gobban's Church (the smallest in Ireland), the Carrick-a-Rede rope bridge, and a generous scattering of bays, beaches, islets, arches, and sea stacks in between.

59
HÆRVEJEN

Jutland, Denmark

The Hærvejen has seen a lot of history. This ancient road across Jutland follows a glacial ridge created at the end of the last ice age. On this higher ground, there were no rivers to cross, making it the easiest route for those on foot. Consequently, humans have used this passage since prehistoric times, and in the Middle Ages it flourished as a drovers' route. These days it's a Y-shaped, 310-mile (500km), two-pronged hiking trail heading south from Hirtshals or Frederickshavn. The prongs merge at Viborg (one of Denmark's oldest cities) and continue to Padborg on the German border, via Stone Age dolmens (tombs), Viking sites, and the horse-drawn cart tracks of travellers past.

GLACIER NORTH CIRCLE

Glacier National Park, Montana, United States

{ Take a seriously cool hike through a pristine, icy wilderness – while the ice is still there . . . }

Need to know

- *Point in time: 2 million years ago (glaciation of Glacier National Park during an ice age)*
- *Length: 65 miles (105 km); 7 days*
- *Difficulty: Moderate – remote; cold nights; insects and bears*
- *Best months: July–Sept*
- *Top tip: Backcountry camping permits required*

It's a sad fact that Montana's Glacier National Park could soon be without its glaciers. When the park was first designated in 1910, 150 of these sparkly white tongues of ice oozed amid its mountains. Today, just twenty-five remain. Some experts predict that all of them may be gone by 2020 – a true tragedy, as it was ice that sculpted this magnificent landscape. Two million years ago, the area was buried under a mile-deep (1.6km) ice cap, which gnawed away at the rock below. When most of the ice melted, 12,000 years ago, today's features were revealed.

The North Circle trek (also called the Highline Trail or the Ptarmigan Tunnel Loop) is the best way to explore the resulting wilderness. Begin at Many Glacier (accessible by public transport), considered by many people to be the heart of the park. From here a clockwise ambulation leads past fir forests and wildflower meadows, glaciers and cascades, impossibly blue lakes, deep glacial troughs, and more peaks than you can count. Indeed, Fifty Mountain claims to give views of fifty mountains.

There's also the chance to hike through the Ptarmigan Tunnel, a 76m (250ft) long passage, blasted at an elevation of 2,195m (7,200ft) into the looming Ptarmigan Wall. Plus there are ample opportunities to spot nimble mountain goats, marmots, moose, elk, bighorn sheep, and grizzly bears. You can even tick off another country – stride north from Goat Haunt into Waterton Lakes National Park and you're in Canada.

RIGHT: Visit icy lakes and steep, snowy mountainsides carved by ice age glaciation.

61
Käsmu Nature and Culture Trail

Lahemaa National Park, Estonia

Walk amid forest, bogs, and erratic boulders carried over the Baltic Sea from Finland by ice age glaciers. The 2.6-mile (4km) Käsmu Trail visits Matsikivi Erratic Boulder, the biggest rock of the lot.

62
Ice Age Trail

Wisconsin, United States

Wind among Wisconsin's glacial landscapes on the Ice Age Trail. It runs for 1,200 miles (1,931km), from Interstate State Park to Potawatomi State Park, via ice age sculpting at its best.

BIBBULMUN TRACK

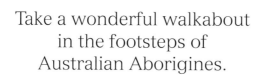

Western Australia

Take a wonderful walkabout
in the footsteps of
Australian Aborigines.

Need to know
- *Point in time: At least 45,000 years ago (known history of regional indigenous peoples)*
- *Length: 600 miles (966km); 6–8 weeks*
- *Difficulty: Strenuous – long; wild and remote*
- *Best months: Apr–Nov*
- *Top tip: Take a fuel stove – open fires are not permitted at all camps*

The indigenous Noongar people have lived in the southwest corner of Western Australia for at least 45,000 years. Archaeological evidence found in caves near Margaret River dates back even further. The Noongar people lived in dispersed families, each surviving off their immediate surrounds. Those near modern-day Perth fished from the sea. Those near Albany hunted turtles. Those in the southeast gathered from the great karri forests, vast expanses of endemic *Eucalyptus diversicolor* trees. But they also came together, walking hundreds of miles across the bush to trade goods and to partake in ceremonial gatherings. The Bibbulmun were a subgroup of the peripatetic Noongar, and Western Australia's greatest long-distance hiking trail is named in their honour.

The Bibbulmun people lived in harmony with the land, and today's Australian Aborigines still believe that everything is connected. Their creation stories and ancestor spirits are deeply entwined with every animal, rock, star, and tree. The precise routes that the Bibbulmun took are not known, but the Bibbulmun Track attempts to give today's walkers a taste of that oneness with nature.

Certainly, thru-hiking the Bibbulmun offers a major wilderness immersion. The trail runs for 600 miles (966km) from Kalamunda in the Perth Hills to Albany on the south coast. There are good maps, guidebooks, and frequent yellow waymarkers, which depict the Waugal (the rainbow serpent of the Aboriginal Dreaming). There are also forty-nine basic campsites en route. But this remains a proper bush experience. For instance, the track passes settlements where you can resupply, but they are few and

far between. As an example, the hike from the start at Kalamunda to the next town of Dwellingup takes about twelve days.

What a hike the Bibbulmun is, though. The start is only 15 miles (24km) east of the state capital of Perth but immediately plunges into the Darling Range, via a mix of jarrah, marri, and wandoo forests with some far-reaching lookouts. Sunset atop Abyssinia Rock is a pinch-yourself moment. After Dwellingup, there are tempting dips in the Murray River, flocks of black cockatoos, and easy walking along old railways that once hauled timber. The next town is charming Collie. Soon after that you'll reach the Mumballup Forest Tavern (a very welcome watering hole) and the pristine Preston Valley. Then fuel up in Balingup, which has a good range of restaurants if you're hankering for a change from camp-stove cooking. South of here, the emergence of towering karri trees – which exist nowhere else on earth – marks the midway point.

Some steep hauls must be overcome to reach the historic mill town of Donnelly River, where you'll be rubbing shoulders with semi-tame emus and kangaroos. From here, the trail follows the actual Donnelly River, from which the town gets its name. The route surmounts the area's most

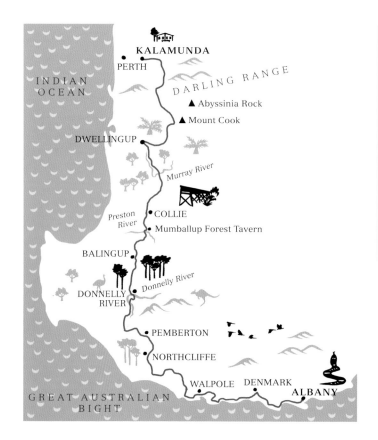

64
Walking with the Bushmen

Kalahari, Botswana

Walk the endless, sandy, and wildlife-rich Kalahari Desert with a local guide. The San people (Bushmen) have long lived off this harshest of lands, and know it better than anyone else.

challenging hills but pays out with waterfalls, railway history and, from August to October, a blaze of wildflowers. Pemberton is home to some of the finest karri trees, while the next, truly wild stretch from Northcliffe to Walpole offers the first views of the ocean. Tough walking, tempered with kangaroo-dotted heathland, beaches, and tingle trees (giant, buttressed eucalyptus, endemic to southwest Western Australia), leads to laid-back Denmark. From here, the end point at Albany is a simple, yet spectacular, coastal walk away.

You don't have to do the whole Bibbulmun in one go. There are many day-long and multi-day options, for those who want a taster. Either way, you start to get a feel for the soil beneath your feet, and a sense of connection to the ancient Bibbulmun people who walked here long ago.

NEANDERLANDSTEIG

North Rhine, Westphalia, Germany

While the 146-mile (235km) Neanderlandsteig opened in 2014, it treads in far more ancient footsteps. In 1856 a fossil discovered near Mettmann (in the Neander Valley) was first recognised as Neanderthal man – a species closely related to modern humans that lived here around 40,000 years ago. To find out more about the landscape occupied by our ancient relatives, follow the seventeen stages of this circular walk. Explore the woody, river-riddled sections around Erkrath and visit the museum in Mettmann encompassing the original Neanderthal man discovery site. The trail also takes in fairy-tale forests and timbered old towns.

66

GOZO COASTAL WALK

Gozo, Malta

The tiny, unassuming island of Gozo, strategically located in the midddle of the Mediterranean, was a hotbed of Neolithic culture. As such, it is home to some of the oldest freestanding structures in the world – the 5,000-year-old Ggantija temples at Xaghra. The most comprehensive way to explore the surfeit of history here is via the 34-mile (55km) Coastal Walk. Where possible, it hugs Gozo's rugged shores for a full circumnavigation. The walk can also be split into four sections, each taking five to seven hours, and uses limestone paths and country roads to explore the island's best parts. Hike from Mgarr Harbour, via rock arches, watchtowers, wildflowers, secluded beaches, Punic-Roman remains, and glimpses of traditional Gozitan life.

67
JATBULA TRAIL

Northern Territory, Australia

The Jatbula Trail follows the western edge of the Arnhem Land Escarpment. This is the route that the Jawoyn people have used to link Nitmiluk (Katherine Gorge) and Leliyn (Edith Falls) for generations. Indeed, indigenous Australians have lived in this region for at least 40,000 years. Primordial, pristine, and raw, the area feels little changed since. A short drive from Katherine, the 39-mile (63km) walk starts with a ferry ride to the east side of 17 Mile Creek. The next five days are an Outback education. Discover rock art on the canyon walls, dip into cool creeks, and camp out under unpolluted starry skies.

68
OFFALY WAY

County Offaly, Ireland

Bogs were beloved of Mesolithic people, who used the rich peatland to preserve food and provide fuel. Boora Bog, created after the last ice age, was no exception. Today, if you follow the 23-mile (37km) Offaly Way from Cadamstown to Lemanaghan, you cross Boora, and can visit the site of an ancient settlement where black chert tools and the charcoal from millennia-old campfires have been unearthed. Elsewhere, the easy trail follows riverbanks and quiet roads, ticking off other time periods. For instance, see a bridge crossed by troops off to the Battle of Kinsale in 1601 and the seventh-century monastic site of Lemanaghan.

69
Chadar Trek

Ladakh, India

India's remote Zanskar Valley has been inhabited since the Bronze Age. Tackle this 47-mile (76km) trek through it from November to March, when the frozen river becomes the only way in.

70
Great Pedestrian Route of Vale do Côa

Portugal

This easy 16-mile (26km) hike from Vila Nova de Foz Côa into Portugal's Côa Valley reveals prehistoric rock art, a Lusitanian castle, and Baroque mansions.

GIANT'S CUP TRAIL

Drakensberg Mountains, South Africa

The indigenous San people have been painting rocks in southern Africa for at least 10,000 years. The Giant's Cup Trail combines glimpses of their artwork with marvellous walking in the Drakensberg Mountains. This 37-mile (60km), five-day hike starts at the Sani Pass road and ends at Bushman's Nek. En route lie a few steepish climbs, but also well-spaced huts offering toilets and a bunk each night. On day one, head into pretty Pholela Valley. On day two, visit Bathplug Cave to see San art. On day three, dip into Killiecrankie Pools. On day four, admire Garden Castle rock. And finally, on day five, cross Mzimunde Valley, see more San paintings, and reflect on a walk well done.

LEFT: Find rock paintings by indigenous San people deep in the Drakensberg Mountains.

GREAT STONES WAY

Wiltshire, United Kingdom

{ Walk in the footsteps of Neolithic people, via the stone circles of Avebury and Stonehenge. }

Need to know
- *Point in time: About 5,000 years ago (age of Stonehenge)*
- *Length: 36 miles (58km) – 53 miles (85km) with optional detours; 4–5 days*
- *Difficulty: Easy – gently rolling countryside*
- *Best months: Apr–Oct*
- *Top tip: Swindon and Salisbury both have railway stations; there are many pubs and B&Bs near the route*

Many features of this patch of South West England remain something of a mystery. Around 5,000 years ago, for reasons we still can't quite fathom, Neolithic people decided to move massive rocks from as far afield as the Preseli Hills of Wales to the chalk downs of Wiltshire – a journey of 160 miles (258km). The stones were then erected in ceremonial circles. Banks and ditches, lines of standing stones, chambered tombs, and long barrows were also constructed at this time.

The Great Stones Way dissects this curious countryside, running from the Iron Age hill fort of Barbury Castle, just south of Swindon, to Old Sarum, just north of Salisbury. Along the official 36-mile (58km) trail lie Bronze Age burial mounds, Roman roads, Norman churches, medieval motte-and-bailey castles, and nineteenth-century white horses etched into the hillside chalk. The trail also extends to a 53-mile (85km) route, which adds on essential detours to Avebury and Stonehenge, the United Kingdom's Neolithic masterpieces.

The circle at Stonehenge is worth seeing but can be overcrowded. You can't actually walk among its menhirs (upright stones). Avebury is a much more interactive prospect. There, a village has grown up around the larger Avebury henge site, which comprises two inner circles inside an outer circle that once numbered ninety-eight stones (although only twenty-seven remain). You can touch the time-worn rocks and explore the surrounding prehistoric landscape – including man-made Silbury Hill. You can then mull it all over with a pint of beer in the local pub.

RIGHT: A 'white horse' etched into the hillside chalk, near the ceremonial stones of Avebury and Stonehenge.

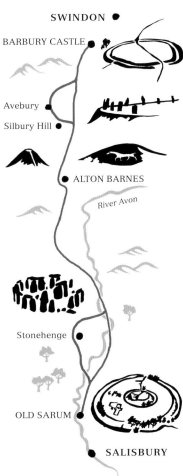

SWINDON ●

BARBURY CASTLE ●

Avebury ●

Silbury Hill ●

● ALTON BARNES

River Avon

Stonehenge ●

OLD SARUM ●

● **SALISBURY**

73
Outer Mountain Loop

Big Bend National Park,
Texas, United States

Make a 30-mile (48km) circuit amid
hardy cacti and rich red canyons
on the Outer Mountain Loop. It's
a great way to explore Chihuahuan
Desert ecosystems and feel the
presence of Native American
ancestors and past pioneers.

74
ACONCAGUA

Mendoza, Argentina

Aconcagua is a beast. This Andean mountain is the highest outside of the Himalayan region, towering 6,962m (22,840ft) above the vine-streaked valleys of Mendoza Province. But despite its monstrous proportions it is, essentially, a trekking peak. This means fifteen to eighteen days on punishing terrain, at breath-stealing altitudes, but with no technical skills required. Most hopeful trekkers head up the Horcones Valley, battling fields of *nieve penitentes* (snow spikes), icy katabatic winds, freezing temperatures, and soul-sapping scree. However, the pay off is looking out over the Andes to the Pacific Ocean, feeling on top of (most of) the world.

75
Los Dientes de Navarino Circuit

Tierra del Fuego, Chile

This tough 34-mile (55km) hike is on Isla Navarino, home to the Yahgan people for more than 10,000 years. The area also purportedly has the highest density of archaeological sites in the world.

76
THE RIDGEWAY

Southern England, United Kingdom

The Ridgeway is Britain's oldest road. It has been in use for at least 5,000 years – by soldiers, drovers, and drifters – and once stretched about 250 miles (402km), from the Dorset coast to easterly Norfolk. Today's route, an abbreviated 87-mile (140km) trail from Avebury to Ivinghoe Beacon, follows the same ancient upland course. It flirts with towns and villages, and occasionally crosses a busy road, but remains surprisingly wild. It takes around six days to complete, plowing northeast from the Neolithic long barrow at West Kennett into bucolic chalk downland. Head further towards the River Thames and there are also hidden valleys, cow-grazed green pastures, and the beech woods of the Chiltern Hills.

77
MONTE TISCALI

Supramonte Mountains, Sardinia, Italy

A hike to Monte Tiscali is a great way to explore the central-eastern Supramonte Mountains. It's also a fascinating insight into Sardinia's indigenous Nuragic civilisation, architects of the 7,000 truncated, conical towers found here. Said to be built around 1800 BC, these beehivelike *nuraghi* have not, to date, been found anywhere else in the world. Follow the half-day trail from the town of Dorgali to explore the Lanaittu Valley. This limestone landscape is peppered with caves and sinkholes. The trail then squeezes through a chasm to reach Tiscali village, a Nuragic settlement just beneath the mountain's summit, where ancient circular houses can still be seen.

78
KUNGSLEDEN

Lapland, Sweden

Lapland is Europe's largest remaining wilderness, a pristine realm of U-shaped valleys, glacial cirques, drumlins, rivers, bogs, and birch forests. The Sami people have been here since prehistoric times, living a peripatetic existence with their huge reindeer herds. For those on foot, the 273-mile (439km) Kungsleden (King's Trail) is the best way to explore the area. It runs south from Abisko, above the Arctic Circle, to Hemavan. There are basic mountain huts every 6–12 miles (10–20km), boardwalks and bridges cross marshes and streams, and ferry services or rowing boats are available for lake crossings. This is Lapland made a little more accessible, but still wonderfully wild.

79
Algarve Way

Southern Portugal

The 160-mile (257km) Algarve Way runs from Alcoutim on the Spanish border to Cabo de São Vicente, Europe's most southwesterly point. Walk it, knowing it has been a sacred area since Neolithic times.

80
METHUSELAH LOOP TRAIL

California, United States

Short, steep, and sweet, the 4.5-mile (7km) Methuselah Loop Trail visits one of the world's most ancient trees. The tree in question – Methuselah – is a Great Basin bristlecone pine, a species native to the western United States and known for its exceptional longevity. Methuselah is nearly 5,000 years old. It grows amid the White Mountains of Inyo National Forest, an area of over 2 million acres (8,000 km^2) of wildlife-roamed peaks, lakes, and streams. The trail starts and ends at Schulman Grove Visitor Center. It's then a 61m (200ft) climb to Methuselah Grove, where several bristlecones stand on the hillside. For its protection, Methuselah's precise identity is kept secret – you have to guess which tree looks almost 5,000 years old.

81
Whitsunday Ngaro Sea Trail

Whitsunday Islands, Australia

The Whitsunday Islands, on Australia's Great Barrier Reef, have been home to the seafaring Ngaro people for over 9,000 years. This network of coastal walks (ranging from 1 to 7 miles / 1 to 11km) visits sites special to Ngaro descendants.

82
Saint-Just Circuit

Brittany, France

Megalithic remnants abound in this area of Brittany. Make an 8-mile (13km) loop from the village of Saint-Just to see menhirs, dolmens, and a prehistoric 'calendar'.

83
Torajaland

Sulawesi, Indonesia

Various short trails here will bring you up close to the unique funeral rites of the Bugis (Toraja), descendants of a Bronze Age people who made an exodus from Vietnam.

RIGHT: Explore the history of the Ngaro people on the Whitsunday Ngaro Sea Trail.

Embark on a five-hour trek up Tenerife's Mount Teide (Spain's highest mountain) via adjacent Montaña Blanca for an intimate encounter with this stratovolcano and the surrounding national park (p. 45).

CHAPTER TWO
THE ANCIENT WORLD

{ Follow in the footsteps of our early
ancestors, from the dawn of
civilisation to AD 600, uncovering
age-old beliefs, myths, and marvels. }

84

JESUS TRAIL

Galilee, Israel

Walk in the footsteps of Christ, from
Nazareth to the Sea of Galilee.

Need to know

- *Point in time:*
  7 BC–AD 33 (purported
  life of Jesus)
- *Length: 40 miles*
  (64km); 3–5 days
- *Difficulty: Moderate –*
  hot; some rugged
  terrain
- *Best months:*
  Feb–May; Oct–Nov
- *Top tip: Walking west*
  to east is easier – the
  route is mostly
  downhill from
  Nazareth to Galilee

The Jesus Trail, a 40-mile (64km) hike in the Holy Land, connects locations relating to Christ. It also crosses the rugged, rocky, surprisingly lush region of Galilee, making it a scenic as well as a spiritual journey.

Followed from west to east, the trail begins in Nazareth, Jesus's purported hometown. It was here that Mary was said to have been visited by the Angel Gabriel and was told she would bear the Son of God. You can visit Mary's Well, reputedly the site of the Annunciation. It was also here that Jesus is thought to have begun his ministry. The current Synagogue Church is allegedly built on top of the temple at which he preached. For an atmospheric step back in time, detour to Nazareth Village, an open-air museum that reconstructs first-century life, complete with wandering goats, biblical refreshments, and fancy dress shepherds.

Leaving Nazareth, the trail then heads northeast, entering Sepphoris (also known as Zippori). This ancient city was the administrative capital of Galilee in the first century. Some scholars believe Mary was born here, and that Joseph worked on its construction. It's now a national park, rich in millennia of archaeological remains – Hellenistic, Jewish, Roman, Byzantine, Islamic, Crusader, Arabic, and Ottoman remnants lie here.

Further on is Cana (Kfar Kana), where Jesus reportedly conducted his first miracle. The town is built on the site of the wedding feast where water was said to have been turned into wine. From Cana to Ilaniya (meaning 'tree') the trail is shaded and green, cutting through oak forest,

ABOVE: The Jesus Trail is a scenic and spiritual journey beginning in Nazareth.

wildflowers, and well-tended farms. This stretch is also home to the ridgetop remains of a Roman road, which Jesus probably used on his own journey from Nazareth to Capernaum.

The trail continues northwestwards via rolling rural landscapes towards the Horns of Hattin, a striking double hill that is actually an ancient volcano. Hattin is also the site of the 1187 battle that saw Islamic forces led by Saladin (then sultan of Egypt and Syria) defeat the Crusader army (Roman Catholic Christian forces from western Europe) and conquer most of Palestine. From here – around the halfway point – the whole Jesus Trail is visible in resplendent panorama. This includes the first views of the Sea of Galilee.

Huddled just beneath the Horns is the shrine of Nebi Shu'eib. The current nineteenth-century complex houses the tomb of Jethro (father-in-law of Moses), a prophet of the Druze religion. It's possible to visit the site, as long as you're modestly dressed. Next, the route heads into the Arbel Valley (or 'Valley of the Doves'), where 213m (700ft) high limestone cliffs, rising at Mount Arbel, are studded with gnarled olive groves, graceful mountain gazelle, and ruined villages. If Jesus did walk this way, he wouldn't have encountered the metal rungs that now aid climbers descending the precipitous slopes.

From here, walkers meet the seashore at Migdal, site of Magdala and home of the Christian figure Mary Magdalene, devoted follower of Jesus. The trail then continues to Tabgha, where the Church of the Multiplication of Loaves and Fishes boasts miracle legends and Byzantine mosaics. Finally, the trail ascends the peaceful, leafy Mount of Beatitudes, where Jesus is thought to have delivered the Sermon on the Mount.

The route finishes in Capernaum, Jesus's base camp during his ministry in Galilee. Capernaum was one of three cities that Jesus cursed due to its lack of faith, declaring: 'And you, Capernaum, will you be lifted up to the skies? No, you will go down to the depths' (Matthew 11:23). True to prophecy, the city was abandoned in the seventh century, and by the 1800s was reduced to nothing but rubble. Now you can visit the ruins and museum, and see Roman-era graffiti – words such as 'Lord' and 'Messiah' – inscribed on the ancient walls.

85
Pilgrim's Way

Wales, United Kingdom

This 130-mile (209km) spiritual trail from Basingwerk to the pilgrimage site of Bardsey Island links churches dedicated to sixth-century saints via hills, valleys, and the sea.

86
CROAGH PATRICK

County Mayo, Ireland

At 764m (2,507ft), Croagh Patrick isn't the biggest mountain in Ireland, but it is the most sacred. It's said that in 441, St Patrick, the country's patron saint, fasted for forty days and forty nights on top of its pointy peak, banishing all the snakes from the Emerald Isle while he was there. Now, each year around a million pilgrims climb the mountain nicknamed 'the Reek', ascending from the base near Westport on Clew Bay. The route runs via the 1920s statue of the saint and up the steep, rocky slope to reach the chapel on the summit. The climb takes around two hours. However, the deeply devout, who ascend barefoot, may take a little longer.

87
ST KEVIN'S WAY

County Wicklow, Ireland

This sixth-century saint probably wouldn't want you to follow in his footsteps. Kevin was an abstemious ascetic, and originally retreated to the isolated valley of Glendalough to live as a hermit. However, the large monastic community that subsequently developed here became the most important in Ireland. It's now the end point of the 19-mile (30km) St Kevin's Way, which begins in the village of Hollywood (also called Cillín Chaoimhín, or 'Kevin's Little Church'). It then wends eastward across the Wicklow Mountains, through the windy 478m (1,567ft) high Wicklow Gap. From there, it travels along the Glendasan River, into glaciated Glendalough, and to the monastery ruins. In parts, old pilgrim road flagstones can still be seen.

88
MOUNT SINAI

Sinai, Egypt

{ Make a sunrise march up to the spot where Moses was said to have met God. }

Need to know
- *Point in time: 548 (St Catherine's Monastery built)*
- *Length: 4.3 miles (7km) round-trip; 5 hours*
- *Difficulty: Moderate – steep; short*
- *Best months: Apr–June*
- *Top tip: The Sinai is a troubled region – check current advice before traveling*

Is this where Moses received the Ten Commandments? Did he and the Israelites gather beneath this mountain to receive the word of God, as the book of Exodus states? Theories are conflicting. Some theologians reckon the Bible's Mount Sinai is actually Mount Al-Lawz in Saudi Arabia; others that it's a hill in southern Israel. However, Egypt's 2,285m (7,497ft) Mount Sinai (also known as Jebel Musa, or 'Moses's Mountain') has staked a strong claim.

The Coptic Christians believed it. In the fourth century, this religious sect founded a church on Mount Sinai, on the spot where God allegedly spoke to Moses as a burning bush. In 548, this developed into St Catherine's Monastery, a sacred church, and a popular starting point for a climb into the past.

Most hikers begin the three-hour ascent from St Catherine's Village at 2:00 a.m., hoping to summit for sunrise. This means walking over rough desert terrain in the dark. Alternatively, you could begin at 2:00 p.m., to summit for sunset.

The Camel Path is the easier route up, gently gaining height to Elijah's Basin. On this plateau, a tree marks the spot where Elijah was said to have heard the voice of God. Then it's a haul up 750 steps to the top. The sunrise, over a sea of sandy, ravine-sliced peaks, feels somehow biblical. To complete a loop, descend via the steeper Steps of Penitence – 3,000-plus knee-crunching steps, looking down on the ancient monastery below.

RIGHT: Climb the steep steps of Mount Sinai to witness a biblical sunrise.

MOUNT ARARAT

Eastern Turkey

Mount Ararat, rising to 5,165m (16,945ft) above the Armenian Plateau, is heaven for altitude-loving hikers. It's one of those rare towering peaks (actually a dormant volcano) that requires no technical skills to climb. The fit and acclimatised can make it to the top and back in four or five days. Access the trailhead from the frontier town of Dogubeyazit. The trek involves camping on the slopes, meeting Kurdish nomads, and cramponing through snow on the last push to the summit. However, Ararat is more than a peak to bag. It's allegedly where Noah's Ark came to rest after the world-rinsing flood, making it both a bucket-list hike and a biblical legend.

90
ISLE OF IONA

Inner Hebrides, Scotland, United Kingdom

In 563 the Irish abbot Columba landed on tiny Iona and brought Christianity with him. The Hebridean island, just 3 miles (5km) long by 1.5 miles (2.5km) wide, became the birthplace of the religion in Scotland, and a renowned seat of Christian learning. It was here that monks created the glorious Book of Kells. Iona remains special. There are no cars on the island, but from the ferry jetty you can explore by foot. In a few hours, you can visit the remains of the latter-day abbey (established in 1200); see the hermit's cell, nestled in the hills; marvel at the old marble quarry; and sink your toes into the white sand of Columba's Bay, where the saint first arrived nearly 1,500 years ago.

91
VIA DOLOROSA

Jerusalem, Israel

The Via Dolorosa, or 'Way of Suffering', is less than 0.5 mile (1km) long but historically mighty. This short shimmy through old Jerusalem is said to be the path Jesus walked to his crucifixion. The route has fourteen Stations of the Cross, beginning at the place where Pilate condemned Jesus (now the Al-Omariya School). It continues under the Roman Ecce Homo arch and via commemorative churches. This includes the small Polish chapel located where Jesus fell for the first time, and the Monastery of St Charalambos, where he consoled the lamenting women. The final four stations are inside the Church of the Holy Sepulchre, culminating in the small chamber, considered to be the location of Jesus's tomb.

92

ABRAHAM PATH

Turkey, Jordan, Palestine, and Israel

The Abraham Path – which, for over 600 miles (970km), retraces the notional journey of the biblical patriarch – isn't just a historical hike, it's a contemporary hand of friendship. As the Bible tells it, Abraham was renowned for his hospitality, and one aim of this trail is to engender a similar spirit in the unsettled Middle East. The path is divided into non-continuous sections across fifteen regions. It runs from Mount Nemrut in southeast Turkey, via Israel and Palestine – taking in Bethlehem, Urfa, and the Negev Desert – to Petra in Jordan. The Hebron section gets closest to Abraham. A shrine in the city sits on top of the cave where he was allegedly laid to rest.

93

ISRAEL NATIONAL TRAIL

Israel

The landscape along the 620-mile (1,000km) Israel National Trail is biblical and beautiful in equal measure, from the shimmering Sea of Galilee to the timeless bleakness of the Negev Desert. The trail traverses the entire country, starting in Dan on the Lebanese border and heading south to Eilat, on the Red Sea. En route it passes the baptismal Jordan River and the striking inselberg of Mount Tabor, where Barak and 10,000 Israelites defeated the Canaanites. It hugs the Mediterranean near Tel Aviv and ascends Mount Carmel. And it lays out a spread of other treats, including wildflower meadows, Nubian ibex, gall oaks, and semi-nomadic Bedouin roaming the plains.

ST PAUL TRAIL

Western Anatolia, Turkey

{ Amble into the rugged splendour of old Asia Minor, on the trail of the apostle St Paul. }

Need to know
- *Point in time:* AD 5–67 *(life of St Paul)*
- *Length: 310 miles (500km); 24–27 days*
- *Difficulty: Moderate/ strenuous – remote; rugged*
- *Best months: Mar– June; Sept–Oct*
- *Top tip: Lodging is available in village houses and small guesthouses; on some sections, camping is necessary*

95
Cosán na Naomh

Mount Brandon, Ireland

Climb the pilgrim's path up 953m (3,127ft) Mount Brandon, named in honour of St Brendan the Navigator (484–577), for views over the Atlantic coast.

Jesus may have founded Christianity, but it was St Paul – born in Tarsus, south-central Turkey, around AD 5 – who spread the word. Following a vision of the resurrected Christ, he began to preach, first in Damascus (Syria), then farther afield in modern-day Cyprus, Turkey, Greece, Italy, and possibly beyond. It was St Paul who ensured Jesus's message left the Holy Land.

The 310-mile (500km) St Paul Trail, which leads inland from the Mediterranean just east of Antalya (either from Perge or Aspendos) to Yalvaç, northeast of Lake Egirdir, loosely traces the apostle's first route into Asia Minor (largely modern-day Turkey). It uses a mix of Roman roads, forest tracks, and well-worn footpaths, dipping into remote villages, forests of oak and cedar, gaping canyons, and the high Taurus Mountains. It passes Roman aqueducts and amphitheatres, Byzantine towns, Ottoman backstreets, and fascinating ruins that don't even have names. Although you'll see few other hikers on the trail, you'll be left in no doubt that people have travelled this way for millennia. The evidence is all around.

The highlights are numerous. Visit the mountaintop site of Selge, where a small village has emerged amid Roman ruins. Follow shepherds' trails through Köprülü Canyon or gaze down into Çandir Canyon. Cross Lake Egirdir by fishing boat. Hike alongside the Roman aqueduct into Yalvaç. But mostly, enjoy the warm hospitality of the Turkish people in the villages, guest houses, homestays, and cafés en route.

The ancient ampitheatre at Selge is just one of the highlights along the St Paul Trail.

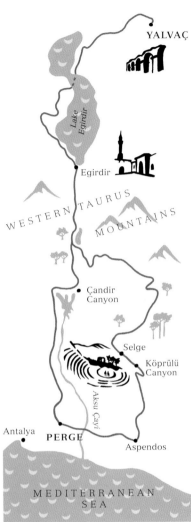

YALVAÇ

Lake Egirdir

Egirdir

WESTERN TAURUS MOUNTAINS

Çandir Canyon

Selge

Köprülü Canyon

Aksu Çayi

Antalya   PERGE

Aspendos

MEDITERRANEAN SEA

96
Lebanon Mountain Trail

Lebanon

Hike 273 miles (440km) from Qbaiyat to Marjaayoun – a trail rich not only in biblical resonance but scattered with Greek, Roman, Ottoman, and Byzantine relics too.

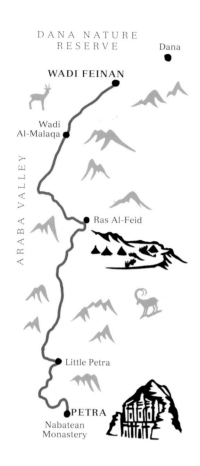

DANA NATURE
RESERVE
Dana

WADI FEINAN

Wadi
Al-Malaqa

ARABA VALLEY

Ras Al-Feid

Little Petra

PETRA
Nabatean
Monastery

97
The Prophet's Trail

Ajloun, Jordan

A 5-mile (9km) path through the oak, pear, and oriental strawberry trees of Ajloun Forest Reserve leads to Mar Elias. Dedicated to the Bible's prophet Elijah, this is one of Jordan's oldest churches.

RIGHT: The best way to arrive at Petra's monastery is on foot.

98
DANA–PETRA TREK

Jordan

{ Avoid the other tourists at the incredible rock-cut city by trekking there via Bedouin trails. }

They call this trek the 'Inca Trail of the Middle East', which is no overstatement. Though the terrain couldn't be more different from the Peruvian Andes, this desert hike is a wild wilderness route with a similarly iconic landmark at its end.

The city of Petra was hewn from the rock of western Jordan around 2,000 years ago. It was built by the secretive Nabateans, a Semitic civilisation that grew wealthy from trading in silk, spices, and gems. At Petra, they constructed mighty tombs, colonnaded streets, altars, temples, and grand facades amid the rose-red canyons. The city continued to thrive until AD 363, when it was rocked by an earthquake. The quake, combined with changes in trade routes, led to the city's downfall. By the middle of the seventh century Petra appears to have been 'lost' to all but the local Bedouin. It wasn't 'found' again until Swiss explorer Jean Louis Burckhardt rediscovered it in 1812.

The best way to arrive at Petra these days is like Burckhardt did: on foot. The Dana–Petra Trek uses a range of old hunters' trails and mule tracks to get from Dana Nature Reserve to World Heritage–listed Petra in four to six days. En route, you can camp in Bedouin-style tents, or under the stars.

Dana Nature Reserve is dramatically varied with high sandstone cliffs, low valleys, prolific plants, and rare wildlife, including ibex and mountain gazelle. Many treks start at Wadi Feinan, from where pathways lead south over rocky desert, through deep canyons, into green valleys, and up to far-reaching lookouts. Finally you reach the massive Nabatean Monastery to access Petra via the back door.

Need to know
- *Point in time: 100 BC–AD 100 (peak of the city of Petra)*
- *Length: 28 miles (45km); 4–6 days*
- *Difficulty: Easy/ moderate – rugged; camping only*
- *Best months: Feb– Apr; Oct–Dec*
- *Top tip: Sturdy footwear is required to cross the rocky desert*

99
Aksum Northern Stelae Field

Ethiopia

Take a short walk amid the leftovers of the kingdom of Aksum. This stelae field is littered with 120 carved, grey-granite obelisks, built in AD 300–500 for purposes still unknown.

100
IHLARA GORGE

Cappadocia, Turkey

Cappadocia looks like something out of a fairy tale. And perhaps this strange, honey-hued landscape of soft tuff rock *did* feel like a dream for the monks who first sought refuge in its caves in the fourth century; they went on to preach Christianity from its underground churches. The 10-mile (16km) walk from Ihlara to Selime, along the crimson-walled Ihlara Valley, is a lesson in the area's gloriously weird geology, the local flora and fauna (from falcons to frogs), and its Byzantine backstory. En route, descend around 360 steps to visit a cluster of subterranean churches, some in a state of disrepair, others displaying ancient yet still vivid frescoes.

101
SAN AGUSTÍN TRAILS

Southern Colombia

Not a lot is known about the civilisation responsible for the ancient settlement of San Agustín. It flourished from around AD 100 to 800 and, during that time, created an abundance of burial mounds, funerary monuments, and strange stone statues. These are scattered across the eastern Andean foothills, with more than 100 curious carvings to be found on walks within the San Agustín Archaeological Park. There are also trails to more widely spread relics, such as a 2-mile (3km) path to La Chaquira, a dramatic spot overlooking the Magdalena Valley, and a 5-mile (8km) route to La Pelota, where the statues are painted with natural dyes.

102
GREAT WALL WALK

China

Hike short, crumbling sections of the Great Wall to get a flavor of this gargantuan fortification.

First, a disclaimer. It is impossible to walk all of the Great Wall of China. This is because no one really knows where it all is. This isn't one wall. It is many walls, a multitude of defensive strands built over 2,000 years by successive paranoid Chinese dynasties to protect themselves from the 'barbarians' to the north. Its construction was started in the Warring States period and continued right up to the time of the Ming dynasty in the seventeenth century.

It's common to quote a total wall length of around 3,100 miles (5,000km). This is due to the wall's nickname since the Qin dynasty (221 to 206 BC): Wan-Li Changcheng. This translates as 'a wall that measures 10,000 half kilometres', which is around 3,100 miles (5,000km). However, centuries of additions and renovations expanded the wall significantly and, in 2012, following a five-year survey, China's State Administration of Cultural Heritage declared the wall to measure a mighty 13,170.7 miles (21,196.18km). Another misleading figure, as some chunks of newer wall were built on top of old parts, so were effectively counted twice. Isolated segments of state-boundary fortifications – therefore, not technically part of the Great Wall – were also included in the final total.

Perhaps all you really need to know is that the Great Wall of China is very long indeed, stretching primarily from Jiayuguan, in the country's wild, wild west, to Shanhaiguan, on the shores of the Bohai Sea. It started life as a mud-and-rock barricade, though little of this rudimentary design remains. The majority of the Great Wall that is visible today (which isn't very much) is courtesy of the Ming dynasty's

Need to know
- *Point in time: 400–200 BC (period when wall was first constructed)*
- *Length: Around 3,100 miles (5,000km); 15–20 months*
- *Difficulty: Moderate/ strenuous – steep; rough; often nonexistent*
- *Best months: Mar– May; Sept–Oct*
- *Top tip: Avoid the first week of October – a national holiday; every major site will be busy*

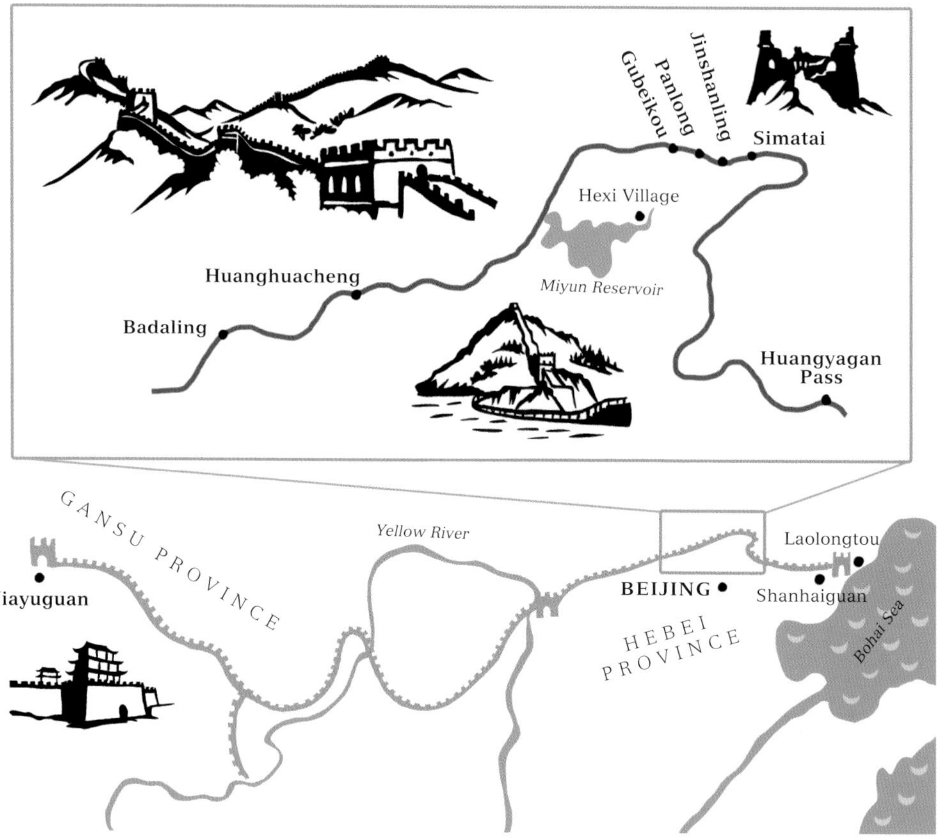
Jinshanling
Panlong
Gubeikou
Simatai
Hexi Village
Huanghuacheng
Miyun Reservoir
Badaling
Huangyagan Pass
GANSU PROVINCE
Yellow River
Laolongtou
Jiayuguan
BEIJING
Shanhaiguan
HEBEI PROVINCE
Bohai Sea

master builders. They used more durable stone to erect a supersize stockade looming up to 8m (26ft) high and measuring 7m (23ft) wide. It was during the reign of this dynasty (1368 to 1644) that the barrier acquired its iconic watchtowers, which served as signaling stations and storerooms. Each watchtower was spaced two arrow shots apart, so that no area was left undefended.

A hardy few have walked the whole wall (or their approximation of it), but hiking short sections is the most realistic option. Some of the best-preserved parts are easily accessible from Beijing. The wall at Badaling, 43 miles (69km) north of the capital, is the most popular, and thus the most crowded. It has also been so perfectly reconstructed as to look a bit like a theme park. However, the sight of the glorious grey edifice snaking away over forested hills is undeniably impressive. Perhaps it is better to tackle the Jinshanling–Simatai stretch (68 miles / 110km

RIGHT: The sight of the Great Wall of China, snaking away into the distance, is impressive in all seasons.

north of Beijing), a 7-mile (11km) hike along authentically crumbling, unreconstructed wall, dotted with obstacles and oval watchtowers. It's steep and rugged, but the moderately fit and sure footed should complete it in three hours. Alternatively, tackle the less-visited portion at Huanghuacheng (37 miles / 60km northeast of Beijing), which traces a ramshackle but generally deserted 7.5-mile (12km) stretch from Huanghua Road to the eighth guard tower. A longer hike is possible along the dilapidated but atmospheric walls at Gubeikou and Panlong. Stay at a farmhouse in Hexi Village to spend a day on each section.

It's possible to visit the wall's extremities too. Walk the rather grand 2.5 miles (4km) from Shanhaiguan to Laolongtou (Old Dragon Head), where a dragon sculpture marks the point where wall meets water. This is the wall's easternmost point. Alternatively, head to Gansu province, culturally more central Asian than Chinese, as the prevalence of Turkic-speaking Uyghur people attests. Stroll around Jiayuguan Fort – known as the 'Impregnable Defile Under Heaven' – which is the westernmost point of the Great Wall. From here, gaze out at the encroaching desert and all the terrifying unknown that two millennia of Chinese emperors were so keen to keep at bay.

103
Ling Canal

Guilin, China
Walk alongside part of one of the world's oldest canals, built in 214 BC by Emperor Qin. This canal is flanked by cobbled streets and offers a taste of ancient China.

MOUNT OLYMPUS

Macedonia, Greece

{ Commune with ancient Greek deities on the top of mythical Mount Olympus – a truly divine realm. }

Need to know
- *Point in time: 500–300 BC (Greek Classical era)*
- *Length: 13.5 miles (22km); 2–3 days*
- *Difficulty: Moderate/ strenuous – remote; variable weather; precipitous drops*
- *Best months: June–Oct*
- *Top tip: Refuges (hostels) should be booked in advance*

Mount Olympus is no ordinary summit. This 2,917m (9,570ft) peak, rising right by the waters of the Aegean Sea, is said to be the home of the ancient Greek gods. According to mythology, the mountain has been that way since around 1680 BC. This is purportedly when Zeus and eleven young upstart deities decided to wage war against the older Titans, the incumbent gods, who were led by Kronos and based on lowlier Mount Othrys. After years of battling, Zeus and his cohorts were victorious, and set up their seat of power at Mytikas, Olympus's highest point. Here, each of the Dodekatheon – the twelve Olympians, including Poseidon (god of the sea), Aphrodite (goddess of love), and Hera (goddess of women) – had their own palace. They spent their days guzzling nectar and ambrosia, gathering with their god-friends, and deciding on the fates of the tiny humans toiling down below.

It's a good story, laid down by one of the world's greatest ever civilisations, which particularly flourished from around 500 to 300 BC. This brief period – known as Classical Greece – gave us unprecedented advances in art, architecture, literature, and mathematics. It gave us Hippocrates and Socrates, Aristotle and Plato. It is because of these creative, inventive, groundbreaking two centuries that the ancient Greeks are generally considered to be the founding fathers of Western culture.

These days, Mount Olympus is less a literally divine realm, and more of a hikers' heaven. The tallest peak in Greece, it sits swaddled in a blanket of dense, green forest

ABOVE: Mount Olympus is the tallest peak in Greece, and said to be the home of the ancient Greek gods.

and rampant wildflowers. More than 1,700 plants are found here, 25 per cent of all Greek flora. There are plenty of creatures too: wolves, jackals, foxes, golden eagles, and a flurry of butterflies. This makes for attractive exploring in the greater Mount Olympus National Park. However, the real prize is standing on top of the peak itself and communing with those deities – in spirit at least.

A satisfying summit circuit can be made in two or three days. Start from the uninspiring town of Litohoro, just east of the mountain. From here it's an 11-mile (18km) taxi ride to the trailhead at Prionia (1,040m / 3,412ft). This is a scenic spot huddled in forest, with views up to more forbidding

craggy cliffs. Heading in a clockwise direction, via beech and black pine woodland and magnificent views across the Mavrolongos ravine, you should hit Refuge A after around three hours. At the refuge, hot meals, log fires, and bunk beds await, while the stars can be spectacular.

Make an early start the next morning to see the sun rise over the glittering Aegean Sea and to make the most of the day. The peaks are often shrouded in cloud or shaken by thunder by lunchtime. The safest way to ascend is up the stark, vertiginous Kaki Skala valley, which leads to the summit ridge. Around two hours after leaving the refuge, you'll arrive at Mytikas itself. A little disappointingly, you'll find a flag and a trig point amid the boulders, rather than the castles of ancient Olympians.

You could retrace your steps to get back down, but circuiteers should try the alternative option. Take the Loúki Couloir, seemingly stepping out into thin air to descend via the northeast face of fearsome Stefani (known as the 'Throne of Zeus'). Then walk beside the Plateau of the Muses to reach Giosos Apostolidis (2.5 hours). There's the option to spend another night here on the mountain, extending your sojourn in the land of the gods. Or carry straight on to the finish at Dhiakladhosi, a 7-mile (11km) downhill trip via the grassy knoll of Skourta. This takes you back to the trees and meadows – and back to the world of mortals.

**105
Kidapawan Trail**

*Mount Apo,
Philippines*

The Bagobos people believe gods live on top of Mount Apo (2,954m / 9,690ft), the Philippines' highest peak. It's a three-day hike – via lakes, geysers, and exotic flora – to its sacred summit.

106
APHRODITE TRAIL

Akamas Peninsula, Cyprus

The 5-mile (8km) Aphrodite Trail follows a mythical route taken by Aphrodite, Greek goddess of love, desire, and beauty, and her lover Adonis. Aphrodite was supposedly born from the waves off Cyprus and used to do her ablutions at a greenery-fringed grotto on the western Akamas Peninsula. The walk starts just above these baths, climbing amid boulders and wild shrubland to the medieval monastery ruins at Pyrgos tis Regainas (Queen's Castle). The trail then heads higher still to a rocky plateau, from where the views across Cape Arnaoutis and the Paphos Forest are quite befitting the goddess of gorgeous things. A truly romantic route.

107
MOUNT AGUNG

Bali, Indonesia

Hinduism had arrived in Indonesia by 600, which means – if you believe the legend – so too had Mount Agung. The 3,148m (10,308ft) stratovolcano is purported to be a fragment of Mount Meru (the universe's central axis), brought to Bali by the first Hindus. The island's biggest and most revered temple, Pura Besakih, sits high on Agung's flanks, at around 914m (3,000ft). As well as being a holy Hindu site, the temple is the starting point for a challenging five-hour climb to the mountain's summit. Most hikers set off at midnight to reach Bali's highest point in time to see sunrise, with the whole island laid out below.

AMATHOLE TRAIL

Eastern Cape, South Africa

{ Hit the heartland of the Xhosa
people for a walk with waterfalls,
wildflowers, and a hobbit or two. }

Need to know

- *Point in time:
  AD 100–500 (Xhosa
  people migrated south
  from central Africa)*
- *Length: 60 miles
  (100km); 6 days*
- *Difficulty: Moderate/
  strenuous –
  mountainous;
  self-sufficient*
- *Best months: Mar–
  May; Sept–Nov*
- *Top tip: There are
  basic huts along the
  trail; hikers need
  to bring bedding,
  cookware, and food*

The Amathole Trail is generally billed as one of South Africa's toughest treks. It starts near the missionary-founded settlement of King William's Town and ends at the fairy-tale village of Hogsback, which perches 1,300m (4,265ft) up in the mossy mountains like something out of *Lord of the Rings*. Between these two points, the trail climbs and falls amid rolling hills, ridgetops, indigenous forest, and innumerable waterfalls. Yet, while the terrain might seem tough to today's hikers, it's been traversed by the Xhosa people for millennia.

The Xhosa were part of the Nguni migration, which saw cattle herders from central Africa spread south around 2,000 years ago. King William's Town itself was a military base during the colonialists' nineteenth-century Xhosa wars, and has an excellent museum. Also, traditional Xhosa *rondavels* (round thatched huts) and cow herds can be seen along the trail.

The route begins in the species-rich Pirie Forest, passing giant worm hills and old sawmill relics. It then follows a valley ridge, swapping the canopy for dense macchia grasslands, wildflowers, and waterfalls. From Geju Peak (1,850m / 6,070ft) there are sweeping views across the Amathole Range, then a descent into a gorge followed by the hike back up. Next are pools and cascades (many ideal for bathing), before the magical woodland of the Hogsback Mountains. J.R.R. Tolkien did indeed vacation here, and it's easy to imagine hobbits hiding behind every tree.

RIGHT: Trek the Amathole Trail, from the Pirie Forest to the fairy-tale village of Hogsback.

STRANDLOPER TRAIL

Eastern Cape, South Africa

Hike with the spirits of the long-gone 'Strandlopers' (Afrikaans for 'Beach Walkers'), the name given to a subgroup of the indigenous Khoi people by colonial Dutch settlers. The Khoi fished and foraged on the Eastern Cape coast long before the Dutch arrived. The four-day, 37-mile (59km) Strandloper Trail runs through the Khoi people's former heartland, from the eco-centre at Kei Mouth to the town of Gonubie. It links high cliffs, bird-rich forests, challenging headlands, seaside hamlets, and wild waves where dolphins might be seen. There are also numerous shipwrecks (including a Portuguese carrack that foundered here in 1593). And there are a scatter of ancient middens, the rubbish dumps of those beach-walking hunter-gatherers who lived here centuries ago.

TOUBKAL CIRCUIT

High Atlas Mountains, Morocco

{ Delve into Berber territory to summit North Africa's highest peak. }

Need to know

- Point in time: 1300–200 BC (Berbers arrived in the area)
- Length: 45 miles (72km); 4–6 days
- Difficulty: Moderate/strenuous – hot; high altitude
- Best months: Apr–May; Sept
- Top tip: A winter climb (Nov–Feb) is possible, but crampons and ice axe are necessary

The zenith of Morocco's Atlas Range, 4,167m (13,670ft) Mount Toubkal is also the highest peak in North Africa. It took until June 1923 for the first official ascent to be recorded, by thrill-seeking Frenchman Marquis René de Segonzac. However, it's almost inconceivable that this was the first time anyone had climbed Toubkal's flanks.

The Maghreb – the region of coastal plains and mountains between the Atlantic and Egypt – has been home to nomadic peoples for over 10,000 years, pushed north by the desertification of the Sahara. The Amazigh people, more commonly known as Berbers, have certainly been around since about 1300 BC. The fiercely independent Berbers have an aversion to outside control, and are masters of self-reliance, even when faced with inhospitable mountains or deserts. As such, it seems improbable, if not impossible, that no one had climbed Toubkal until 1923.

Hiking up and around the mountain is as much an insight into Berber culture as it is a peak-bagging expedition. This circuit begins in the highland village of Imlil, 37 miles (60km) south of Marrakech. The Imlil Valley is home to subsistence farmers, traditional Berber houses, walnut groves, cherry orchards, and now a thriving trekking industry. On the main street you'll find cafés serving mint tea to hikers dressed in Gore-Tex, shops selling food and toilet paper, and the Bureau des Guides. And there are touting muleteers, hoping to persuade you to use their beasts to carry your burdens. Imlil is also home to the Kasbah du Toubkal, a former citadel that is now a comfortable hotel.

RIGHT: Hire a guide to help you reach the tripod-marked summit of Mount Toubkal.

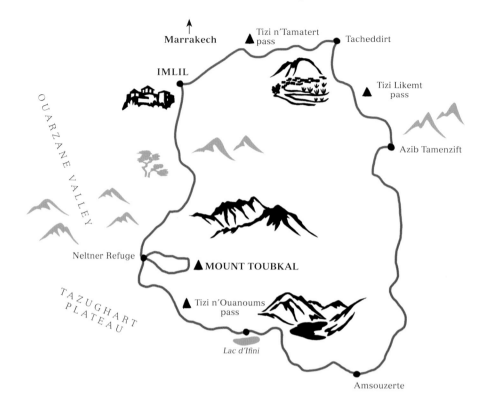

Hire a guide in Imlil and hike eastward to circuit the trail in a clockwise direction. The first challenge is the long, zigzagging climb up to the 2,286m (7,500ft) Tizi n'Tamatert pass, via small terraced fields and mud-brick houses. The views from the pass are impressive, as are lookouts across the ridges and tidy fields to the village of Tacheddirt. There's a refuge here, or you could camp nearby.

The next few days are wild, wonderful walking, first along the tussocky valley floor to the 3,554m (11,660ft) Tizi Likemt pass. The route then takes you via Berber hamlets clinging to slope sides, scattered *azibs* (shepherd shelters), and the odd enterprising local selling warm sodas. If you're feeling brave (or just dirty), a detour from Azib Tamenzift leads to a waterfall with a refreshing, if icy, plunge pool.

From the valley-hidden village of Amsouzerte, the route veers west towards Lac d'Ifni. The trail here is lined with neat, irrigated terraces that contrast starkly with the barren upper slopes and blocks of lava. You'll pass a mosque and welcome cafés before the lake, where it's possible to camp by the shore on a little beach.

**111
M'Goun Massif
Circuit**

Morocco

Walk through the cultural landscapes of the Berber on a four- or five-day hike from the Aït Bougoumez Valley to 4,071m (13,356ft) Jebel M'Goun. This is North Africa's second-highest peak.

Mount Toubkal is now in reach – though between you and the peak lie a rugged gorge and plains carelessly strewn with unwieldy boulders. It's a tough scramble up the 3,663m (12,017ft) Tizi n'Ouanoums pass, but the Neltner Refuge – Toubkal base camp – isn't far ahead. Sleep well at Neltner and rise early for the final summit slog to the roof of North Africa. The South Col ascent is the most used route. It's an often-chilly, three-hour grind up scree and around boulders to the tripod marker on top. But the panorama makes the effort worthwhile.

To complete the loop, there's a fine hike back to Imlil. It's a mix of ups and downs, of scattered shepherds' huts, and wind-twisted juniper trees. There's also one last view back to Toubkal, as well as across the Ouarzane Valley and to the cliffs of the Tazughart Plateau. All in all, the circuit is a tough but manageable hike through sometimes stark, always spectacular terrain. This is a landscape that feels completely wild, but which the hardy Berber have managed to make their own.

112
Reef Bay Trail

St John, United States Virgin Islands

Follow this 3-mile (5km) deep-valley trail to the ruins of a beachside sugar factory. Take a side spur to see some ancient Taino petroglyphs en route.

113
PUEBLOS MANCOMUNADOS

Oaxaca Province, Mexico

In the forested highlands of Mexico's Oaxaca Province sit the Pueblos Mancomunados, eight villages teetering above 2,200m (7,220ft) and connected by a 62-mile (100km) network of hiking trails. These united communities are the domain of the Zapotec people, an indigenous civilisation that sprang up here around 700 to 500 BC, and which remains today. Walking in this region – a striking ripple of canyons, caves, pines, and waterfalls – is a window into an enduringly traditional way of life. Hike into the sierras, looking for mushrooms and spider monkeys, before returning to a village to simmer in a *temazcal* (Mexican sauna). Then tuck into tortillas, swing in a hammock, and listen to the donkeys bray.

HADRIAN'S WALL PATH

Northern England, United Kingdom

{ March along Emperor Hadrian's
ancient barrier, built two millennia ago
to keep the barbarians at bay. }

Need to know
- *Point in time:* AD *122
  (Hadrian's Wall was
  started)*
- *Length: 84 miles
  (135km); 6–7 days*
- *Difficulty: Easy/
  moderate – short
  ups and downs*
- *Best months: May–Oct*
- *Top tip: Do not walk
  on top of the
  masonry wall*

Hadrian was one of ancient Rome's 'Five Good Emperors', a coin termed by Italian political theorist Niccolò Machiavelli in 1503. As emperor, he was an astute military strategist, and travelled extensively to visit his domain's vulnerable north and east extremes. But he was also a humanist, an art collector, and a lover of architecture (Rome's Pantheon was one of his commissions). In total, he ruled for twenty-one years, from AD 117 to 138. Unusually for Rome, it was a time of relative stability and peace.

However, in order to maintain that peace, he had to defend his borders. Which brought Hadrian to Britannia. This outpost of the empire, only invaded by the Romans in AD 43, was not fully conquered. The south of Britannia was largely under control, but what to do about the barbarians in the north? For several years legionnaires were embroiled in skirmishes among the Caledonian wilds. When Hadrian came to power, he decided to give up on mastering the unruly Scottish Highlands. Instead, he drew a literal line in the ground, demarcating the empire's limits and creating a mighty barrier and lookout post. From there he could keep an eye on those troublesome Pict tribes.

Hadrian chose the comparatively narrow neck between the River Tyne on the east coast – at what is now the city of Newcastle – and the Solway Firth on the west. In between lay the rolling hills and craggy escarpments of the Tyne Valley, dramatically stark moors, rich pasture, shimmering lakeland, wildflowers, and wildlife-rich salt marshes. He picked quite the spot.

ABOVE: Hadrian's Wall was built to keep an eye on the unruly Picts.

When originally constructed, the wall was a part-stone, part-turf barrier. Built for defence, it averaged around 5m (15ft) high, often with deep *vallums* (ditches) on either side. Building on high ground also helped secure the best vantage points. Consequently, this ancient barricade is now not only a path through history, it also affords fine views along its entire length – down to the Pennines mountain range, up into Scotland, and out to sea. Windshields Crags (345m / 1,131ft), on the great tabular cliff of Whin Sill, offers the best outlook of all.

The wall took up to 15,000 troops around six or seven years to build, and was bolstered by sixteen forts. Segedunum Roman Fort (at Wallsend) marks the eastern end of the 84-mile (135km) national trail that now traces Hadrian's border. Segedunum has been heavily excavated; you can see the barracks' foundations and commander's

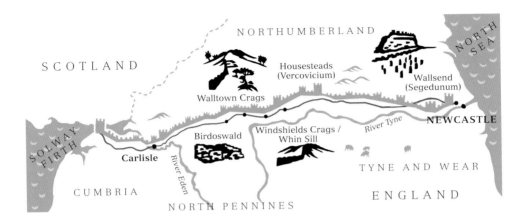

house, a reconstruction of the luxurious Roman baths, and a stretch of original wall.

But this is only the beginning. Although the rampart no longer stands in its entirety, the way is peppered with tantalising segments that practically echo with the sandal-slaps of legionnaires past. One of the finest is at Walltown Crags, where a long, snaking section of 2m (6.5ft) high stone undulates over the Northumberland Hills like a low-key Great Wall of China. It's still punctuated by two turrets and two milecastles – small fortlets that once marked every Roman mile and acted as gateways to allow trade between north and south.

The well-preserved fortress ruins at Housesteads (known as Vercovicium, or 'Place of Good Fighters', to the Romans) still look fortlike, and have identifiable granaries and latrines. The wall near here is also dramatic, dragon-backing along green ridges, in between the sheep. The stronghold at Birdoswald offers some of the most sweeping vistas, plus on-site accommodation if you're in need of a rest. There are subtler relics too. You'll soon come to realise that all those grassy lumps, bumps, and gullies aren't Mother Nature's doing, but rather man-made ancient earthworks.

To be granted unhindered access to such a swathe of World Heritage–listed structures is quite unprecedented. Therefore, walkers must tread lightly and obey basic rules. For instance, at only one point is walking on the wall allowed. That way, Hadrian's handiwork may be enjoyed for another 2,000 years.

**115
Hermannshöhen
Trail**

Germany

This 140-mile (226km) hike through the Teutoburg Forest from Rheine to Marsberg passes the monument to the battle of AD 9, when Germanic tribes trounced the Roman legions.

116
Fort Ancient

Ohio,
United States

Short trails lead around this extensive hilltop site of Native American earthworks, built by the Hopewell peoples between 100 BC and AD 500.

117
Nine Dragon Stream Scenic Area

Dehang, China

Stroll through idyllic countryside, rich in the culture of the Miao people, who have lived here for about 2,000 years. Try the hour-long hike to Liusha, where you can walk behind the waterfall.

118
Hittite Trails

Corum, Turkey

Seventeen trekking routes, covering 239 miles (385km), connect Bogazkoy-Hattusa, Alacahoyuk, and Sapinuva. The trails follow old roads and caravan routes used by the Hittites, the local superpower around 1600 BC.

119
The Corniche

Alexandria, Egypt

Promenade the 16-mile (26km) seafront walkway that hugs the second most important city of the ancient world. Alexandria was once home to the Pharos lighthouse, the Great Library, and Cleopatra.

120
LYCIAN WAY

Southern Turkey

The 335-mile (540km) Lycian Way was Turkey's first official trekking route, waymarked in 1999. However, its roots stretch back much further. The democratic but pugnacious Lycian people lived and traded on the Tekke Peninsula from around 3000 BC. Alexander the Great marched through in 334 BC. Today's hikers follow the footpaths and mule tracks he used, plus roads laid by subsequent Roman rulers. The Lycian Way trail runs from Oludeniz to Antalya, often tracing the craggy-cliffed azure coast, and seeking shade amid the carob, strawberry, and juniper trees. It also passes hidden historic sites, from Roman ruins to crumbling Byzantine monasteries, sunken cities, and Lycian graves.

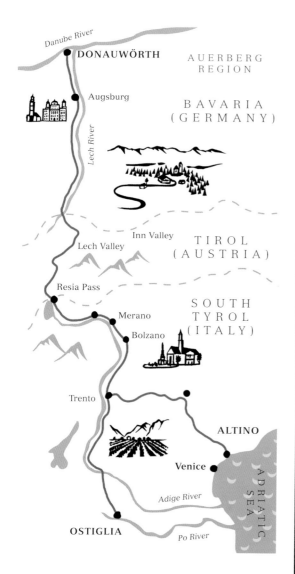

DONAUWÖRTH

Danube River

AUERBERG
REGION

Augsburg

BAVARIA
(GERMANY)

Lech River

Inn Valley

TIROL
(AUSTRIA)

Lech Valley

Resia Pass

Merano

SOUTH
TYROL
(ITALY)

Bolzano

Trento

ALTINO

Venice

ADRIATIC
SEA

Adige River

OSTIGLIA

Po River

RIGHT: Explore the Alps in the footsteps of Romans, on a journey along the ancient Via Claudia Augusta.

VIA CLAUDIA AUGUSTA

Germany, Austria, and Italy

{ Cross the Tyrol, the Alps, and Bavaria, following in Roman legionnaires' footsteps. }

It took the Romans sixty years to build the Via Claudia Augusta, their first real road through the Alps. It was designed to connect either the Adriatic port of Altinum (now Altino) near Venice, or the Po River in Ostiglia to Augusta Vindelicorum (Augsburg) near the Danube, at that time the Roman Empire's northern frontier. Given that this ancient highway measures around 400 miles (644km), had to tackle the mountains, and was constructed using first-century AD technology, sixty years doesn't seem bad.

The confusion regarding the road's Italian terminus is due to the two rare Roman milestones, found at Rablà and Cesiomaggiore. These commemorative markers provide helpful information about the road: its name, its length, when it was completed (AD 46–47), and by who. But each stone documents a different end point.

Historians do agree on the Claudia Augusta's path north from Trento. It led into the South Tyrol (via pretty Bolzano and Merano), over the 1,504m (4,934ft) Resia Pass, into Austria's meadowy, mountainous Lech and Inn Valleys, and on to the Bavarian city of Donauwörth on the Danube.

Romans mostly travelled on foot, with rest stations a day's march apart. Today's hiking trail is similarly designed, split into twenty-nine sections of four to six hours, each combining cultural intrigue with natural splendour. This includes the peaceful hills of the Auerberg region (inhabited since Roman times), the snow-dusted Tyrol, and the vineyard-lined plains of the Adige.

Need to know
- *Point in time: AD 46–47 (Via Claudia Augusta completed)*
- *Length: 373 miles (600km); 29 days*
- *Difficulty: Easy/ moderate – varied terrain*
- *Best months: May–Oct*
- *Top tip: Both German and Italian are spoken in South Tyrol; most places have two names (one Germanic, one Italian)*

122
Confucius Forest

Qufu, China

Hike in the home town of the Chinese philosopher Confucius. From the Confucius Temple, it's a twenty-minute walk to the cemetery where he was buried in 479 BC.

123
KALASHA VALLEYS

Chitral, Pakistan

In a remote valley in the Chitral region of northern Pakistan live a little-known tribe called the Kalash. It's alleged that these pale-skinned, fair-haired people are descended from the armies of Alexander the Great, who marauded into the Hindu Kush mountains in the fourth century BC. A two-day trek from Batrik to Balaguru, covering around 7 miles (11km), crosses the Donson Pass and enters the Kalasha valleys of Bumboret and Rumbur. En route it passes cedar forests and meadows, with views up to the snow peaks of Tirich Mir and Noshaq. It also visits the settlements of the enigmatic Kalash people themselves.

124
PEDDARS WAY

Norfolk, England, United Kingdom

In AD 60–61, in an early example of girl power, Queen Boudicca (leader of the Iceni tribe) led an uprising against the occupying Romans. She was ultimately defeated, but shook the Roman Empire enough to prompt them to build a road into Iceni territory – they needed to keep a watchful eye on the rebels. Today, that road is the Peddars Way. It runs for 46 miles (74km) from Knettishall Heath in Suffolk to Holme-next-the-Sea, on the north Norfolk coast. It is a flat march via river valleys, wild heath, rare round ice age pingo ponds, a Norman castle, and a deserted medieval village.

125
Carian Trail

Southwest Turkey

Follow in the footsteps of the Carian civilisation, which arose around 1100 BC. This 510-mile (820km) trail connects sea and mountains, ancient sites, and tiny villages.

126
Aurelian Walls

Rome, Italy

In AD 270, Emperor Aurelius decided to wrap Rome in imposing brick ramparts, 12 miles (19km) long and 6.5m (21ft) high. Today, you can trace its crumbling but impressive remains.

127
VIA APPIA

Rome, Italy

Back in 250 BC, the almost pin-straight Via Appia (one of the first Roman roads) stretched 350 miles (560km), from Rome to the port of Brindisi. These days, the first 10 miles (16km) are protected within the Appia Antica Park, and are easily traceable from the Italian capital. This is especially true on Sundays, when the area is closed to traffic. The Appia officially starts at Porta Capena and leads through the Aurelian Walls to Frattocchie (ancestral home of the family of Julius Caesar). Walking on time-worn basalt paving stones, you'll pass ruined Roman villas, aqueducts, and Christian catacombs. You'll also see the Domine Quo Vadis Church, which marks the spot where Peter allegedly had a vision of Jesus.

128
ARISTOTLE'S WALK

Halkidiki, Northern Greece

The great Greek philosopher Aristotle was into everything – from physics to theatre, zoology to walking. He was born in 384 BC in Stagira, and possibly thought many great thoughts while strolling the mountains of the Halkidiki Peninsula. This 20-mile (32km) trail in Aristotle's name wends through the landscapes of his youth. It links the small port of Olympiada to the ruins of ancient Stagira. Here you can see the remains of old houses and the *agora* (meeting place). It finishes in the modern village of Stagira, via a sweep of herb-infused hilltops, chestnut trees, and sparkling Aegean views.

129
Sabine Hills

Central Italy

Notorious for the abduction of the Sabine women (750 BC), when Romans came here to grab wives, this rolling countryside is perfect for a multi-day hike. It also produces delicious wine and olive oil.

130
Col de Clapier Pass

France and Italy

Trace the elephant prints of Carthaginian commander Hannibal. This 2,491m (8,173ft) pass between Savoy and Piedmont might be where he crossed the Alps during his 218 BC march on Rome.

NEBAJ–TODOS SANTOS

Cuchumatanes Mountains, Guatemala

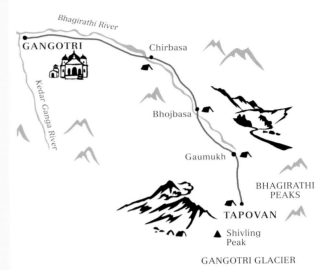

Bhagirathi River

GANGOTRI

Chirbasa

Kedar Ganga River

Bhojbasa

Gaumukh

BHAGIRATHI PEAKS

TAPOVAN

▲ Shivling Peak

GANGOTRI GLACIER

For an authentic taste of Guatemala's Mayan culture, take a hike across the Sierra de los Cuchumatanes. These high, remote mountains were largely left alone by the conquering Spanish. Subsequently, Mayan traditions remain strong here, albeit with some adulterated Catholicism thrown in. A four-day, 36-mile (58km) traverse between the villages of Nebaj and Todos Santos takes in the lushness of forests, cow pastures, and cornfields as well as the stark, alien *altiplano* (high plain). Homestays and village stops allow interaction with local people, while an ascent of 3,870m (12,697ft) La Torre – the highest nonvolcanic peak in Central America – offers an impressive panorama of more volatile spluttering cones.

PILGRIMAGE TO THE SOURCE OF THE GANGES

Uttarakhand, India

{ Walk along Hinduism's most sacred river, deep in the Himalayas. }

The origins of Hinduism are a little hazy. However, the spiritual texts known as the Upanishads – written in around 500 BC – were key in the religion's development, and in elevating the role of the creator-destroyer god Shiva. Shiva is one of the Hindu pantheon's greats. Among other things, he tamed the goddess Ganga. When she descended to earth, she was too powerful and could have washed away the country. Shiva calmed her, and released her waters gently, via his hair. A more scientific soul might argue that India's most sacred river actually issues from the Himalayas' Gangotri Glacier. But that doesn't stop Hindus from making a pilgrimage to the Ganges' source.

The trek begins in the town of Gangotri (3,046m / 9,993ft), where pilgrims visit the Ganga shrine before joining the trail. It follows the river through diminishing forest into the valley beyond, where colourful *dhabas* (restaurants) dot the route. The trail runs via Chirbasa to Bhojbasa, the upper valley's widest point, with views of the sharp Bhagirathi Peaks. Beyond, shards of ice may start to appear in the water – this is a sign that the glacier's snout at Gaumukh (3,969m / 13,022ft) is close. The brave or devout strip off to take a chilly dip here. Finally, the trail ends at Tapovan (4,463m / 14,642ft), where you can stand at the base of thrusting 6,543m (21,467ft) Shivling Peak – Shiva's *lingam* (penis) – to pay your respects to the god himself.

Need to know
- *Point in time: 500 BC (Upanishads written)*
- *Length: 28 miles (45km) round-trip; 4–5 days*
- *Difficulty: Easy/ moderate – high altitude*
- *Best months: Sept–Oct; May–June*
- *Top tip: Buses to Gangotri run from Uttarkashi, which is served by buses from Haridwar*

LEFT: Follow the sacred Ganges from Gangotri to Shivling Peak.

133
VIA EGNATIA

Albania, Macedonia, and Greece

The ancient Romans loved building roads, and the Via Egnatia was one of their greatest, linking the Adriatic Sea at Dyrrachium (now Durrës in Albania) to mighty Byzantium (Istanbul). Parts of this old highway can still be seen (at Radozda and Kavala) and, while the Via Egnatia's precise footprint isn't known, a conjectured 295-mile (475km) route across the Balkans from Durrës to Thessaloniki has been mapped for hikers. It's quite an undertaking, but the rewards are an epic, barely trodden trail via Lake Ohrid, Ottoman Peqin, ancient Greek Heraclea Lyncestis, and Pella, birthplace of Alexander the Great. Along the way you will encounter mountains, valleys, villages, and old bazaars.

134
Antonine Way

Scotland, United Kingdom

Built in AD 142, the Antonine Wall briefly marked the Roman Empire's most northern frontier. Traces of it can still be seen along this 37-mile (60km) trail from Bo'ness to Old Kilpatrick.

135
The Roman Walls of Lugo

Galicia, Spain

Some 1.3 miles (2km) long, and boasting seventy-one towers, the third-century fortifications around Lugo are the best-preserved Roman walls in the world. They are also navigable on foot.

136
Roman Way

England, United Kingdom

This 174-mile (280km) trail traces a triangle of Roman roads between Chesterton (Oxfordshire), Cirencester (Gloucestershire), and the Roman walled town of Silchester (Hampshire).

137
Tai Shan

Shandong, China

It's said that those who climb this 1,545m (5,069ft) mountain – holiest of China's five Taoist peaks – will live to be a hundred years old. It's worth a try. The hike, via 6,660 steps, takes eight hours round trip.

138
SIGIRIYA

Central Highlands, Sri Lanka

Looking at this massive magma plug rearing 180m (590ft) out of the jungle, you have to admire the chutzpah of King Kassapa I (ruler of Sri Lanka from 477 to 495), who decided to build a fortress on the top. It's a climb of 1,200 steps, taking fifty to eighty minutes, to surmount Sigiriya (Lion Rock). Starting from the lower palace's Boulder Gardens, you zigzag up steps to the rock-cut gallery of the Mirror Wall. Here, a spiral staircase twists up to risqué frescoes, which once wound right around the rock. The final ascent is via the Lion Gatehouse, where huge stone paws guard the entrance to the summit's sanctum and its far-reaching views.

139
HUASHAN

Shaanxi Province, China

One legend states that Lao Tzu, sixth-century BC founder of Taoism, used to preach from Huashan's 2,154m (7,070ft) South Peak, the mountain's highest point. Regardless of whether this is true, this giant of the Qin Mountains is one of China's five sacred Taoist summits, and has attracted pilgrims for millennia. Many people still brave the climb, despite its dangerous drop-offs and narrow, rickety ledges. The traditional route runs from Jade Spring Temple, via a gauntlet of souvenir sellers and the challenging Eighteen Bends to reach North Peak. From here, follow the Green Dragon Ridge to circuit the remaining four peaks. The whole hike takes around eight hours. You will need a head for heights.

ADAM'S PEAK

Central Highlands, Sri Lanka

Join a stream of pilgrims of all faiths for a nighttime climb to a sacred footprint.

Need to know
- *Point in time: 563–483 BC (lifetime of Buddha)*
- *Length: 4.5–7 miles (7–11km) one way; 3–7 hours*
- *Difficulty: Easy/ moderate – steep in parts; bad weather possible*
- *Best months: Dec–early May*
- *Top tip: It can be cold and windy at the top – dress appropriately*

Adam's Peak (also known as Sri Pada) is many things to many people. Spearing up from the lushness of Hill Country, at 2,244m (7,362ft) it is Sri Lanka's fifth-highest mountain. It is also the country's premier pilgrimage destination. On the summit is a large, 173cm by 79cm (68in by 31in) dent or *sri pada* (sacred footprint), which has been appropriated by a range of different faiths.

Hindus say the impression was left by Lord Shiva during his creation dance. Christians believe it was made by St Thomas, who supposedly first brought their religion to Sri Lanka. Muslims think it is the mark of the prophet Adam, who was forced to stand here on one foot for 1,000 years, in penance for being banished from the Garden of Eden. However, it is the Buddhist belief that is most powerful.

It's alleged that Siddhartha Gautama, the Buddha, came to the peak on his third visit to the country in the fifth century BC and left the print behind. One legend states that he trod on top of Sri Pada with his left foot, then strode right across the Bay of Bengal to Thailand, where he planted his right one.

Although it's not a long climb, it takes pilgrims far more than one footstep to reach the top, as it has done for millennia. It's said the first person to find the footprint was the exiled King Valagambahu (104 to 76 BC), who was led there by a deity in the guise of a stag. This opened the floodgates, and since then everyone from peasants to royals, as well as legendary travellers Ibn Battuta and Marco Polo, have paid a visit to this sacred spot.

ABOVE: Buddha supposedly left his mark on mist-swirled Adam's Peak.

There are several routes to the top. The short, popular 4.5-mile (7km) Hatton Route leads up from the village of Dalhousie, around 93 miles (150km) from the capital of Colombo. Most pilgrims set off at around 3:00 a.m. This allows them to reach the summit at sunrise, and to see the mountain's great cone cast a triangular shadow onto the mist-wreathed plains below. Because most people walk at night, the route is lit the whole way, previously by flickering lanterns and now by a string of electric bulbs. However, the way is illuminated only during pilgrimage season (December to May). Outside these months, it's a darker prospect. Make sure you take a torch.

The climb begins gently through a tea estate, and travels past Buddhist shrines. It then steepens as it enters the higher wilderness sanctuary, with sections of steps and handrails. Fortunately, taking a break is no problem. There are many *madam* (resting places) and all-night tea shops serving chai

tea to the mass of devotees. It can be crowded, but the soundtrack of spiritual songs and excitable chatter adds to, rather than detracts from, the hike.

The toughest test is the final haul up the Mahagiridamba (Great Rock Climb), but this ends with the ultimate payoff – exquisite views and the chance to pay your respects at the tiny temple housing the footprint itself. First-time climbers or pilgrims (known as *kodu karayo*) should take a fragment of pure white cloth to put on the sacred sole before worshipping it. Pilgrims should also ring one of the two bells, one chime for every time they've summited the peak.

If you want to earn more karmic points, opt for the longer, tougher Ratnapura Route (7 miles / 11km), known as the 'Classic' or 'Father's Path'. It starts from the trailhead at Siripagama, near the village of Ratnapura. This wilder path begins steeply, leading through a thick canopy of tall trees and then into cloud forest, an area rich in butterflies and birds. En route you'll face rugged, uneven steps, some dating back to the eleventh century. You'll also have to climb seven peaks, the seventh peak being mighty Sri Pada itself.

141
Babaji's Cave

Uttarakhand, India

Some say Guru Babaji was born in AD 203. Others say that he's still alive. Either way, you can hike to this cave 2 miles (3 km) from Kukuchina, where he allegedly passed on the teachings of Kriya yoga.

142
EMEI SHAN

Sichuan Province, China

China's very first Buddhist temple was built on the summit of Emei Shan in the first century AD. Now, the 3,099m (10,167ft) peak is one of China's four sacred Buddhist mountains. More than thirty temples – some very old – are scattered amid Emei Shan's forests and crags, adding a strong spiritual element to a climb. The ascent from Declare Nation Temple, via Long Life Monastery and Elephant Bathing Pool to the Golden Summit Temple, is around 24 miles (39km). The descent, via Magic Peak and Venerable Trees Terrace, is about the same but arguably more spectacular. Allow three to four days, and stay at the basic but atmospheric monasteries en route.

143
MOUNT DAMAVAND

Alborz Mountains, Iran

Mount Damavand is a dormant volcano and the highest peak in Iran. It's also home to a three-headed dragon, doomed to be chained here until the world's end. This is the story according to Zoroastrianism, which began in Iran 3,500 years ago, and was Persia's official religion from 600 BC to AD 650. If the beast doesn't interfere, it takes three to five days to conquer 5,671m (18,605ft) Damavand from the Gardeneh-Sar trailhead, east of Tehran. It's not a technical climb, but it's lung-scrapingly high, and requires a crunch over snow to reach the summit. Here, views to the jungly north, the capital's urban sprawl, and the Caspian Sea await.

144
GOLDEN ROCK PILGRIM PATH

Southeast Myanmar

{ Climb up to a glittering, teetering boulder, allegedly kept in place by one of Buddha's hairs. }

Need to know
- *Point in time: 563–483 BC (lifetime of Buddha)*
- *Length: 7 miles (11km); 4–5 hours*
- *Difficulty: Moderate – short; steep*
- *Best months: Oct–Apr*
- *Top tip: Hikers must dress respectfully, with legs and shoulders covered*

Such is Buddha's transcendental power that he can stop the fall of an enormous boulder with just one hair. On 1,100m (3,609ft) Mount Kyaiktiyo, a huge, gilded rock teeters on the summit's brink, perfectly balanced (reputedly) by a single sacred strand, which is kept in a pagoda on top.

The hair was brought here by a hermit in the eleventh century, and pilgrims have been trooping to this precarious spot ever since. You can cheat your way to the top. Crowded trucks ply the road up to Yathetaung, a mile (1.6km) from the summit. But the more traditional option is to hike the 7-mile (11km) Pilgrim Path from the village of Kinpun.

The route is well marked, leading up via Buddhist *stupas* (shrines) and stalls selling drinks and coconuts, past red-robed monks and barefoot pilgrims. It's a stiff climb, though mercifully tree-lined most of the way for shade. The rewards include views over jungle-tufted hills that seem to stretch on forever.

Kyaiktiyo's peak is peppered with shrines and, in high pilgrimage season (November to March), crowded with people variously consulting monks, lighting incense, meditating, and making offerings of rice. Men can cross a bridge over to Golden Rock itself, and even buy sheets of gold leaf to stick to its shimmering sides. Women must stay further back. Summiting for sunset is particularly atmospheric, as the peak heaves with pilgrims and candles flicker in the fading light.

RIGHT: Follow the Pilgrim Path up Mount Kyaiktiyo to one of Myanmar's most sacred Buddhist sites.

MOUNT KYAIKTIYO /
GOLDEN ROCK

Kkin Mon Chaung

Yathetaung

GOLDEN ROCK
MOUNTAIN ROAD

KINPUN

145
Banaue Rice Terraces

Luzon, Philippines

Walk amid the great, green agricultural staircases cut into the cordilleras here by the Ifugao people. They have been farming these slopes for over 2,000 years.

EL MIRADOR

Maya Biosphere Reserve, Guatemala

{ Delve into the deep jungle to walk along Mayan roads between a handful of hidden cities. }

Need to know
- *Point in time: 300 BC–AD 150 (Late Mayan Preclassic period)*
- *Length: 37 miles (60km); 5 days*
- *Difficulty: Moderate/ strenuous – remote; jungly; humid*
- *Best months: Feb–June*
- *Top tip: Hire an official guide*

Guatemala's headline attraction is the Mayan city of Tikal. From 600 to 900, it was one of the ancient Mesoamerican civilisation's most powerful capitals, and the apogee of Mayan masonry. Spread over a vast area, it comprised huge stepped pyramids, plazas and ball courts, temples, tombs, and altars. However, this grandeur, coupled with the site's tour-bus accessibility, means that it won't be just you and the toucans exploring here. Tikal gets very crowded.

But there is another option. Centuries before Tikal rose to prominence, another Mayan city flourished to the north. In its golden age (between 300 BC and AD 150), El Mirador was twice the size of Tikal, possibly home to more than 100,000 people and dominated by the 72m (236ft) La Danta pyramid. This is the tallest pyramid that the Maya ever constructed. Over time, however, the city was abandoned and swallowed by the jungle. It was only 'rediscovered' by pilots in the 1930s. Now it sits amid a concealing canopy of ramón, sapodilla, mahogany, and cedar trees. It is only 20 per cent excavated and still a long way from any roads.

Unless you hire a helicopter, hiking is the only way to reach El Mirador. It's a wild hike – a five-day circuit via straggly lianas, seasonal swamps, nasty chechen trees (which have toxic sap), and a field-guide-full of creatures including jaguars and fer-de-lance snakes. The climate can be hot and humid, cold at night, or very wet, and the bugs can be out in force. But it's the most intimate way to marvel at the ancient Maya.

RIGHT: Travel deep into the Guatemalan jungle to discover the 'lost city' of El Mirador.

Carmelita is the main trailhead. Here you can hire official guides from the local cooperative, as well as *arrieros* (muleteers) who will load their beasts with the essentials. This includes gallons of water, bags of rice, cans of beans, tortilla flour, camping equipment, and hammocks. From here it's a three-hour trek to the ruins of La Florida. This is a small settlement dating to the same period as Tikal, where you can see 2,000-year-old pottery and make camp for the night, serenaded by the jungle chorus.

The next day is spent negotiating the forest, looking (or listening) for screeching howler monkeys, en route to Nakbé. This ruined city was superseded by El Mirador, as the latter offered a more advantageous location, on the edge of an escarpment. Nakbé is a fascinating place to explore, with its crumbling platforms, temples, and *chultún* (deep holes used for storage). There is also a *sacbe* (causeway), one of the Maya's plastered 'white roads', which were raised several feet off the ground and measured over 20m (65ft) wide. The *sacbe* here travels the 7.5 miles (12km) to El Mirador.

Following this ancient chalky highway, you'll reach the ruins the next day, a bush-encroached spread of temples, passageways, giant carved faces, and high terraced plazas. Above it all, a little to the east, is La Danta. It's believed this pyramid was used for coronations and special religious ceremonies. It's also reckoned that it took 15 million worker-days of labour to build. The climb to the top is steep and precarious, but the views over the seemingly never-ending jungle make you wonder how many other 'lost cities' might lie out there.

After a night camping near the researchers' buildings (archaeologists work here in the wet season, May to September), the next day's 12-mile (19km) hike is to El Tintal. Again, this is along a causeway, and is a vast Mayan site, second only in size to El Mirador itself. Here there is an enormous ball court, a red sandstone *stela* (stone column), and a 49m (160ft) high pyramid. This is the perfect place from which to watch a final sunset sink into the sea of green, before hiking back to Carmelita – and civilisation – the next day.

Crete, Greece

The Europe-spanning E4 trail ends with a flourish in Crete. Here, a 200-mile (320km) section traverses the island, via its sparkling coastline, rugged mountains, and Minoan relics.

148
RWENZORI CIRCUIT

Uganda

Ptolmey's *Geographia*, written around AD 150, was the first text to claim that the Nile's source lay in the 'Lunae Montes'. Exactly where those 'montes' were was unclear, but the fact remained undisputed for centuries. Uganda's Rwenzoris (the fabled 'Mountains of the Moon') are the strongest contender, their glaciers dripping into the Nile basin. They make for interesting, offbeat trekking too, with a 30-mile (48km) loop from Nyakalengija encompassing lakes, peaks, squelchy bogs, and a range of climatic zones. It's a hike that's rich in giant lobelia, thick forest, colobus monkeys, and 290 species of birds. Enlisting a local guide and Bakonzo porters is advised.

149
ROTA VICENTINA

Alentejo, Portugal

The rural Alentejo region encompasses more than a third of Portugal, yet is home to just 4 per cent of the population. Also, its Atlantic-bashed coast sees few visitors compared to the Med-facing Algarve. Which all makes it a wild, wonderful, empty place for a walk. Various strands of the Rota Vicentina cut through the Sudoeste Alentejano e Costa Vicentina Nature Reserve, taking in rugged cliffs, time-untouched villages, and ancient cork forests – vital, since Roman times, for the all-important plugging of wine bottles. Opt for the 143-mile (230km) Historical Way, which starts at Cape St Vincent and veers inland to Santiago do Cacém.

150
VALLE DELL'INFERNO

Mount Vesuvius, Italy

{ Hike up one of the world's most
dangerous volcanoes, which once
engulfed a whole city. }

Need to know
- *Point in time: AD 79
(Vesuvius erupted,
burying Pompeii)*
- *Length: 6 miles
(10km); 4–5 hours*
- *Difficulty: Moderate/
strenuous – rough
terrain; steep*
- *Best months: Mar–
June; Sept–Oct*
- *Top tip: Trains run
from Naples to
Ercolano, from
where there are
buses to Vesuvius
National Park*

Mount Vesuvius is no historical artifact. This 1,282m
(4,205ft) stratovolcano, glaring over the Bay of Naples, is
best known for its cataclysmic antics in AD 79. This is when
it erupted with serious ferocity, spewing ash 20 miles
(32km) into the air, vomiting molten rock, and burying its
surrounds in a hot, deadly pyroclastic flow. The Roman
cities of Pompeii and Herculaneum were engulfed.
However, still-active Vesuvius remains a clear and very
present danger. It has blown at least thirty-five times since
the first century (most recently in 1944), and is likely to do
so again. Worryingly, around 3 million people now live in
its firing line.

This does give a walk on the volcano a certain frisson,
however. There are several hiking options. Nine trails,
totaling 33.5 miles (54km), explore Vesuvius National Park.
The 6-mile (10km) Trail 1: Valle dell'Inferno route ventures
up the mountain's eastern flank into the valley between
Mount Somma and Vesuvius, which was deluged by lava in
1944. The hike begins in Ottaviano, and climbs via pine
forest and a series of hairpin bends to an open area flooded
with pyroclastic deposits. It then joins the Strada Matrone,
the path used to reach the top in the 1920s. Up on the bleak,
scorched, strangely spectacular summit area it's possible to
add on the remainder of the 2.5-mile (4km) Gran Cono
circuit, a loop around the caldera, before heading back
down to safety.

RIGHT: Take one of nine
trails up Mount Vesuvius,
plus a loop around its
vast caldera.

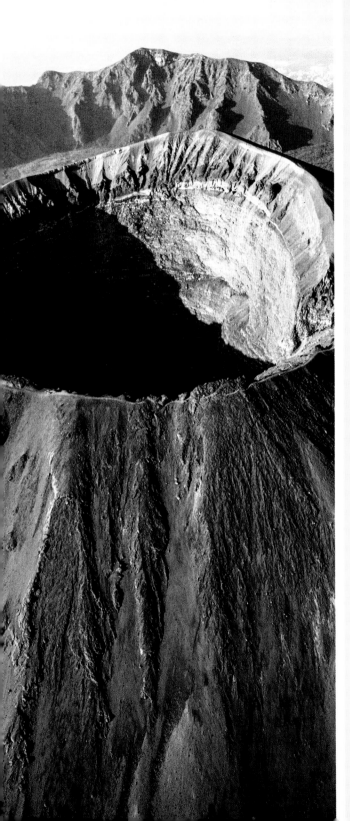

SAMARIA GORGE

Crete, Greece

Crete was home to Europe's earliest advanced civilisation – the ahead-of-their-time Minoans, who lived here from 2000 BC. The Minoans even inhabited the island's Samaria Gorge, a 10-mile (16km) gash running south through the White Mountains to the Mediterranean; they built the city of Tarrha at the gorge's mouth. The hike from the inland trailhead of Xyloskalo to coastal Agia Roumeli takes four to six hours. It passes small churches, pine forest, and, with any luck, Cretan ibex. At first the way is wide, but after an abandoned village the ravine narrows until, at the Sidiroportes (Iron Gates), its walls are just 3.5m (11.5ft) apart. Squeeze through to finish and celebrate with a dip in the sea.

MOSELSTEIG

Moselle River, Germany

Drink to the Romans on this wine-soaked walk along the twistiest of rivers.

Need to know
- *Point in time: 16 BC (Romans established Augusta Treverorum)*
- *Length: 227 miles (365km); 24 days*
- *Difficulty: Easy/moderate – mostly low-level walking; excellent facilities*
- *Best months: Apr–Oct*
- *Top tip: The Moseltalbahn railway provides transport to sixteen of the twenty-four trail stages*

Let's all raise a glass to those ancient Romans. For without them the Rhineland would be a far less intoxicating place. It was the grape-loving Romans who first brought viticulture to the Moselle Valley, 2,000 years ago. They believed that drinking wine daily was an absolute essential, for everyone from peasant to king. So, when the Roman legions forged north into what was known as Germania, establishing Augusta Treverorum (modern-day Trier) in 16 BC, the generals needed to ensure that their men had a steady, readily available wine supply. Importing from elsewhere was costly, so the sensible option was to plant vines right there.

It caught on. Two millennia later, it seems that the whole Moselle Valley is cloaked in neat, serried ranks. Even the sharpest slopes have been cultivated – the Calmont vineyard, just outside Bremm, dips at a 65-degree angle, making it the steepest in the world. The sections of the riverbank that aren't growing grapes are dotted with towns, villages, and hamlets selling wine, offering tastings, flinging open their cellars, and generally celebrating the joy of the drink.

This makes the Moselsteig (Moselle Path) a very well-watered walk, in every sense of the word. The 227-mile (365km) hiking trail, which wends south to north from the Germany/France/Luxembourg border at Perl to the Moselle's mouth at Koblenz, follows the entire German stretch of the river. Indeed, it barely lets the waterway out of its sight.

It's a drunkard of a route. The Moselle lurches in great switchbacking curves, as if it's had one too many of its own fine wines. For instance, via the meander-hugging

Moselsteig, it's a two-day, 21-mile (34km) hike between the towns of Bernkastel-Kues and Traben-Trarbach. As the crow flies, using a direct, field-crossing trail, it's about 4.5 miles (7km).

But where's the fun in shortcutting? The pleasure of the well-waymarked, largely genteel Moselsteig is savouring it like you might a light, crisp Riesling wine. The trail is broken down into twenty-four stages, measuring between 7 miles (11km) and 15 miles (24km), with buses and trains providing convenient access to the starting points. Along the way lie all kinds of historical references. To stick with the Romans, hike legs four and five. Four starts in Konz, one-time summer home of Emperor Valentinian, and finishes in Trier, where the huge Porta Negra (Black Gate) and old amphitheatre nod to the city's founders. Leg five heads onward to Schweich, via the Römische Weinstrasse, a former trade route through forests, meadows, and vineyards. Alternatively follow leg seventeen, from Ediger-Eller to Beilstein, which detours to the Nehren Roman graves.

Beilstein is a good stopping-off choice for anyone. It is the most fairy-tale village on the Moselle, a tight, narrow cluster of medieval, half-timbered houses that looks like it could be home to the Brothers Grimm. It is actually home to the twelfth-century hilltop ruin of Metternich Castle.

Indeed, there are castles in various states of dilapidation all along the river, from the twin-towered bastion at Thurant to the glorious nineteenth-century reconstruction at Cochem. Grevenberg Castle, above Traben-Trarbach, is particularly ruined. It was mostly destroyed by French invaders in the eighteenth century, but now shelters a café.

Taking time out at cafés and seasonal wine-tasting houses is one of the greatest pleasures of this trail. It's also wonderful to learn about the wine. As you walk amid myriad vines you will see how they are grown. Notice how the fields are overlaid with the area's Devonian slate to trap more heat, and how the vines are often trained in the traditional way, looped in a heart shape on a single post. These are ancient skills, passed down the generations, which ensure that walkers here can end each day in the most delicious of ways.

153
Anbo and Okabu Trails

Yakushima, Japan

Hike amid Yakushima Island's most precious forests. This 6.5-mile (10.5km) route passes Meotosugi – two embracing cedars. It also passes Jomonsugi, Japan's oldest tree.

154
Sentiero degli Dei

Campania, Italy

For centuries, walking was the only way to reach villages on the sheer Amalfi coast. The cliff-hugging 7.5-mile (12km) 'Walk of the Gods' remains the best way to explore.

155
Il Sentiero del Viandante

Lake Como, Italy

'The Wayfarer's Trail' runs for 28 miles (45km) from Abbadia Lariana to Colico along the eastern side of Lake Como. This is a route used by traders, tramps, and pilgrims for centuries.

156
Arif Karkom Trek

Negev Desert, Israel

Navigate 38 miles (61km) of old trade routes used by the Nabatean people around the third century BC. Look out for rock art, desert shrines, arches, craters, ancient wells, and oryx.

157
STROMBOLI

Aeolian Islands, Italy

Stromboli has been in a bad mood for more than 2,000 years, spewing, rumbling, and bubbling almost continuously since the time of Christ. It stands stark against the turquoise Mediterranean, its black, ashen flanks rising 924m (3,031ft) out of the sea. Remarkably, people live on the island and, despite the volcano's hyperactivity, climbing to the top is possible. It's a strenuous three-hour hike up. Guided trips depart in the late afternoon, to ensure you arrive for sunset, or after dark, to better see Stromboli's pyrotechnics against the night sky. Watch the magma spurt, smell the sulphur, and feel the ominous trembling of the ground beneath your feet.

TASH RABAT PASS

Tian Shan Mountains, Kyrgyzstan

{ Trace a strand of the Silk Road from
a mountain-nestled caravanserai
in remote central Asia. }

Need to know
- *Point in time: 200 BC
  (start of the Silk Road)*
- *Length: 8–10 hours*
- *Difficulty: Strenuous –
  remote; wild; steep*
- *Best months: July–
  Aug*
- *Top tip: Tash Rabat is
  320 miles (520km)
  from Bishkek; there is
  no public transport*

The Silk Road had many strands. This ancient trade route, along which precious goods and ideas were transported, wasn't a single road but a network of highways, squiggling between Chang'an (Xi'an), in the east, and Constantinople (Istanbul), on the edge of Europe. Transborder commerce had existed for centuries, but the Silk Road came to fruition in 200 BC, when China first made contact with the West.

Hiking the whole road – around 4,970 miles (8,000km) – isn't really practical, but the climb to southern Kyrgyzstan's Tash Rabat Pass gives an atmospheric insight into the challenges those early traders faced. The pass is in the Tian Shan (Celestial Mountains), close to the Torugart Pass into China. From here, merchants would have been heading to or from Kashgar's massive market.

The starting point for a tough eight-hour trek is the fifteenth-century Tash Rabat caravanserai. It's a fine example of the staging posts that lined the Silk Road, a complex of rooms where traders would have rested and resupplied. From here the hike follows an old caravan route alongside the river, climbing a meadow amid a scatter of nomads' yurts. As the valley narrows, the trail navigates river crossings and crags before revealing the At-Bashy Range. At the 3,968m (13,018ft) Tash Rabat Pass itself, there are views over the snowcapped Tian Shan, Lake Chatyr-Kol, and the Taklamakan Desert. Today, it's a magnificent vista. For ancient travellers, it would have been a forbidding sight.

RIGHT: Follow the Silk
Road through the Tian Shan
Mountains, taking in the
view at Tash Rabat Pass.

GR7

Andalusia, Spain

This GR7 hike is part of the almost 6,500-mile (10,500km) E4, which eventually winds its way to Crete. However, this 435-mile (700km) stretch is a good and manageable start. It begins in Tarifa, on the Straits of Gibraltar, and leaves the southern Spanish province at Puebla de don Fadrique, following trade routes used by the ancient Romans. However, as Andalusia is the physical and cultural frontier between Europe and Africa, walking here reveals a mix of influences and legacies, from Moorish towns to the tumbling white Berber villages of the Alpujarras. This walk is a great way to explore them all.

160
GEMMI PASS

Bernese Alps, Switzerland

Gazing at the sheer rock wall behind the Alpine village of Leukerbad, it seems impossible there could be any way through. But since Roman times – and even perhaps before – intrepid travellers, traders, troops, and pilgrims have used a niche here to get over the mountains. The Gemmi Pass is 2,270m (7,448ft) high. It's a relentless, winding climb of nearly 1,000m (3,000ft) to get to the pass and its eerie plateau of rugged rock and scree, murky lakes, and an inn once renowned for bandits. After crossing this netherworld, plunge back down into cow-grazed green, descending swiftly through pine trees to the Kander Valley. You will have mastered this mountainous obstacle in the space of 12 miles (19km).

POLAND

KRAKÓW

Wisla River

Wieliczka
Salt Mine

Váh River

▲
TATRAS MOUNTAINS

Vlkolínec •

SLOVAKIA

Banská Štiavnica
Gold Mine

Danube Bend

Esztergom

BUDAPEST

HUNGARY

161
AMBER TRAIL

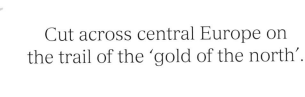

Poland, Slovakia, and Hungary

{ Cut across central Europe on the trail of the 'gold of the north'. }

As far back as the sixteenth century BC, amber was big business. This honey-coloured fossilised resin was desired for jewellery and decoration. The ancient Egyptians even believed that it protected mummies against decay. So, to satisfy the likes of the pharaohs, the amber had to be transported from its source in the Baltic region, across Europe and beyond. The Amber Road, like the Silk Road, wasn't one distinctive trade route but a transportation web. The most direct route is thought to have been from the Baltic coast to the Adriatic Sea, between Gdansk in Poland and Pula in Croatia.

Part of this prehistoric gemstone trail – between Kraków (Poland) and Budapest (Hungary) – has been more recently organised into a 192-mile (307km) greenway, although the waymarking is far from complete. It heads to Poland's Wieliczka Salt Mine, where chapels have been carved from the salt. It visits the old gold-mining town of Banská Štiavnica, a scatter of wooden Slovak churches, and passes near the fourteenth-century village of Vlkolínec. It crosses the border at Esztergom, one of Hungary's oldest towns. It also traverses fine natural countryside, from meadows and pastures to the high Tatras Mountains and the great Danube Bend. This is a route to dip into. Just be sure to visit traditional towns and villages en route, where craft markets still sell trinkets made from the 'gold of the north'.

Need to know
- *Point in time: 1600 BC (amber trade thrived)*
- *Length: 192 miles (307km); 15–18 days*
- *Difficulty: Moderate – varied; not well marked*
- *Best months: Apr–Oct*
- *Top tip: Non-EU nationals will need a Schengen visa to cross borders*

162
Selma Plateau

Eastern Hajar Mountains, Oman

A two-day hike up Wadi Bani Khalid canyon to arid Selma Plateau and down to cool Wadi Tiwi accesses the heart of the Hajar Mountains. These peaks have been crossed by traders for millennia.

Visit China's very first Buddhist temple, built on the summit of Emei Shan in the first century AD. Scattered amid Emei Shan's forests and crags are more than thirty temples, adding a strong spiritual element to a climb here (p. 119).

CHAPTER THREE
THE MIDDLE AGES

{ Explore the 'dark' epoch from 600 to 1500, a time of pilgrimage, conflict, conquest, and crusades. }

MOUNT KAILASH KORA

Tibet, China

{ Make a spectacular circuit around Mount Kailash, one of the world's most sacred summits. }

Need to know
- *Point in time: 650 (Buddhism introduced in Tibet)*
- *Length: 33 miles (53km); 3–4 days*
- *Difficulty: Moderate/ strenuous – high altitudes; remote*
- *Best months: May– June; Sept–Oct*
- *Top tip: Accommodation options are basic pilgrim rest houses and camping*

'This is a place in the Himalayas where one can barter life for endless bliss.' So said the Buddhist hermit Milarepa of mighty Mount Kailash, an unmistakable pyramid of a peak looming over western Tibet. Its clout is both physical and spiritual. Mount Kailash is isolated and enormous, standing at 6,714m (22,028ft), and it is also a religious heavyweight, sacred to four separate faiths.

Hindus believe Shiva, the creator-destroyer god, resides here. To Jains, Kailash is where their first prophet achieved enlightenment. The Bon (the pre-Buddhist animistic religion of Tibet) think the 'Nine-story Swastika Mountain' is the centre of all spiritual power. But Kailash is best known as a Buddhist mountain. Although the Buddhist religion only entered Tibet from around AD 650, it is said that Siddhartha Gautama (the Buddha himself) visited Kailash in the fifth century BC.

Allegedly, it was on this holy peak that Buddhism replaced Bon as Tibet's main faith. In the late eleventh century the aforementioned Buddhist hermit Milarepa challenged Bon leader Naro-Bonchung to a race up Kailash. Naro-Bonchung set off on a magic drum, while Milarepa sat meditating below. When Naro-Bonchung was almost at the summit, Milarepa overtook him, riding on the sun's rays.

There's no such celestial shortcut these days. Indeed, summiting the sacred mountain is not permitted. But performing a *kora* (circumambulation) is allowed, and pilgrims hope doing so will earn them karmic points. One circuit around Kailash's base – a journey of 33 miles (53km) –

ABOVE: Perform a *kora* around the base of Tibet's holy peak, Mount Kailash.

is said to wash away the sins of your current lifetime. You need to do 108 circuits to scrub off the sins of *all* of your lifetimes. The devout walk the route in one day. The extremely devout don't walk at all, but rather prostrate their way round – a cycle of kneeling and praying – which takes four weeks and immense faith. Most foreign trekkers settle for one simple revolution, on foot, completed in two to four days.

Reaching Kailash is the first challenge. The village of Darchen (4,600m / 15,092 feet), trailhead for the *kora*, is a four-day drive from the Tibetan capital of Lhasa. However, it's a spectacular road trip, via the monastery town of Gyangtse and Lake Manasarovar. In Darchen you can hire yaks, buy basic supplies, and spin prayer wheels for good luck before you begin.

Pilgrims walk clockwise, leaving town to hike up past *mani* walls (rocks daubed with mantras), to a wide plain flecked with sheep, goats, and nomads' tents. The trail traverses the craggy red walls of the Lha Chu Valley, with Kailash's summit sneaking into view. It then stays with the river, negotiating forbidding canyon walls, the odd grassy spot, and dramatically stark hillsides. Next, it's a rocky and boulder-strewn hike up to the prayer-flag-fluttered Drolma-la pass (5,660m / 18,570ft), the *kora*'s highest point. Finally, it's a

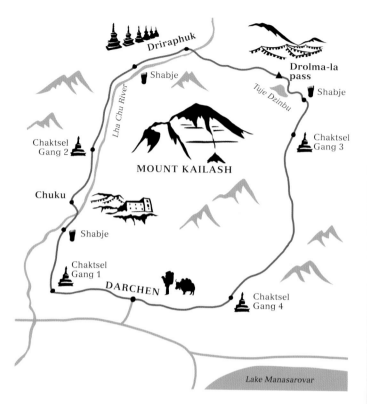

164
Lingkhor

Lhasa, China

This 5-mile (8km) circumambulation of the Tibetan capital, Lhasa, has been practised for at least 1,000 years. The circuit visits the Potala Palace, and Chakpori and Jokhang temples.

165
St Cuthbert's Way

Scotland and England, United Kingdom

This 62-mile (100km) trail links Melrose in the Scottish Borders (where seventh-century St Cuthbert began his religious life) to Holy Island, off Northumberland's coast. This was his final resting place.

steep descent via a sacred lake into a lovely long valley, to rejoin the plain and return to Darchen. The scenery is raw, hostile, impressive, and breathtaking, with each step offering a slightly different perspective on the holy mountain at the centre of it all.

Scenery is just one aspect of the Kailash *kora*, however. Ultimately this is a human trail, where multiple faiths hike in harmony. There are monasteries en route. Chuku, teetering on a mountainside, was founded in the thirteenth century by the sage Gotsangpo, who is credited with finding the *kora* route. Driraphuk monastery, built around caves where Gotsangpo once meditated, gazes at Kailash's icy north face. It also has a rest house, for those who prefer not to camp.

There are other sacred spots, such as the four *chaktsel gang* (devotional sites), where pilgrims prostrate, and the three *shabje*, rocks where Buddha allegedly left his footprint. The whole route is like a physical prayer – busy with pilgrims, festooned with blue, white, red, green, and yellow flags, and serenaded by the sound of mantras floating on the wind.

166
HUANG SHAN

Anhui, China

Mist-swirled, pine-pocked, jagged-granite Huang Shan is the Chinese mountain that launched a billion dreamy landscape paintings. Since the eighth century, when a legend named it home of the 'elixir of immortality', Huang Shan has loomed large in the national psyche. There are two ways to hike up it, via the Eastern Steps from Cloud Valley Temple (a tough 4.5 miles / 7.5km), or via the Western Steps from Flying Rock (a tougher 9 miles / 15km). The western route cuts amid the mountain's most glorious geology, negotiating 'Gleam of Sky' chasm to reach 1,873m (6,145ft) 'Lotus Flower Peak'. From there, it's easy to see why Huang Shang is often called 'the loveliest mountain of China'.

167
BOROBUDUR PILGRIMAGE

Java, Indonesia

The pilgrimage to the ninth-century hilltop Borobudur Temple is traditionally made on Waisak, Buddha's birthday. Saffron-robed devotees flock by the thousands to walk there from Mendut Temple, via Pawon Temple – a straight line of 2 miles (3km). Mendut is the oldest of the three temples, housing a fine statue of Buddha flanked by two *bodhisattvas* (spiritual beings). Smaller Pawon is thought to be the grave of a Javanese king, and a place for pilgrims to purify their minds before reaching Borobudur itself. The vast complex of Borobudur is built in three tiers, topped with a monumental stupa, and decorated with 672 relief panels and 504 Buddha statues. This is the biggest Buddhist monument in the world – a worthy finish.

88 TEMPLE PILGRIMAGE

Shikoku, Japan

{ Circumnavigate an entire island in the footsteps of a peripatetic Buddhist saint. }

Need to know
- *Point in time: 774–835 (lifetime of Kobo Daishi)*
- *Length: 670 miles (1,100km); 40–50 days*
- *Difficulty: Moderate – some climbs; long*
- *Best months: Mar– May; Sept–Nov*
- *Top tip: The route is largely on asphalt – comfortable shoes are required*

Kobo Daishi liked to walk. Born in 774, the priest trudged all over Shikoku, Japan's fourth-largest island, before gaining enlightenment at a cave in Kochi-ken. He then founded Shingon Buddhism. This 670-mile (1,100km) pilgrimage around the circumference of Shikoku is a fitting tribute.

Many *henro-san* (pilgrims) start their journey on the island of Kansai, paying their respects at Koya-san, one of Japan's holiest mountains. This is where Daishi founded his first temple. Pilgrims then travel over to Shikoku, where the hike begins. The goal is to visit the eighty-eight temples that represent the eighty-eight evils as described by Shingon Buddhism. The starting point is not important, as long as a full circuit is completed. That said, most pilgrims begin at Ryozenji, which happens to be numbered Temple 1. Most walk in a clockwise direction.

Henro-san stand out a mile. They traditionally wear a short, white vest and a conical straw hat, inscribed with the words *dogyo ninin,* meaning 'we go together'. Pilgrims also carry walking sticks. This represents the priest Kobo Daishi, and also helps with the steep ascents and descents.

The temples themselves (some of which offer accommodation) are simple, unfussy structures. Sometimes they're several days apart, sometimes several are clustered close together. The scenery between them varies too, from testing mountains and rural idylls to flat, lonely coastline and drab city suburbs. But this hike isn't really about the view or even the temples – it's about the path itself.

RIGHT: Zentsuji Temple (number 75) is the largest of Shikoku's 88 temples.

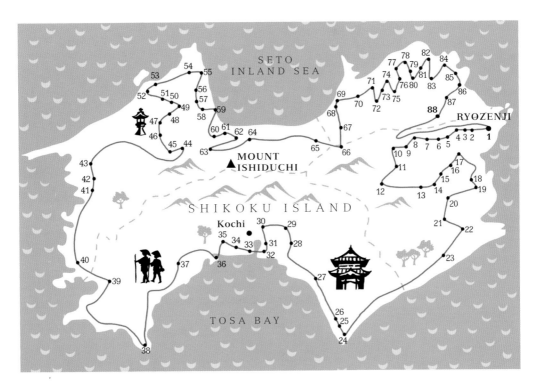

CAMINO DE SANTIAGO

France and Spain

{ Follow centuries of pilgrims to reach one of Christendom's holiest tombs – and the 'End of the World'. }

Need to know
- *Point in time: 830 (first church built on the current site of Santiago Cathedral)*
- *Length: 485 miles (780km); 30 days*
- *Difficulty: Moderate – long; regular facilities; varied terrain*
- *Best months: May–Oct*
- *Top tip: Hikers require a credencial (pilgrim's passport) to stay in pilgrim hostels en route*

There are as many reasons to hike the Camino de Santiago as there are *peregrinos* (pilgrims) hiking it. Walkers on this trail from St Jean Pied de Port in France to Santiago de Compostela in the northwesterly Spanish province of Galicia come in all shapes, nationalities, and motivations – as they have done for centuries.

The origin of it all was James the Apostle. It's alleged that this follower of Jesus preached in Galicia before returning to the Holy Land and that, in the first century AD, after his martyrdom, his bones found their way back to Spain. The first church to house these beatific remains was built around 830. Within 100 years, pilgrims had started to visit. Within 300 years, Santiago de Compostela was medieval Europe's premier pilgrimage site.

As *peregrinos* travelled from all over the continent (and still do), there isn't really one definitive *camino*. 'Ways of St James' spider out in all directions. There are threads spinning to Portugal, Germany, Norway, and beyond. However, the route to Santiago from the Pyrenean town of St Jean Pied de Port – more correctly called the Camino Frances – is the trail most commonly taken.

And it's a scenic one. Waymarked by golden scallop shells (the Christian symbol of St James), the *camino* first surmounts the Pyrenees to cross quickly into Spain. Walkers traditionally stop at Roncesvalles, a small village with a huge abbey where a pilgrims' mass is held daily at 8:00 p.m. The route then veers west through the provinces of Navarra and La Rioja, where limestone hills are streaked

RIGHT: St James reputedly rests within Santiago de Compostela's baroque cathedral.

with neat ranks of vines. Next, the *camino* inches between two sierras to hit Castile and León's seemingly endless *meseta*, a vast, high plateau, wavy with wheat fields. It then hauls over the Cordillera Cantábrica into the lush (i.e., rainy) valleys of Galicia.

En route are many cities worth pausing in: Pamplona, infamous for its bull running; historic Burgos, its old centre packed with architectural gems and tapas bars; León, with its magnificent Gothic cathedral; Astorga, where Roman ruins add extra depth to the walled medieval town. Then of course there's Santiago de Compostela itself, a World Heritage–listed labyrinth of cobbled streets leading to the ostentatious baroque cathedral, inside which St James reputedly rests. Each day at noon a pilgrims' mass here welcomes the new batch of weary arrivals.

However, the Camino Frances is as much about the journey as the destination. Its real joys are the people you meet along the way, the stories shared, the bread broken, the blisters nursed, the lows overcome, the highs communally celebrated. This is not a trail for those who like alone time, though hiking in winter can offer a more solipsistic experience.

Much of this camaraderie is fostered at the *albergues*, the simple pilgrim hostels dotted liberally along the route. These offer cheap accommodation for *peregrinos*, usually in mixed-sex dormitories. In order to stay in the *albergues*, you must have a *credencial* (pilgrim's passport), which will be stamped at the hostels. To qualify for a *compostela* (certificate of completion) at the end of your hike, you need to show a *credencial* with stamps to prove you've walked at least the last 60 miles (100km) of the route.

Of course, you could carry on. While St James's tomb and the delights of Santiago seem a fitting end, the *camino* isn't necessarily over. From the Plaza de Obradoiro, in front of the cathedral's elaborate main facade, a less-followed strand continues west for 56 miles (90km) to Cape Finisterre, the 'End of the World'. Here, Europe disappears into the crashing Atlantic, leaving pilgrims nowhere left to walk.

170
Sufi Path

Turkey

Follow the spiritual trail of the Sufi mystic Rumi. This route leads north for around 60 miles (100km) from Karaman to Konya, where Rumi was buried in 1273.

171
GUDBRANDSDALEN PATH

Norway

King Olaf II was, according to legend, a brutal man. But he's also credited with Christianising Norway. Following his death in 1031, rumors spread of miracles occurring at his tomb. He was canonised a century later, and his grave in Nidaros (now Trondheim) became a key pilgrimage site. The 400-mile (643km) Gudbrandsdalen Path was the main route north to Trondheim from Oslo. It still resonates with pilgrims' footsteps. Cutting through a wilderness of ancient forest and unpeopled mountains, the path passes ruined *sælehus* (old pilgrim rest houses) and 'Olavskilder' springs (purported to have healing effects). It also visits sites such as Bønsnes's medieval church and the Granavollen Runestone, inscribed with an early Christian prayer.

172
VIA FRANCIGENA

England, France, Switzerland, and Italy

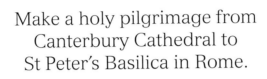

Make a holy pilgrimage from
Canterbury Cathedral to
St Peter's Basilica in Rome.

Need to know
- *Point in time: 990
  (pilgrimage by
  Archbishop Sigeric
  on Via Francigena)*
- *Length: 1,100 miles
  (1,700km); 80 days*
- *Difficulty: Moderate/
  strenuous – varied
  terrain; many climbs*
- *Best months: Apr–Oct*
- *Top tip: A credencial
  (pilgrim's passport) is
  required to prove
  pilgrim status; it
  may be stamped at
  churches and refuges
  en route*

In 990, Archbishop Sigeric undertook an on-foot pilgrimage from Canterbury, then the religious epicentre of England, to Rome, the heart of the Christian church. He was far from the first. The Via Francigena had been in use since Roman times, being the shortest way to travel between the empire's capital and the North Sea. Helpfully, however, Sigeric recorded his precise route, making it easier for keen hikers to follow more than a millennium later.

The Via Francigena leaves Canterbury's colossal cathedral, heads across fecund Kent – the 'Garden of England' – and sails across the English Channel from the White Cliffs of Dover. In France it plunges south, via Napoleonic and First World War battlefields, and the vineyards of Champagne. It enters Switzerland via the Jura Mountains, skirting around Lake Geneva to cross the Alps into Italy. From here it's straight down, traversing the castle-dotted Aosta Valley, the Apennines, and the romantic Tuscan hills to Rome.

The Via Francigena (Road from France) had fallen out of favor by the seventeenth century, but recently interest has resurged. In 2004, the Council of Europe declared it a 'Major Cultural Route'. Its infrastructure is not nearly as well developed as that along the more famous Camino de Santiago. However, the route is now largely waymarked and the Italian section has a good network of *spedales* (pilgrim hostels). This means following the Francigena is viable again, for the first time in almost 500 years.

150   *The Middle Ages*

LONDON
Dover
Canterbury
Calais
Bruay
ENGLISH CHANNEL
Arras
Lyon
Reims
UNITED KINGDOM
PARIS
Bar-sur-Aube
SWITZERLAND
Besançon
ALPS
Lausanne
FRANCE
Lake Geneva
Vercelli
Aosta
Piacenza
Massa
San Gimignano
MEDITERRANEAN SEA
Siena
Viterbo
ROME
ITALY

LEFT: The Via Francigena passes landmarks such as Montalto Dora's castle in northwest Italy.

173
Klosterrute

Denmark

The Danish Monastic Route uses old pilgrim trails to link a wealth of medieval abbeys right across Denmark, from Helsingør to Frederikshavn. In total it is 1,118 miles (1,800km) long.

174
LOUGH DERG PILGRIMAGE

Donegal, Ireland

Pilgrims have walked this 7.5-mile (12km) route alongside Lough Derg since the twelfth century, drawn by the story of St Patrick's Purgatory. It's said that Christ told Ireland's patron saint that a pit on the lake's Station Island could purge the sins of all who spent the night there. Nowadays, monastery-dominated Station itself is largely off limits, but this trail follows the old road pilgrims took to get there. From the visitor centre, the path passes St Brigid's Well, to hit the lake shore opposite the island. Here, foundations of the bridge that once delivered devotees to hoped-for salvation can still be seen.

175
TEMPLAR TRAIL

France to Israel

In 1096, God-fearing Godfrey of Bouillon set off on the First Crusade. At the request of the pope, he assembled an army to march east from France, with the aim of freeing Jerusalem from its Muslim invaders and reclaiming it for Christianity. It was a really long trip, covering over 2,500 miles (4,023km) and taking four years. Today's unwaymarked Templar Trail, blazed by two hikers in 2006, is an attempt to follow Godfrey's mission. It starts in Dijon and loosely traces the old Roman way to the Holy Land via Switzerland, Germany, Austria, Slovakia, Hungary, Serbia, Bulgaria, Turkey, and Cyprus, before reaching Israel.

176
Nakahechi

Wakayama, Japan

In 900, the Nakahechi – the 'Imperial Route to Kumano' – was Japan's pre-eminent pilgrimage. The 19-mile (30km) section between Takijiri Oji and ridgetop Hongu shrine is a historic taster.

177
Dharamsala

Himachal Pradesh, India

Various walks wend from this Himalayan haven on the Kangra Valley's upper slopes. Dharamsala is the home of the in-exile Dalai Lama, whose lineage traces back to the thirteenth century.

178
VIA SACRA

Lower Austria

The Via Sacra is Austria's Holy Road, linking Vienna to the pretty city of Mariazell so that pilgrims can pay homage to a statue of the Virgin Mary. In 1157, the Benedictine monk Magnus was praying to this little Madonna effigy in the woods of Styria when the boulder blocking his path magically split. A chapel was built for it. Pilgrims followed. The Via Sacra is still a wonderful walk, running for 75 miles (120km) via the vineyard-cloaked Wienerwald, traditional valleys, wide woods, and wayside shrines. It also takes in sacred Annaberg Mountain and the monasteries of Heiligenkreuz, Klein-Mariazell, and Lilienfeld. At the end is Mariazell's Chapel of Miracles, housing the icon itself.

179
SENTIER DU MONT SAINT-MICHEL

Northern France

The tidal island of Mont Saint-Michel sits off the Normandy coast like a giant wedding cake, its tiers topped by a Benedictine abbey. The first monastic complex was founded here in 709, and soon attracted *miquelots* (pilgrims). The 155-mile (250km) Sentier du Mont Saint-Michel is the trail to the abbey from Paris. Starting from Notre Dame Cathedral, the route heads west. It passes near Louis XIV's Palace of Versailles, continues into the Avre Valley, and heads across green and fruitful (yet battle-scarred) Normandy. It then hits the sea at Avranches for the coast-hugging approach to the island.

180
Kawa Karpo Pilgrimage

Yunnan, China

This tough 150-mile (240km) Buddhist pilgrimage makes a clockwise circuit of Yunnan's Kawa Karpo range, from Yangtsa to Meilixi. It travels via alpine meadows and high passes.

181
Pulemelei Trail

Savai'i Island, Samoa

Hack through the palms of Letolo Plantation for about 3 miles (5km) to reach overgrown and enigmatic Pulemelei. This is the largest stone mound in Polynesia, dating from between 1100 to 1400.

TIGER'S NEST MONASTERY

Paro Valley, Bhutan

{ Climb up to an improbably perched
monastery to commune
with a Buddhist guru. }

There are easier ways to reach the Himalayan monastery of Taktshang Goemba (Tiger's Nest) than hiking there – perhaps. It's said that Guru Rinpoche, the great teacher who introduced Buddhism to Bhutan in the eighth century, flew to its perilously cliff-perched location on the back of a tigress. He then meditated in a cave there for three months, and a monastery was subsequently built to mark the spot. However, if you don't have a flying feline, you will have to walk.

From the town of Paro, it's a short drive down a verdant valley to reach the trailhead, already at a breathy 2,600m (8,530ft). The route first climbs steeply through a forest of oak and blue pine that's draped in old man's beard and fluttering prayer flags. It then switchbacks to a ridge where a small café provides tea – and spectacular views of the monastery. It's a sharp onward climb, via a spring and a sacred cave, to the official observation point at 3,140m 10,300ft). From here, the cascading, whitewashed complex of Taktshang Goemba looks within arm's reach – though there's still a plunging chasm in the way.

If you have a permit, it's possible to clamber down a set of precipitous steps and back up the other side to enter the Tiger's Nest. Inside you can visit the inner *chorten*, the deity-daubed main temple, and the holy Dubkhang – the cave where Guru Rinpoche himself once sat and meditated.

183
Mount Athos

Northern Greece

The Autonomous Monastic State on this hilly peninsula has been an Orthodox spiritual centre since 1054. Various trails link the holy mountain's monasteries – which are accessible to men only.

184
Meteora

Greece

Six Byzantine monasteries (and many more ruins), dating from 1050 onward, perch atop sandstone pillars on the Plain of Thessaly. A network of ancient trails riddles between them.

LEFT: Climb through pine forest to gaze at cliff-perched Taktshang Goemba.

185
Régordane Way

France

This 140-mile (211km) trade route from Puy-en-Velay, near the Loire, to St Gilles, by the Mediterranean, was repurposed by ninth-century pilgrims flocking to Gilles's revered relics.

186
Cammino di Assisi

Central Italy

Follow superstar saint Francis (1182–1226) on this religious, relic-strewn, 186-mile (300km) route. It runs from the hermitage of Dovadola, Emilia-Romagna, to his birthplace in Assisi, Umbria.

187
Cheonnyeon Bulsim-gil Trail

Suncheon, South Korea

A 7.5-mile (12km) hike beside ecologically rich Suncheon Bay takes in two temples: Seonamsa, with its picturesque stone bridge, and Songgwangsa, established by a Zen master in 1190.

188
Hammond Canyon Trail

Utah, United States

This 9-mile (15km) out-and-back trek in the Manti-La Sal National Forest is littered with archaeological sites. This includes Three Fingers Ruin, an Ancestral Puebloan cliff dwelling built around 900 to 1200.

189
EAST MEKET TREK

Northern Ethiopia

In the late twelfth century, eleven churches were painstakingly hewn from the rock at Lalibela in Ethiopia by a king trying to create a 'New Jerusalem'. Over 800 years on, it feels as if the region has barely changed since. Life in northern Ethiopia's Wollo Highlands feels medieval. The time-untouched ravines, plateaus, and stark escarpments are dotted with ox carts and round, thatched *tukul* huts. Amid all this, a sustainable tourism organisation runs scenic, community-focused, village-to-village hikes. The rugged, three-day East Meket Trek is a good choice, with its unique rock-cut chapel, giant heathers, boulder scrambling, gelada baboons, and a chance to share *injera* pancakes with the locals.

190
PHNOM KULEN TREK

Siem Reap, Cambodia

Mahendraparvata was the first great capital of the Khmer Empire, founded by Jayavarman II in 802 on the slopes of Phnom Kulen, the holy 'Mountain of Lychees'. However, over the centuries, its great temples and stone carvings have been subsumed by the jungle. It was only in 2012 that archaeologists proved the identity of the forgotten site. This gives an 'Indiana Jones' feel to a trek here. A two-day hike, accessed from Siem Reap, negotiates the tropical forest to search out towers and pagodas, sandstone elephants, a reclining Buddha, and a riverbed carved with 1,000 phallic *lingas* (symbol of Hindu creator-god Shiva).

191
BAGAN

Central Myanmar

There are more than 4,000 temples scattered across the plains of Bagan. From the eleventh to the thirteenth centuries, this royal capital, by the Irrawaddy River, was one of the world's most populous cities. Now it's virtually uninhabited. There's no set walking trail, but as the site spreads over 16 square miles (40km²), there are plenty of opportunities for leg-stretching. The densest cluster of temples is in Old Bagan. Here, walk between revered Ananda Pahto, well-proportioned Mingalazedi (Blessing Stupa) and Shwesandaw Pagoda, a popular sunset spot. Walk south to Myinkaba for ancient stupas. Head east for the offbeat temples of Minnanthu.

NORTH COAST TRAIL

Easter Island, Chile

{ Hike amid mysterious *moai*, big stone heads carved by an intriguing Polynesian civilisation. }

Need to know
- *Point in time: 700–1200 (island first inhabited by Polynesians)*
- *Length: 11 miles (18km); 5–7 hours*
- *Difficulty: Easy – largely flat; short*
- *Best months: Nov–Feb*
- *Top tip: Do not walk on the ahu (ceremonial platforms) – it is considered disrespectful*

This trail on Rapa Nui (the indigenous name of Easter Island) may not be the longest hike, but it's perhaps the most mysterious. How any humans ever made it to this Pacific-marooned outpost is baffling enough. Rapa Nui, the surface-breaking summit of a subterranean volcano, sits about 2,300 miles (3,700km) off the South American mainland. Its nearest inhabited neighbour, minuscule Pitcairn Island, is still 1,180 miles (1,900km) away. But some humans *did* make it here. It's thought that the island was first settled by Polynesians, who landed in double-hulled canoes between 700 and 1200, possibly earlier. No one quite knows.

However, what these new arrivals did over the subsequent centuries is even more intriguing. As society developed on this remote little island, the Rapa Nui people started to sculpt. Using the landscape's volcanic origins to their advantage, they made tools from the tough basalt and sharp obsidian, and set to work on the softer tuff (rock made from volcanic ash). From this porous rock they carved a range of *ahu* (ceremonial platforms) and *moai* (huge heads). Some of them are up to 65 feet (20m) high. Even more astonishingly, they whittled these massive monuments from the tuff at Rano Raraku, a volcanic crater in the southeast of the island. They then transported the finished articles to coastal sites. It's not a big island – just 64 square miles (117km²). However, this was quite a feat for a civilisation lacking heavy machinery, yet driven by some strange purpose.

ABOVE: The best way to see the *moai* of Easter Island is to hike one of its trails.

Rapa Nui's small scale is an advantage for today's hikers, as it was for those early engineers. It would be easy enough to walk right across it, and several trails lead to the most interesting sites. For instance, a dramatic 3-mile (5km) track from the capital of Hanga Roa leads to the Rano Kau crater lake and Orongo ceremonial village, seat of the island's odd Birdman cult. And a 5-mile (8km) trail from Ahu Akivi, with its rare sea-facing *moai* (most *moai* look inland), leads up 511m (1,677ft) Maunga Terevaka, the island's highest point.

Perhaps the most spectacular option is the trail from Anakena Beach to the ceremonial site of Tahai, just outside Hanga Roa. This traces the wild, undeveloped north coast. Taxis run along one of the island's few roads, which links the capital to Anakena. The walk's start is behind the white sand beach. This is thought to be where Hotu Matua, legendary king of the first Polynesian settlers, landed. He's said to have lived in one of the bay's caves. The large single *moai* here was toppled by warring tribes, but has been

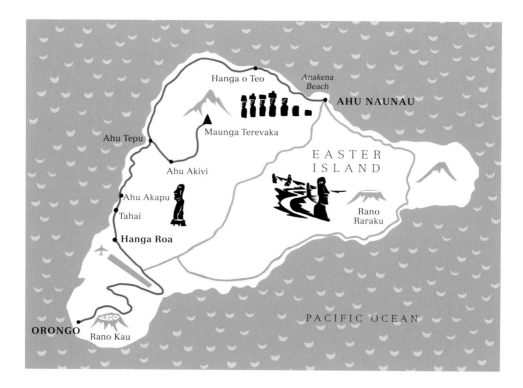

re-erected. You will also find Ahu Naunau, a line of seven statues, four of which sport *pukao* (topknots). These are curious later additions to the carvings.

The trail leads along the shore, undulating between the ocean to the right and fields of oxen-dotted green to the left. After a couple of miles, you come to Hanga o Teo, site of a ruined village. A little further on lies a burial ground, where macabre ditches are scattered with bones.

Continuing to cling to the coast, the track affords views up to Maunga Terevaka and out to the little isle of Motu Tuatara, and runs steadily downhill to join a quiet road. It's hard to miss the old settlement of Ahu Tepu, with its *manavai* (stone enclosures), crumbling houses, and broken *moai* strewn corpse-like on the ground. From the tall, solitary sculpture at Ahu Akapu, it's then not far to Tahai, one of the oldest *moai* sites. It comprises three *ahu*, one of which, Ko Te Riku, has restored white and black eyes. Tahai is particularly photogenic at sunset, when the silhouettes of the *moai* gain a backdrop of darkening seas and fiery skies.

**193
Kyrenia Mountain
Trail**

*North Cyprus,
Turkey*

This 143-mile (230km) trail runs along the rugged Kyrenia range to the tip of the wild Karpaz Peninsula. It passes a vanguard of three crag-top Crusader castles en route.

194
ANGKOR WAT

Siem Reap, Cambodia

The five-towered, relief-carved masterpiece of Angkor Wat – built by Khmer king Suryavarman II in the twelfth century – is merely the headline act of the vast Angkor Archaeological Park. Hundreds of temples, dating from 900 to 1500, are scattered across the jungle-clad countryside. Start by walking anticlockwise around Angkor Wat's 3-mile (5km) moat. Then, from the grand western entrance, head north, following the ceremonial avenue across the demon- and goddess-flanked causeway into Angkor Thom. This mighty ruin was the last Khmer capital, and is home to the three-tiered Baphuon Temple, and the strange smiling heads of the Bayon. Take Angkor Thom's east exit to find the tree-strangled ruins of Ta Prohm.

195
LAIRIG GHRU

Cairngorms, Scotland, United Kingdom

The first official record of a drover passing through the gaping, glacial scoop of Lairig Ghru dates to 1359. However, this 19-mile (30km) pass through the Cairngorms would undoubtedly have been used for centuries before, by all kinds of people trying to get between Deeside and Speyside. While the Lairig is a useful thoroughfare, it is not an easy option. This is wild, unsheltered terrain, snowbound in winter, rising to 843m (2,765ft), and very remote. The pay off, however, is a dramatic Scottish walk via broken cliffs, hidden glens, sparkling *lochans* (small lakes), and gurgling burns (streams), watched over by deer and eagles.

RHEINSTEIG

Rhine River, Germany

> Trace the illustrious Rhine River
> via a profusion of medieval castles.

Need to know
- *Point in time: 1100s (Marksburg founded)*
- *Length: 200 miles (320km); 21–23 days*
- *Difficulty: Moderate – well waymarked; steep sections; undulating*
- *Best months: Apr–Oct*
- *Top tip: The trail is well marked; signposts bear a white 'R' on a blue background*

The Rhine is one of the world's greatest rivers, and has been used as a transportation superhighway since prehistoric times. Now, the Rheinsteig hiking trail means travellers can follow its meanders on foot. The right bank of the mighty watercourse can be traced for 200 miles (320km), between the German cities of Wiesbaden and Bonn.

However, it's not just the rippling river, medieval villages, and slopes of vine-lined green that make this such an appealing walk. It's the profusion of fairy-tale castles. In the Middle Ages, this region wasn't one country but a scatter of fractious states with paranoid or pugilistic rulers. A frenzy of fortress-building ensued. Consequently, the Upper Rhine, between Bingen and Koblenz, is peppered with fortifications.

Many of the castles that the Rheinsteig passes have been reduced to romantic ruins. For instance, there's the remains of twelfth-century Stahleck at Bacharach, which sits above the Lorelei Valley. There's ledge-perched Burg Katz, which was stormed by Napoleon in 1806. There's the squat bulk of Rheinfels, the largest castle on the Rhine, and the two neighbouring forts of Liebenstein and Sterrenberg, known as the 'hostile brothers'. However, Marksburg, which lords over the town of Braubach, is the odd one out. Founded in 1100, and boasting a *bergfried* (free-standing defensive tower), turreted ramparts, and Gothic additions, it's the only medieval castle on the Rhine never to have been destroyed. It has been staunchly defending its patch for over 800 years.

BONN
Bad Godesberg
Niederdollendorf
SIEBENGEBIRGE
Bad Honnef
Unkel
Bad Hönningen
WESTERWALD
Rhine River
Leutesdorf
Bendorf-Sayn
KOBLENZ
Bad Ems
Braubach
HUNSRÜCK
Kestert
▲ Lorelei
TAUNUS
Rheinfels
Kaub
Stahleck
RHEINGAU
Kiedrich
Schlangenbad
Bingen
Mainz
WIESBADEN

199
VINHAS DA CRIAÇÃO VELHA TRAIL

Pico, Azores, Portugal

The nine islands of the Azores lie adrift in the mid-Atlantic, 850 miles (1,360km) west of their Portuguese motherland. The archipelago's origins are volcanic, which the inhabitants of Pico Island have long put to good use. Since the fifteenth century, farmers here have planted vines in the fertile lava grounds and built long, linear walls to protect their grapes from the Atlantic elements. The 4-mile (6.5km) Vinhas da Criação Velha Trail, from Porto do Calhau to Areia Larga, affords fine views of this World Heritage–listed viticultural landscape. It passes through an intriguing succession of small *currais* (rectangular plots), divided by black-rock walls, with the crashing sea beyond.

197
Rila Mountains

Bulgaria

Trace numerous trails amid the lake-speckled Rila Mountains (Bulgaria's highest), finishing at striking, striped Rila Monastery. This was founded in the tenth century by the hermit Ivan of Rila.

198
Mount Popa

Central Myanmar

It's a steep climb up 777 steps to Taungkalat Monastery, perched on top of Mount Popa. This volcanic plug is home of the Nats, thirty-seven animist spirits, instituted in the eleventh century.

OL DOINYO LENGAI

Northern Tanzania

{ Scramble to the explosive summit of the Maasai 'Mountain of God'. }

Need to know
- *Point in time: 1400 (arrival of the Maasai people to the area)*
- *Length: 6 miles (10km); 7–10 hours*
- *Difficulty: Strenuous – hot; steep; slippery*
- *Best months: May– Sept*
- *Top tip: This is an active volcano – seek local advice before climbing*

It's not difficult to believe that Ol Doinyo Lengai is the 'Mountain of God'. When it glows angry red, belches smoke, and spits a fury of jet-black lava, it certainly seems like some powerful deity must be at its summit. According to the Maasai people, this peak is home to Engai, creator of everything, who communicates his anger via such pyrotechnic displays.

As mythologies go, it's relatively recent. The Maasai people, a proud Nilotic group originating from Sudan, first moved south from around the fifteenth century. They spread into the Rift Valley to find better pastures for their beloved cattle. But 2,962m (9,718ft) Ol Doinyo Lengai, rearing up from the plains of northern Tanzania, must have quickly caught their attention.

That's no surprise. This youthful cone is one of Africa's few active volcanoes, and its eruptive episodes (or messages from a god, depending on your point of view) are regular occurrences. It's also the only volcano on the planet that spews natrocarbonatite lava, a type of igneous rock rich in sodium. Because of its unusual chemical makeup, this lava is very fluid – almost like oil – and cools quickly to a white powder, leaving Ol Doinyo Lengai's eerie, alien summit looking like it is dusted with snow.

Incredibly, given the geothermal sprightliness of this mountain, it is possible to climb it, although an experienced local guide is essential. The remote volcano is hard to access independently, and it would be easy to get lost on the gullied lower slopes. The steam vents, lava channels,

RIGHT: The youthful cone of Ol Doinyo Lengai is one of Africa's few active volcanoes.

and cracked and fragile ground can also be hazardous to those not in the know.

Ol Doinyo Lengai sits south of flamingo-dotted Lake Natron and north of Ngorongoro Crater, one of East Africa's greatest wildlife-watching destinations. Access to the mountain's base is gained via the Rift Valley villages of Engaruka and Ngare Sero. Camp nearby because climbs require an early start. It's best to begin between midnight and 2:00 a.m., both to avoid the searing heat of the day and to summit for a panoramic sunrise. Climbing under a full moon is particularly atmospheric.

The foot of the mountain is thick with 2m (6.5ft) high elephant grass, but this soon disappears as you begin to ascend, hiking onto slippery, frustrating ash and scree. Here, you seem to take two steps forward, one step back. Deep, soft-sided crevasses scour the slopes too, and must be traversed with extreme caution. As the gradient steepens to an angle of around 45 degrees, the terrain becomes a slightly more secure pavement of stones and rocks. The going is still precarious, however. You also need to look out for any strange swirls of air. The brownish dust devils are fairly benign, but white puffs of steam could indicate an imminent volcanic eruption, requiring a very speedy descent.

Passing through the Pearly Gates – two tall, white lava towers, which are remnants of an ancient explosion – a slope leads up toward the volcano's rim. There are two craters at the top, the inactive southern crater and the active northern one. In all, it's a spooky, other-worldly realm, the air tinged with eggy sulphur, the cracked ground a swirl of pitch black, ashen yellow-brown, and bright sodium white. Small *hornitos* (cones) pierce the craters and can act like fountains, shooting hot gas and that unique, muddy-looking natrocarbonatite lava from their tops. These are best seen in the dark, when you may be able to discern a fiery glow. It feels as though you have landed on another planet.

The views will assure you that you're still earthbound, however. As the sun rises, the Great Rift Valley spreads out below, with the Ngorongoro Escarpment, Lake Natron, Mount Gelai, and Mount Kitumbeine all peeking up from the plains. This is a sight to truly cherish, before making the speedy, scree-sliding hike back down.

201
Borgarfjörður Valley

East Iceland

A 7.5-mile (12km) trek into this ethereal landscape passes Alfaborg Mound (Elves' Castle). The area is laced with *Hudufolk* (Hidden Folk) legends, brought here by Norse settlers in the ninth century.

202
Havasupai Trail

Arizona, United States

Take an 8-mile (13km) hike into Havasu Canyon, a gorgeous side gorge of the Grand Canyon. This has been home to the Havasupai people for the past 800 years.

203
LA ARISTA DEL SOL

Iztaccíhuatl, Mexico

According to the Aztecs – Mexico's dominant force from 1200 to 1500 – Iztaccíhuatl was a princess who fell in love with the warrior Popocatépetl. She killed herself, thinking that he was dead. He returned and tried to revive her but he died too. God turned the tragic pair into volcanoes, which loom near Mexico City. The 5,230m (17,160ft) extinct massif of Iztaccíhuatl, known as the 'Sleeping Woman', can be climbed in six hours along the Arista del Sol (Ridge of the Sun). The trail from La Joya ascends via a craggy peak – 'the Feet' of the slumbering maid. It then scrambles up 'the Knees' and along to 'the Breasts'. From here, still-active Mount Popocatépetl can be seen smoking away.

204
MOUNT BROMO

Java, Indonesia

Start the 2-mile (3km) hike up Mount Bromo before dawn. That way you will reach the summit of this active 2,329m (7,641ft) volcano in time to see sunrise over the wide, dusty Tengger Crater. You can see ash-spewing Gunung Semeru just beyond. Don't be surprised if you see someone toss something into Bromo's smoking bowels. In the fifteenth century, childless King Seger and Queen Anteng asked the gods to help them to conceive. The gods obliged, on condition that the couple's twenty-fifth baby be thrown into the volcano as a sacrifice – or they would face its fiery wrath. The annual Kasada festival sees locals throw in offerings to continue to appease the peak.

205
BESSEGGENTUREN

Jotunheim, Norway

Take a dramatic ridge hike in Norse mythology's 'Land of the Giants'.

Need to know
- *Point in time: 1220 (Prose Edda written; Norse mythology popularised)*
- *Length: 10.5 miles (17km); 5–7 hours*
- *Difficulty: Moderate – sheer drop-offs; steep sections*
- *Best months: July-Aug*
- *Top tip: Buses run to Gjendesheim from the town of Fagernes*

It was the *Prose Edda*, written by Icelander Snorri Sturluson around 1220, that popularised Norse mythology. In it, he established the 'Nine Norse Worlds'. One of those was Jotunheim, 'Home of the Giants', an untamable, wintry realm of ice-crusted rocks, mountains, and deep, dark forest. The Norwegian national park that has assumed this name isn't so very different. There are no fearsome *jotuns* (giants), but plenty of glaciers, peaks, and pristine wilderness.

There are several hiking trails within the national park, located in western-central Norway. The standout trail is the Besseggenturen, which follows the Besseggen Ridge for

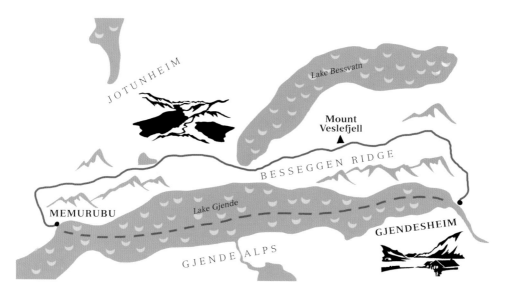

10.5 miles (17km) between Gjendesheim and Memurubu. Playwright Henrik Ibsen wrote that the ridge 'cuts along an edge like a scythe', and it certainly looks hazardously steep and narrow from a distance. In fact, it's never less than 10m (33ft) across. The drop-offs to the lakes below may still test the vertiginous, however.

A popular option on this trail is to take a ferry to Memurubu and hike back to the hut at Gjendesheim. From Memurubu, the trail climbs steeply before levelling and descending to pass between two lakes: navy blue Bessvatn and emerald Gjende. The trail then heads back up onto the increasingly skinny ridge, to the top of 1,743m (5,719ft) Veslefjell. This is the hike's highest point, affording views over the endless Gjende Alps. It's then downhill to the finish – unless a giant gets in the way . . .

CIUDAD PERDIDA

Sierra Nevada, Colombia

{ Blaze through the steamy
jungle to reach the 'Lost City'
of the Tayrona people. }

Need to know
- *Point in time: 800
  (Teyuna built)*
- *Length: 28 miles
  (45km); 5 days*
- *Difficulty: Moderate –
  hot and humid; some
  climbs*
- *Best months: Dec–Mar*
- *Top tip: Santa Marta,
  gateway to the Sierra
  Nevada, is a four-hour
  bus ride from
  Cartagena*

Just as the Inca hid Machu Picchu amid the Andes, the
Tayrona people secreted their own Ciudad Perdida (Lost City)
deep inside Colombia's Caribbean-coast jungle. However,
they did this about 600 years earlier. The Sierra Nevada
settlement, also known as Teyuna, was built around 800.
Its houses, plazas, staircases, and ceremonial sites are
thought to have supported up to 10,000 people. Then,
with the arrival of Spanish conquistadores, Teyuna was
abandoned, forgotten, and reclaimed by the bush. It was
rediscovered only in the 1970s and, long off limits due to
guerrilla activity, only recently opened to trekkers.

The Ciudad Perdida trek begins with a bumpy drive from
Santa Marta to the trailhead, at the village of Machete Pelao.
From here the route largely leaves behind civilisation, winding
via smallholdings, coffee plantations, a few taxing climbs, and
trees alive with twittering birds. There are many rivers to
negotiate – some crossing points have stepping-stones, others
require a wade or swim. There's also the chance to meet the
ethnic Wiwa and Kogui people, who live among these hot hills,
and who offer fresh fruit to hungry hikers.

The final trek to Teyuna itself follows the Buritaca River.
It then ascends 1,200 mossy steps to reach the ancient city's
circular stone terraces, perched up at 1,300m (4,265ft) in the
mountains. The Tayrona people are long gone, but a handful
of soldiers keep it safe for today's jungle adventurers.

207
Kjalvegur

Iceland

This wild, 27-mile
(44 km) route follows
ancient horse trails
used by Vikings
to cross the
inhospitable interior
of Iceland in the
Middle Ages. It's
said to be haunted
by them still.

RIGHT: Find the 'Lost City' of Teyuna deep in the Colombian jungle.

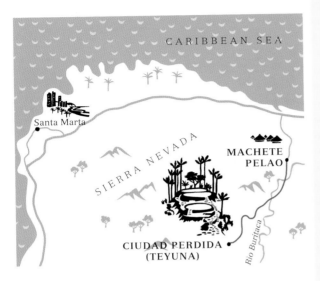

GR221: DRY STONE ROUTE

Mallorca, Spain

The Serra de Tramuntana, the northern spine of Mallorca, is an attractive mountain range. It's also a cultural landscape that tells the story of the medieval Mediterranean. Amid its ridges and sheer-sided peaks is a network of smallholdings, orchards, and olive groves. It is divided by old stone walls, and irrigated by ancient canals. Here, Moorish water-harvesting techniques and Christian land management combined, as Mallorca changed religious allegiances around the thirteenth century. The 84-mile (135km) GR221 Ruta de Pedra en Sec (Dry Stone Route) links southwest Port d'Andratx to northwest Pollenca, via the cobbled paths and drystone walls of those early agriculturalists. There is plenty of spectacular natural scenery too.

RAKIURA TRACK

Stewart Island, New Zealand

{ Make a loop around part of this southern isle via native forest, abundant birds, and Maori history. }

Need to know
- *Point in time: 1200 (first Polynesians arrived on Stewart Island)*
- *Length: 20 miles (32km); 3 days*
- *Difficulty: Easy/ moderate – well- maintained; boardwalked sections; variable weather*
- *Best months: Nov– Mar*
- *Top tip: Huts and campsites must be booked in advance*

While the Toltec Empire was falling in Mexico, the samurai clans were warring in Japan, and Genghis Khan was uniting the Mongol tribes, uninhabited New Zealand was only just welcoming its first humans. This remote archipelago, hidden at the southwestern edge of the vast Pacific, was the world's last large land mass to be settled. Intrepid Polynesians, paddling their *waka* (canoes), finally found it in around 1200.

This means New Zealand was left to its own devices for a long time. It was formed 540 million years ago, part of the ancient supercontinent of Gondwana. However, according to the legends of the newly arrived Maori, the country's origins were somewhat different. They believed South Island was the canoe of their demigod Maui, North Island was the fish Maui pulled from the sea, and Stewart Island was the anchor that secured the canoe as Maui hauled up the fish.

Stewart Island, a 650-square-mile (1,680km^2) outpost floating 19 miles (30km) off South Island's bottom, is probably the part of New Zealand least changed since the days of those early pioneers. The manuka shrubland, muddy swamps, and podocarp and hardwood forests remain. The flora, fish, and birdlife that first drew the Maori is still abundant. Although it's been 800 years since Stewart Island's discovery, fewer than 400 people call it home.

This makes a tramp here like time travelling, with plenty of natural and cultural history en route. The Rakiura Track is the simplest option, a well-marked three-day loop from

ABOVE: Walk the Rakiura Track on Stewart Island to visit ancestral Maori lands.

the island's main town of Oban. It takes in wild coast, pristine bush, and stories of settlers past. Sections of the trail cross ancestral Maori lands. Rakiura is the Maori name for the island, and roughly translates as the 'Land of the glowing skies'. This may be a nod to the Aurora Australis (Southern Lights), which sometimes dance and dazzle above on dark nights.

Tiny, sleepy Oban, also known as Halfmoon Bay, is a short flight or ferry ride from South Island. The Rakiura Track's official trailhead, Lee Bay, is a one-hour walk from the town centre. The route starts by dipping into bush, crossing the Little River, and descending onto the white sand of Maori Beach. This was once the site of a Maori village, and in 1913 a sawmill was built for logging rimu trees (a rusty steam boiler can still be seen). There's a campsite here, but it's better to continue over the hill and towards Magnetic Beach to stay at Port William Hut. This has long been a popular spot. The Maori established a *kaika* (hunting camp) here, and later the settlement of Pa Whakataka. In the nineteenth century, sealers and whalers utilised the sheltered harbour, and a profitable oyster bed was found offshore.

STEWART ISLAND

FOVEAUX STRAIT

Port William Hut
Magnetic Beach

Port William/Potirepo

Wooding Bay

Lee Bay

Maori Beach

Little River

RAKIURA NATIONAL PARK

Horseshoe Bay

North Arm Hut

Oban

Halfmoon Bay

Sawdust Bay

Kaipipi Bay

Prices Inlet

PATERSON INLET (WHAKA A TE WERA)

Ulva Island

210
Robin Hood Way

England, United Kingdom

Starting in Nottingham and delving into Sherwood Forest, Thieves Wood, and the Robin Hood Hills, this 107-mile (172km) hike visits sites associated with the legendary medieval bandit.

211
Olkhon Island Trail

Lake Baikal, Russia

Trace the northwest coast of this island in Siberia's Lake Baikal. A 47-mile (75km) trail reveals the culture of shamanistic Buryat people, resident since the thirteenth century.

Day two starts with a quick backtrack before heading west and inland, climbing hills and passing podocarp forest feathered with ferns. In parts the trail follows old tramlines from the tree-milling days. The trees that remain are a haven for native birds, including tiny tomtits, vibrant-green parakeets, kaka (a large parrot), and pipiwharauroa (the shining cuckoo). Home for the night is North Arm Hut. This offers glorious views over Paterson Inlet, known to the Maori as Whaka a Te Wera, a place of sacred significance and natural bounty.

Day three wends around the headland to Sawdust Bay, hugging a coast where green-lipped mussels cling to the rocks and seabirds dabble. The track cuts through lush native forest, emerging at Kaipipi Bay, a key sawmill site in the 1860s. The old logging road leads almost all the way back to Oban, where a plate of oysters at the South Sea Hotel provides the perfect finale.

212
JHOMOLHARI TREK

Western Bhutan

This classic nine-day trek into the pristine Himalayas centres on 7,314m (23,995ft) Jhomolhari, a giant of a mountain straddling the Tibet-Bhutan border. According to legend, the peak is home to the goddess Jomo. She was asked to protect the land and its people by the Buddhist teacher Guru Rinpoche in the eighth century. On a clear day, the mountain can be seen from the trailhead at Drukgyel Dzong. From there, it takes three days to reach Jangothang (4,080m / 13,385ft), Jhomolhari's base camp, which gives the very best vantage. Continue for six more days of virgin forest, yak pasture, high passes, and marvellous mountain views.

213
CINQUE TERRE HIGH TRAIL

Liguria, Italy

People have lived in the five cliff-clinging fishing villages of Cinque Terre for over 1,000 years. The medieval settlements of Monterosso al Mare (the oldest one, founded in 643), Vernazza, Manarola, Corniglia, and Riomaggiore somehow balance on the Ligurian Riviera – their audacious construction results in ridiculous picturesqueness. The 7.5-mile (12km) Blue Trail is the easiest way to walk between them, following centuries-old paths along the coast. Tougher and quieter is the 25-mile (40km) High Trail, which starts in the village of Portovenere, to the south of Cinque Terre, and traces the coastal range north to the town of Levanto. En route, at Punta Mesco, you can look down on all five villages at once.

214
SENTIER CATHARE

Southern France

{ Trek into the castle-dotted hills where a group of so-called heretics once ran for their lives. }

Need to know

- *Point in time: 1100–1300 (Cathar era)*
- *Length: 155 miles (250km); 12 days*
- *Difficulty: Moderate/strenuous – varied; steep sections; good infrastructure*
- *Best months: May–Oct*
- *Top tip: The trail is easier to follow from east to west (from Port-la-Nouvelle to Foix)*

215
Historic Oxen Trail

Northern Germany

Walk for 310 miles (500km) from Wedel, near Hamburg, to Viborg, in Denmark, following old trade roads and medieval pilgrimage routes.

The Catholic Church didn't like the Cathars. This religious sect, which dared to question the theology of Rome, was considered a bunch of heretics. So, in one of the most brutal acts in the history of Christianity, Pope Innocent III ordered their eradication.

The Cathars had sprung up around the twelfth century, particularly flourishing in the liberal Languedoc region of France. As the Catholic Crusaders advanced, the Cathars fled to castles in the foothills of the Pyrenees, in an attempt to escape annihilation. It didn't work. By the late fourteenth century, they'd been virtually wiped out.

It's a grim tale, but one that played out against some of France's most magnificent countryside, as the Sentier Cathare (Cathar Way) proves. This twelve-stage, 155-mile (250km) trail leads inland from Port-la-Nouvelle on the Mediterranean coast to the uplands town of Foix. It ventures amid lonely limestone outcrops, vineyard-striped hills, high meadows and plateaus, and deep, craggy gorges, with a backdrop of snow-tinged Pyrenees. It also links several former Cathar hideouts. These include the dramatic peak-perched ruins of Quéribus Castle, the cliff-side stronghold of Roquefixade (dating to the fourteenth century, but built on an earlier Cathar refuge), and the prow-like fortress of Peyrepertuse, never attacked by the Crusaders but surrendered nonetheless. Hilltop Montségur Castle was the site of the Cathars' last stand – in 1244, after a ten-month siege here, they finally gave up.

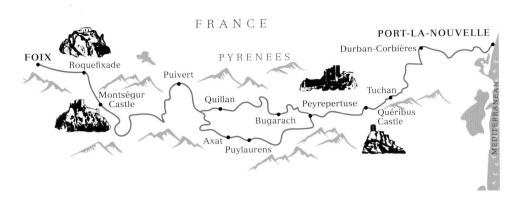

FRANCE

PYRENEES

FOIX
Roquefixade

Montségur
Castle

Puivert

Quillan

Bugarach

Axat
Puylaurens

PORT-LA-NOUVELLE

Durban-Corbières

Tuchan

Peyrepertuse

Quéribus
Castle

MEDITERRANEAN

Hike past Cathar castles
such as Peyrepertuse.

Hungary's National Blue Trail affords spectacular views of Balaton, central Europe's largest lake.

216
NATIONAL BLUE TRAIL

Hungary

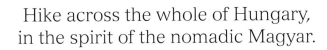

Hike across the whole of Hungary,
in the spirit of the nomadic Magyar.

There is no better way to get to know a country than to march right across it. And that's exactly what Hungary's National Blue Trail does, inching from Irottko Mountain, on the western border with Austria, to the village of Hollohaza, on the eastern border with Slovakia. This is a journey of 700 miles (1,128km). The current size of this landlocked nation was decreed in 1920, but its foundations were laid far earlier. The notion of 'Hungary' dates back to 895, when nomadic Magyar tribes, freshly united under Prince Arpad, arrived from the east and decided to stay.

The Blue Trail – Europe's oldest long-distance hiking trail – showcases the landscapes that attracted the Magyar. It drops from the Köszeg Mountains to the 700-year-old town of the same name, a riot of Gothic, Renaissance, and Baroque architecture. The trail then crosses the Little Hungarian Plain, tickles Lake Balaton, and wends among the Transdanubian Mid-Range Mountains. It hits Budapest and the Danube at its halfway point.

Veering north from the capital, the trail crosses the river at the Danube Bend, to run along the Northern Mid-Range Mountains. It climbs 1,014m (3,327ft) Mount Kékes – Hungary's highest peak – and continues to the dripstone caves of Aggtelek. Finally, it reaches Hollohaza, an Arpad-era settlement, where a monument marks the walk's end. En route are 147 checkpoints where hikers can collect stamps. Only those with a full booklet can officially say they've completed the Blue Trail.

Need to know
- *Point in time: 895 (Magyar tribes arrived from the east)*
- *Length: 700 miles (1,128km); 55–60 days*
- *Difficulty: Moderate – varied terrain*
- *Best months: June–Oct*
- *Top tip: Pack a booklet and a small ink pad to collect stamps en route*

217
Old Salt Road

Liguria, Italy

La Via del Sale crosses the Apennines and the fertile Lombardy Plains for 80 miles (129km). It shadows the salt-toting mule herders who used these routes 1,000 years ago.

218
VIA JACOBI

Switzerland

There are many Ways of St James, wiggling across Europe toward Santiago de Compostela. This is the Swiss one. The numbers of foreign pilgrims heading to Spain's holy shrine increased from the eleventh century. Those travelling from Scandinavia and Germany took the Via Jacobi through Switzerland. The trail runs for 218 miles (350km) from Lake Constance, on the country's German-Austrian border, to Geneva, on the border with France. It's as typically Swiss as you want it to be: meticulously waymarked, and lined with Alpine peaks, lakes, meadows, and pretty towns, such as St Gallen, Interlaken, and Spiez. And good cheese and chocolate are never hard to find.

219
CAMINO DEL INCA

Central Highlands, Ecuador

Peru doesn't have a monopoly on Inca trails. The civilisation's empire extended far beyond that country. This 25-mile (40km) trek in Ecuador, from Acchupallas to Ingapirca, follows part of the Incan Royal Road that once linked Cusco with Quito. Winding over the Andean *páramo*, it's an easy tramp. It does reach an altitude of 4,800m (15,700ft), however, which increases the challenge. The trail finishes up at Ingapirca, Ecuador's own answer to Machu Picchu. Far less dramatic perhaps, but the well-preserved site has a fine Sun Temple and ruined *acllahuasi*, the dwellings where sacrificial virgins once lived.

220
Lake Waikaremoana Track

Te Urewera, New Zealand

This 29-mile (46km) 'Great Walk' explores North Island's less-visited Te Urewera National Park. It follows the lake's western side for fine forest hiking and Maori history.

221
Richard III Trail

Leicester, England, United Kingdom

Take a stroll around Leicester, visiting sites relevant to the hunchbacked King Richard III. Killed in 1485, his remains were found under a car park in 2012.

INCA TRAIL

Cusco Region, Peru

{
Take the famed four-day trail
through the Andes to the 'lost'
mountainside city of Machu Picchu.
}

Need to know
- *Point in time: 1200–1550 (period of the Inca civilisation)*
- *Length: 28 miles (45km); 4 days*
- *Difficulty: Moderate/ strenuous – high altitudes; steep sections*
- *Best months: May–Sept*
- *Top tip: Trail is closed in February*

The tenure of the Inca was short but sweet. This South American civilisation seemingly emerged from nowhere, in around 1200 (when founder-king Manco Cápac allegedly rose from Lake Titicaca). Over the following 300 years, it grew to rule the largest empire that the continent has ever seen. It stretched around 3,400 miles (5,500km) north to south, and built a wealth of finely engineered roads, temples, and terraces. However, by the mid-sixteenth century, after the Spanish conquistadores had done their worst, the Inca had been virtually wiped out.

Wiped out, but not forgotten. The Inca left quite a legacy. Their masterful stonework still dominates much of Peru's Sacred Valley. Their paved paths still fan out across the region. Indeed, there are multiple 'Inca Trails' that you can follow, in Peru and beyond. But none is better known, nor more iconic, than the Classic Inca Trail to the World Heritage–listed ruins of Machu Picchu. It is not known for sure, but this 28-mile (45km) hike may have been a pilgrimage route to the holy citadel. Certainly, walking here feels like treading on sacred ground.

The trail is incredibly popular. The drier months (May to September) are the best times to tackle it. Independent walking is not allowed, permits are mandatory (and can sell out well in advance in high season), and numbers on the trail are limited to 500 a day, which includes guides and porters. Even with these restrictions, camp stops still get crowded. Despite this, the Inca Trail remains one of the world's greatest walks – an enduringly alluring hike

through high mountains and deep valleys to reach a city that was 'lost' for centuries.

From the traditional start at KM88 (a stop on the Cusco–Aguas Calientes railway), the trail weaves amid the high Andes. Here, the Urubamba River churns, ethereal mist swirls, and condors soar. En route lie some testing passes, including 4,200m (13,800ft) Abra de Huarmihuañusca – known as 'Dead Woman's Pass'.

There's also a succession of increasingly impressive ruins, each site a stepping stone to Machu Picchu itself: Runcu Raccay, an observation point and rest stop for the *chasqui* (relay runners) who conveyed messages around the Inca empire; Sayacmarca, a guard post surrounded by nosediving cliffs; and the wide terraces, elaborate masonry, and ceremonial baths of Huinay Huayna.

Then there's the grand finale. After days of hiking, you climb through cliff-draped cloud forest to reach the stone gate of Intipunku, in time for sunrise over mountain-teetering Machu Picchu. You can also see the pyramidal

ABOVE: Embark on a multi-day trek to reach the 'lost city' of Machu Picchu.

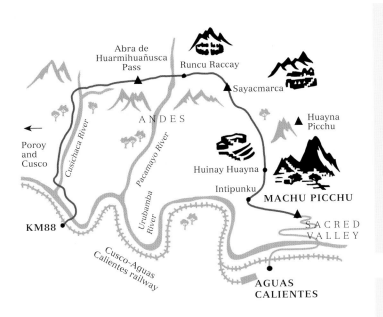

Abra de
Huarmihuañusca
Pass

Runcu Raccay

Sayacmarca

ANDES

Huayna
Picchu

Cusichaca River

Pacamayo River

Poroy
and
Cusco

Huinay Huayna

Intipunku

MACHU PICCHU

Urubamba River

KM88

SACRED
VALLEY

Cusco-Aguas
Calientes railway

AGUAS
CALIENTES

**223
Circuit Jeanne
d'Arc**

Lorraine, France

Some 50 miles
(80km) of tracks
connect sites
associated with
French heroine Joan
of Arc (1412–31).
These include the
house of her birth,
and Vaucouleurs, the
town that armed her.

**224
Licancabur
Volcano**

Chile and Bolivia

It's an eight-hour
slog to the lake atop
Licancabur. At
5,900m (19,400ft),
it is one of the
world's highest
lakes. The Inca
performed rituals
here, and ruins can
still be found.

guardian peak, Huayna Picchu, rearing up behind.
Mystery still envelops this 'lost city'. Was it a coca-
collecting hub, a defensive post, or a refuge for virgins?
Some think it was a holy site. Studies show that Machu
Picchu's Temple of the Sun was used for solstice worship.
Whatever its purpose, it's likely that the remote citadel
was abandoned by the Inca around 1540, when
maintenance would have been of secondary importance
to fighting the Spanish.

The conquistadores never found Machu Picchu. In 1911,
long after they'd gone, American explorer Hiram Bingham
'discovered' it by accident (he was actually looking for
Vilcabamba) and brought it to the attention of the world.
This cluster of ruined warehouses, guardhouses, and
temples clinging to an Andean hillside went on to be voted
one of the New Seven Wonders of the World in 2007. Trains
now run to the site from Poroy, near Cusco, enabling more
people to visit. But the best, most atmospheric, most
satisfying way to get here is still as the Inca did – on foot.

CRYSTAL MAIDEN TREK

Actun Tunichil Muknal, Belize

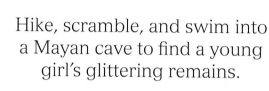

Hike, scramble, and swim into
a Mayan cave to find a young
girl's glittering remains.

Need to know

- *Point in time: 700–900 (Crystal Maiden thought to have been sacrificed)*
- *Length: 5 miles (8km); 1 day*
- *Difficulty: Moderate – short; rugged terrain; scrambling required*
- *Best months: Nov–May*
- *Top tip: Pack kit in dry bags – you will get wet*

**226
Huchuy Qosqo
Trek**

Sacred Valley, Peru

The two-day, 10.5-mile (17km) route from Tambomachay to Lamay, though the Sacred Valley, follows parts of stone-laid Inca pathways that once connected Cusco to Pisac.

Delving into Actun Tunichil Muknal is like descending into the very belly of Xibalbá – the Mayan underworld. Secreted away in the jungle-clad, cavern-riddled mountains, on the edge of Tapir Mountain Nature Reserve, this 'Cave of the Stone Sepulchre' was only rediscovered in the past few decades. It has a long and ghoulish past, however. The grottoes hereabouts were used by the Maya for various functions: as water sources, larders, hiding places – and ceremonial sites of sacrifice. Actun Tunichil Muknal seems to have been the latter.

From the nearest roadhead, it takes a short hike and three river crossings to reach the cave entrance, where a pool blocks the way. No matter: a quick swim, and you're in. Actun Tunichil Muknal sneaks 5 miles (8km) into the mountains. To find its ultimate treasure requires wading up to your armpits and ducking under crags.

You must then sidle along a shelf, amid a scatter of terracotta pots (all smashed by the Maya to free ancestral spirits). The next stage is the echoing 'cathedral', a hall of stalagmites and calcite curtains. Finally, you have to negotiate a ladder, and squeeze down a narrow passage, before entering a little chamber. There you'll meet the Crystal Maiden, the skeleton of a teenage girl. She was sacrificed more than 1,000 years ago, and now her bones lie coated with calcite, glittering in the gloom.

RIGHT: Squeeze down a narrow passage and into a little chamber to see the glittering Crystal Maiden in her final resting place.

TAKESI TRAIL

Western Bolivia

The Takesi is Bolivia's very own Inca Trail. It is a segment of the massive Qhapaq Ñan Andean Road System – a network of roads that connected all corners of the Inca Empire, from Colombia to Chile. This 25-mile (40km) Bolivian section follows a pre-Columbian thoroughfare from Ventilla, just east of La Paz, to Yanacachi, in the lush Yungas valleys. It starts at an altitude of 3,200m (10,500ft), and ascends quickly to a panoramic pass at 4,600m (15,902ft). Then the trail runs downhill virtually all the way, via high peaks, llama-grazed pasture, and increasingly steamy jungle. There are traditional villages and some still-intact Inca paving en route.

228
Choro Trail

Bolivia

This 43-mile (70km), mostly downhill hike along pre-Hispanic trails cuts through Cotapata National Park's cloud forest from La Cumbre. Inca ruins lie en route.

229
El Misti

Arequipa, Peru

It's a technically easy but lung-gasping climb to Misti's 5,822m (19,101ft) summit where, in 1998, six Inca mummies were found by the inner crater.

230
Viking Way

England, United Kingdom

Vikings first invaded Britain in 793. This 147-mile (237km) trail from Lincolnshire to Rutland crosses their old stomping ground. It explores their legacy, from Danelaw place names to ancient sites.

231
Tipperary Heritage Way

Tipperary, Ireland

Early settlers – including Vikings (800s) and Normans (1100s) – followed the River Suir to access Ireland's best farmland. This 35-mile (56km) trail, from the Knockmealdown Mountains to Cashel, does the same.

232
BURKHAN KHALDUN

Khentii, Mongolia

Genghis Khan, leader of the Mongol Empire and perhaps the world's most notorious warrior, was born on Burkhan Khaldun. It was to this mountain that he came for spiritual guidance. It was also on its 2,354m (7,724ft) summit that, after his death in 1227, he was buried under a large stone cairn. Or so the story goes. Lack of evidence doesn't stop Mongolians from regarding Burkhan Khaldun as a sacred place. It's not a tough climb. Rather, it's a pilgrim trail, doable in a day, that leads up via pine forest and a stony plateau. The hard part is getting there. The trailhead is 125 miles (200km) northeast of Ulaanbaatar, accessible only by four-wheel drive or horse.

233
BARBAROSSA TRAIL

Hessen and Thuringia, Germany

Legend has it that Holy Roman Emperor Frederick I, known as Redbeard or Barbarossa, didn't actually die in 1190. Rather, he's asleep in a cave in the Kyffhäuser Mountains. The best way to find out is by walking the Barbarossa Trail, which runs for 205 miles (330km) from Korbach, in Hessen, to Tilleda, a village in Thuringia. The latter sits just below the myth-swirled Kyffhäuser hills. The trail uses a mix of old royal roads and trading routes to explore a rich, cultural landscape. As well as grandiose monuments, imperial castles, and ancient hermitages, the route is dotted with 150 works of modern art.

234
DUBROVNIK WALL WALK

Dalmatia, Croatia

The walls girdling Dubrovnik have taken a battering since their first erection in the twelfth century. Measuring almost 1.5 miles (2.4km) long and 25m (82ft) high, and fortified by towers, they were built to protect the city against the Turks. It was the 1667 earthquake and the Balkan conflict of the 1990s that did the most damage, however. Still, these walls are remarkably well preserved, and it's possible to climb up and walk a circuit around them. Start from the Pile Gate to stroll past fifteenth-century Minceta Fortress. Pause at Ploce Gate for good views of the port. Then, from the south side, admire the domes and terracotta rooftops of the city of Dubrovnik huddled below.

OFFA'S DYKE PATH

Wales and England, United Kingdom

{ Follow the remains of a little-known king's ancient earthwork as you criss-cross a wild frontier. }

Need to know

- *Point in time: 757–796 (reign of King Offa of Mercia)*
- *Length: 177 miles (285km); 12–14 days*
- *Difficulty: Moderate – changeable weather; undulating*
- *Best months: Apr–Oct*
- *Top tip: The trail is waymarked – follow the acorn symbols*

236
Heaphy Track

Kahurangi National Park, New Zealand

This 48-mile (78km) trail on the South Island was first used by Maori *pounamu* (jade) hunters. They used it to cross the downs and forests between Golden Bay and Westland's jade rivers.

In his day, Offa was quite the man. In 757 this pugnacious Anglo-Saxon became king of Mercia, at that time the largest of England's seven kingdoms. During his reign, he extended his territory, becoming ruler of most of England. Wales, however, was a different matter. Twice King Offa tried to conquer the feisty Celts, but twice he failed. Finally, he built a barrier along the England-Wales border to keep them at bay.

Unlike the Roman emperor Hadrian, who was so keen to defend England's north from the Scots that he built a wall, Offa didn't build his barrier out of stone. Instead he dug a ditch and backed it with a high mound of soil – now known as Offa's Dyke. It's thought that the ditch measured up to 20m (65ft) wide, and the dyke behind rose 2.5m (8ft) high. It's said that a wooden palisade may have sat on top of the embankment for extra defence, although no archaeological evidence has been found. It's also said that the Welsh hanged any Englishmen that they found on their side of the divide. If the English captured trespassing Welshmen, they cut off both their ears. There's no such penalty for crossing the border these days. This is fortunate, as the 177-mile (285km) Offa's Dyke Path, which largely follows the line of the ancient earthwork, hops across the national divide between England and Wales more than twenty times.

Sadly, being largely made of mud, the dyke hasn't survived the centuries completely intact. Along many sections of the hike the fortification can still be seen. Along others it can't, but the far-reaching views and natural contours of the landscape make it easy to imagine why this route was chosen.

From south to north, Offa's Dyke Path runs from the River Severn's Sedbury Cliffs, almost in the shadow of Chepstow's eleventh-century castle, to the Welsh resort of Prestatyn, on the Irish Sea. Between lies a glorious frontier-land of deep dales, crumbling strongholds, burbling rivers, wild mountains, and endless sheep-dotted hills.

One of the first highlights is the romantic ruin of Tintern Abbey, founded by Cistercian monks in 1131 and hidden deep in the Wye Valley. Beyond lie the wild, heather-fleeced Black Mountains: the hike follows their exposed spine, looking down on the dishevelled remains of Llanthony Priory (now an atmospheric hotel). It then drops down to the cute town of Hay-on-Wye (known for its literary festival). Beyond this, the trail follows the River Wye, scaling Hergest Ridge for panoramic views and well-preserved earthworks. It then hits the market town of Knighton (called Tref-y-Clawdd in Welsh, meaning 'the Town on the Dyke'). The following section, which switchbacks through the Shropshire Hills, is

The Middle Ages   **189**

237
1066 Country Walk

East Sussex, England, United Kingdom

Walk with William the Conqueror, who defeated King Harold at the Battle of Hastings in 1066. This 31-mile (50km) route links villages, windmills, castles, and the battle site itself.

238
Kumbhalgarh Fort Walls

Rajasthan, India

Walk 22 miles (36km) of fifteenth-century fort walls, the second-longest continuous barrier on the planet, which protects a complex of more than 300 temples in the Aravalli Hills.

the trail's toughest. It is also home to its highest and best-preserved bit of dyke, on Llanfair Hill, at 408m (1,339ft). Just after, Newcastle on Clun heralds the trail's halfway point.

The route flattens for a while, and frequently flits between Wales and England. It then joins the Montgomeryshire Canal and River Severn before entering the town of Llanymynech, where the national border runs along the high street. Soon hills reappear, most notably Moelydd, offering a picturesque 360-degree sweep over the surrounding mounds. Next, the path hits the Clwydian Range, passing Chirk Castle and crossing the 38m (126ft) high Pontcysyllte Aqueduct. This was designed by Thomas Telford in 1805 and remains an engineering marvel.

After negotiating the limestone Eglwyseg Crags, the route traverses moorland and forest before getting up onto the Clwydian Ridge and passing Iron and Bronze Age hill forts. From here, there are views west to the heights of Snowdonia. Finally, the hills peter out as the trail descends to Prestatyn. Here, walkers traditionally remove their boots to dip their weary, time-travelling feet into the sea.

XI'AN CITY WALLS

Shaanxi, China

{ Circuit the ancient Silk Road city
by completing a lap of its
mighty Ming dynasty walls. }

Need to know
- *Point in time: 1370s
  (Ming walls built)*
- *Length: 8.5 miles
  (14km); 3–4 hours*
- *Difficulty: Easy –
  flat; accessible*
- *Best months: Apr–
  May; Sept–Oct*
- *Top tip: There is an
  entry fee to access
  the city walls*

The Ming-era walls encircling the city of Xi'an are an impressive sight. Built in the 1370s and remarkably well preserved, the 8.5-mile (14km) barrier measures 12m (39ft) high and up to 14m (46ft) wide. The only thing that is more remarkable is that the earlier Tang dynasty walls they replaced were almost three times longer.

The current walls were commissioned by Emperor Zhu Yuanzhang. They're supremely tough, initially made from earth, quicklime, and sticky rice. They are now composed of brick. There are crenellations along the outer edge, lower parapets on the inner side, and a total of ninety-eight sentry towers, spaced two arrow shots apart.

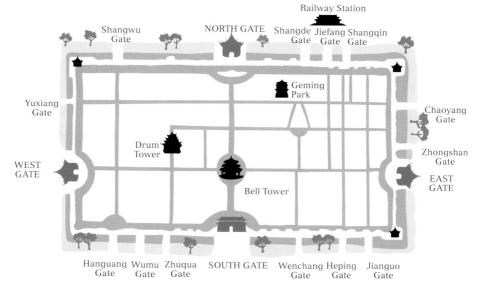

Railway Station

Shangwu Gate   NORTH GATE   Shangde Jiefang Shangqin Gate Gate Gate

Yuxiang Gate

Geming Park

Chaoyang Gate

Drum Tower

Zhongshan Gate

WEST GATE

Bell Tower

EAST GATE

Hanguang Wumu Zhuqua   SOUTH GATE   Wenchang Heping Jianguo
Gate   Gate   Gate   Gate   Gate   Gate

Access the ancient ramparts of the Xi'an City Walls via one of its many gates.

Steps at the four main city gates – North, South, East, and West – provide access to the ramparts. The South Gate is the most revered. However, there are also many smaller gates. These include Chaoyang (Toward the Sun), the first gate to see sunrise, and Wenchang, site of a literature temple.

A moat surrounds the perimeter of the wall, and the leafy strip between wall and water is now the Round-the-City Park. This is a popular retreat for musicians, fan dancers, table-tennis players, and locals 'walking' their pet birds. The best thing about being up on top, however, is the view over the farrago of modern China – the contrast of ancient stone, red lanterns, and traditional swooping roofs with the skyscrapers, smog, and bedlam of the twenty-first century.

240
City Walls of Ávila

Castile and León, Spain

Built from the eleventh century onwards to protect Spanish lands from the Moors, the walkable 1.5-mile (2.5km) walls of Ávila – complete with eighty-seven towers and nine gates – are among the world's best preserved.

241
ROOPKUND TREK

Uttarakhand, India

This glorious trek in the Indian Himalayas is a little bit ghoulish too. Its focus is
Roopkund, a tarn (small lake) nestled 4,800m (15,478ft) up in the shadow of the Trisul
Massif. Here, in the 1940s, a ranger found more than 200 human skeletons floating in
the water, revealed by the melted ice. Experts dated these bones to AD 850, concluding
that they were pilgrims, killed – unbelievably – by iron-hard hail. Don't let this deter
you, as it's a delightfully diverse seven-day hike. Leaving from Lohajung, the trail
passes bird-filled oak and rhododendron forests, green meadows, remote villages,
and a spread of snow-capped peaks before reaching the eerie lake itself.

242
MOUNT RINJANI

Lombok, Indonesia

In 1257 the earth was shaken by a mass eruption, the most powerful of the past
7,000 years. It affected the whole planet's climate, possibly kick-starting the Little Ice
Age. Which volcano was responsible for the eruption has long been a mystery. Now,
scientists think that it was probably Mount Rinjani, the 3,726m (12,225ft) giant on the
island of Lombok. Rinjani remains extremely active, making a two- to four-day trek
here particularly thrilling. Trails run from Senaru and Sembalun Lawang, ascending
through dense forest to the crater rim. This is a realm of medicinal hot springs, scarred
and jagged peaks, and a blue crater lake out of which a boisterous new volcanic cone
has grown.

BAEKDU DAEGAN TRAIL

South Korea

{ Trace the rugged, temple-dotted spine of the country's identity-defining mountain range. }

Need to know

- *Point in time: 826–898 (life of Doseon Guksa)*
- *Length: 460 miles (735km); 60–65 days*
- *Difficulty: Strenuous – mountainous; remote; long*
- *Best months: May–June; Sept–Oct*
- *Top tip: Some of the Buddhist temples on the slopes below the trail offer accommodation*

The Baekdu Daegan isn't just a mountain range. This 'White Head, Great Ridge', which runs for 1,055 miles (1,700km) from sacred Baekdu-san on the North Korea–China border to the peak of Cheonwangbong in southern South Korea, is the life-giving spine of the peninsula.

It was ninth-century Buddhist Zen master Doseon Guksa who developed *Pungsu-jiri* (the Wind Water Earth Principles theory). This is a sort of natural feng shui focused on how topography affects the human condition. Key to this was the notion of Baekdu Daegan as a central nerve supplying *gi* (the energy of existence) throughout the nation, via its network of valleys, furrows, rivers, and streams. The ridge, Guksa believed, was the peninsula's watershed, its anchor to Asia, and its very lifeblood. Inspired by this, devotees from many spiritual schools – including Shamanism, Taoism, and Buddhism – have constructed monasteries, temples, and shrines along the range ever since.

Doseon Guksa traced the source of all Korea's *gi* back to 2,744m (9,003ft) Baekdu-san, the peninsula's highest and holiest mountain, closely linked with the kingdom's creation mythology. Sadly, long-distance hiking in secretive North Korea is not an option, and the mapped Baekdu Daegan Trail covers only the South Korean portion of the ridge. This section runs between 1,915m (6,285ft) Cheonwangbong and the pass of Jinburyeong, just before the Korean Demilitarized Zone (DMZ). This buffer area along the peninsula's thirty-eighth parallel –

RIGHT: Feel the *gi* of the landscape on a spiritual trek through South Korea.

separating North and South Korea – is as far as today's hikers are permitted to go.

Still, that leaves 460 miles (735km) of spectacular, spiritual, waymarked trail that *can* still be accessed. The route visits seven national parks, hundreds of peaks, and innumerable religious sites. Thru-hiking is tough, so most people tackle the Baekdu Daegan in stages. Consequently, the trail is busiest on weekends, although meeting Korean hikers, monks, and shamans en route is part of the pleasure.

From the DMZ, the trail heads south into Seoraksan (Snow Rock Mountain) National Park, a domain of jagged granite and gneiss, and richly diverse flora and fauna. Its forests of pine and oak contain Asian black bears, musk deer, otters, and flying squirrels. Next are the smoother summits and deciduous forests – resplendent in fall – of Odaesan (Five Plateau Mountain). This is also home to the seventh-century temple of Woljeongsa, with its octagonal nine-story pagoda. The trail then follows the east coast all the way to sacred Taebaeksan (Grand White Mountain), dotted with gnarled yew trees, Buddhist shrines, and shamanistic altars.

At this point, the Baekdu Daegan veers west toward central South Korea and into Sobaeksan (Little White Mountain) National Park. This is a section of dense forest and lush valleys, topping out at 1,439m (4,720ft) Birobong. This peak's verdant summit is a riot of royal azaleas in May.

The steep peaks of Woraksan (Moon Crags Mountain) are tickled by waterfalls, and roamed by the rare long-tailed goral (a type of wild goat). Then the trail hits the country's middle at Songnisan (Remote from the Ordinary World Mountain), a secluded fuzz of forested granite that conceals the sixth-century temple of Beopjusa. This is home to a 33m (108ft) high golden Buddha and a vast iron cauldron that was once used to cook for 3,000 monks.

From here the Baekdu Daegan turns south again, arriving at the dramatic valley-gouged Deogyusan (Gentle Mountain with Virtue). This is a little Eden dotted with crystal-clear pools and streams. Lastly it hits Jirisan (Mountain of the Odd and Wise People), the largest national park in Korea and the trail's finale. It's a place of magnificent peaks, pristine virgin forest, numerous

CHINA

BAEKDU-SAN ▲

NORTH KOREA

BAEKDU DAEGAN RANGE

SEA
OF
JAPAN

DMZ Seoraksan ▲
**JINBURYEONG
PASS** Odaesan

SOUTH KOREA

Woljeongsa

Taebaeksan ▲

Woraksan ▲ Sobaeksan
▲ Birobong

▲ Songnisan

Beopjusa

YELLOW
SEA

▲ Deogyusan

▲ Jirisan

CHEONWANGBONG

244
Miners' Ridge and James Irvine Loop

*California,
United States*

This 11.5-mile
(17km) hike in
Redwood National
Park passes massive
700-year-old trees
and a habitat of ferns
that feels primeval.
Finish your walk at
surf-pounded Gold
Bluffs Beach.

245
Quilotoa Traverse

*Central Highlands,
Ecuador*

Link a scatter of
traditional Andean
villages and
volcano-moulded
terrain on a 22-mile
(35km) hike from
Sigchos to Quilotoa.
End at sparkling
blue Quilotoa Crater
Lake, formed 800
years ago.

temples, and ten official 'scenic views'. It's also home to
the peak of Cheonwangbong, where it's said that even
fools can become clever if they stand here long enough –
further proof, if it were needed, of the Baekdu Daegan's
positive powers.

246
PILGRIMS WAY

England, United Kingdom

Pilgrimage was popular in medieval England. And Winchester, home to St Swithun's shrine, was the main destination. However, when Archbishop of Canterbury Thomas Becket was murdered in Canterbury Cathedral in 1170, a new hotspot was born. Many pilgrims began to walk between the two. The Pilgrims Way is 120 miles (193km) long, following pathways used since prehistoric times. It wends via bucolic patches of busy southern England, including Hampshire's Itchen Valley, the wooded hills of the Weald, and the chalk escarpments of the North Downs. Some spots even afford views north to London. The finale is Canterbury's great cathedral. Becket is no longer here (his shrine was destroyed in 1538), but a candle burns in its place.

247
ISLA DEL SOL TRAVERSE

Lake Titicaca, Bolivia

This is where it all began: Isla del Sol is the alleged birthplace of Manco Cápac – father of the Incas – who was sent down by the Sun God to civilise the humans below. There are no cars, or even roads, on this tiny isle floating on ethereally blue Lake Titicaca. A 9-mile (15km) traverse loop is the best way to explore, following the coast path from Yumani to Challapampa, and returning on the upper path. En route, pass neat terraced fields, a sprinkle of pre-Columbian sites, and Puma Rock, the spot where Manco was supposedly born.

248
Hansaweg

Northwest Germany

Linking key cities of the medieval Hanseatic League, the 47-mile (75km) Hanseatic Trail passes Herford, Lemgo, and Hamelin (of Pied Piper fame). It also visits spa towns and the Teutoburg Forest.

249
WAD- EN WIERDENPAD

Netherlands

First, some definitions: a *wad* is a mud flat, a *wierde* is an artificial hill. Together, these words give some insight into the character of the northern Netherlands. The region is a victory of man over nature. From the twelfth century, the Dutch began forming polders – reclaiming land from the Wadden Sea by draining swamps and digging dykes and channels. The 77-mile (123km) Wad- en Wierdenpad trail follows these raised dykes, from coastal Lauwersoog to the spa town of Nieuweschans on the German border. Expect big skies, swaying reeds, bird-filled marshes, and a wealth of windmills in between.

251
Great St Bernard Pass

Valais, Switzerland

In the eleventh century, St Bernard de Menthon established a travellers' hospice on this 2,066m (6,778ft) Alpine pass. The hike over, from Bourg-St-Pierre (Switzerland) to St-Rhémy (Italy), can be done in a day.

250
THINGVELLIR CIRCUIT

Southwest Iceland

Thingvellir is a wild, godforsaken place. This fissure-cracked plain sits inside a rift valley formed by the North American and Eurasian tectonic plates pulling apart beneath. And yet, in 930, this was where the Vikings established the Althing – the world's first democratic parliament. Little physical evidence remains, but the ancient atmosphere is still palpable. An easy, 6-mile (10km) loop of the site starts at the information centre. It passes mossy rocks and craggy lava to reach the knoll-perched farm ruins of Skógarkot and old Thingvellir church. The trail then crosses the river towards the Almannagjá cliffs, beneath which those Vikings once laid down the law of their newly settled land.

Trek southwest Iceland's Thingvellir Circuit in late September, when the bushes are yellow and flaming red, and the mountaintops are capped in snow. This is where the Vikings established the world's first democratic parliament (p. 199).

CHAPTER FOUR
TOWARDS THE MODERN WORLD

{ Enter the era from 1500 to 1800, an age of discovery, revolution, renaissance, and enlightenment. }

HOERIKWAGGO TRAIL

Table Mountain National Park, South Africa

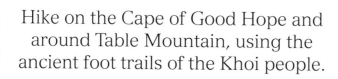

Hike on the Cape of Good Hope and around Table Mountain, using the ancient foot trails of the Khoi people.

Need to know
- *Point in time: 1652 (first permanent colonial settlement at the Cape of Good Hope)*
- *Length: 47 miles (75km); 5 days*
- *Difficulty: Moderate – some steep sections*
- *Best months: Nov– Mar*
- *Top tip: Bush fires have caused trail and camp closures in the past – check before hiking*

The Khoi people have been walking around Table Mountain for close to 1,500 years. They call it Hoerikwaggo, meaning 'Mountain in the Sea'. Their ancient foot trails form the basis of today's Hoerikwaggo Hiking Trail, a long-distance amble around Table Mountain, its eponymous national park, and the wild peninsula on which it sits.

The Portuguese coined the name Cape of Good Hope for this southerly headland in the late fifteenth century. However, they didn't linger. They were simply passing by, en route to lucrative trading in East Africa and beyond. It was much later, in the 1650s, that outsiders actually settled. The Dutch, eager to challenge Portuguese dominance of the surrounding waters, set up the first Cape Colony in 1652. This was the beginning of Kaapstad (Cape Town), and also the beginning of the end for the Khoisan way of life. The Khoi became the first indigenous African people to feel the full force of white colonisation. Within a few hundred years, they had been assimilated as servants, forced from their lands, or killed by European diseases and weaponry.

However, this gloomy backstory shouldn't deter you from a magnificent trail. There's a reason why the Khoi people, the Dutch, and others were attracted to South Africa's now-cosmopolitan Western Cape. The seas and soil are rich, the climate is temperate, and the location – a handy stop-off on the journey around Africa – is strategic.

The scenery is also spectacular. Table Mountain is a fabulous flat-topped mesa, rising up to 1,086m (3,563ft) high and often draped in cloud. Its emerald flanks are

ABOVE: Enjoy an amble around Table Mountain on the Hoerikwaggo Trail.

cloaked in 2,200 species of plants, from fragrant swamp daisies to huge king proteas – the country's national flower. Amid this floral diversity live many creatures, including rabbit-like rock hyraxes, eland antelopes, Verreaux's eagles, and chacma baboons.

The 47-mile (75km) Hoerikwaggo Trail also offers a rather comfortable option for exploring the cape. There is no need to carry tents. Accommodation is in thoughtfully designed permanent camps, all supplied with hot water, comfortable beds, communal bathrooms, and fully equipped kitchens.

Traced south to north, the trail begins at the Cape Point lighthouse car park. It's a short detour to reach the tip of the skinny, sheer-sided promontory itself, which thrusts out into the treacherous, shipwreck-strewn waves. From here, Hoerikwaggo hikers head north, winding along vertiginous cliffs, and between low peaks and profuse *fynbos* – the 'fine bush' shrubland endemic to southern Africa. Camp One is rustic Smitswinkel, tucked above False Bay, alongside a flowering gum plantation. It is the ideal place for a traditional *braai* (barbecue).

The following day is an easy hike via Simonstown – within reach of the Boulders Beach penguin colony – to Slangkop Lighthouse. Here, Slankop Camp huddles within a stand of milkwood trees, right by the Atlantic Ocean. The village of Kommetjie is close if you need supplies. Day three is a tougher test. It begins with a leg-stretch along Noordhoek Beach before the climb up Chapman's Peak, a dramatic shard that drops straight into the ocean; however, the views from the top are worth the effort. Next, the trail falls and rises once more to trace the Silvermine Ridge before dropping to Silvermine Camp. A swim in the dam here is a very welcome refresher.

Ascending from the Silvermine Valley, there are more fine views from Blackburn Ravine. The trail then zigzags along high paths that seem to fall away into Hout Bay before climbing the whale-backed massif of Constantiaberg. Orangekloof, hidden amid Afromontane forest, yet only twenty minutes' drive from downtown Cape Town, is home for the night. Finishing on a literal high, the last day's hike leads, via Disa Ravine (named for the endangered red disa orchid) and the Valley of Isolation, up the western flank of Table Mountain. From this summit end point, the land, seas, and burgeoning city of Cape Town are laid out below.

253
Voyageur Hiking Trail

Ontario, Canada

'Voyageurs' were the seventeenth-century Europeans who canoed Canada to trade fur. This 370-mile (600km) hike from Sudbury to Thunder Bay, via Lake Superior, is named for their pioneering spirit.

254

CAPE FROWARD

Magdalena Island, Chile

It's a wild walk to reach the southernmost point of continental South America, at Cape Froward. The clue to its inhospitable nature lies in its name. 'Froward' means 'difficult', a moniker bestowed on the tip of Chile's Magdalena Island by an English privateer in 1587 (though Portuguese explorer Ferdinand Magellan was the first European here, in 1520). Indeed, the hiking *is* difficult, the weather often rages, and a guide is required for the 26-mile (42km) trek along the Brunswick Peninsula and the Magellan Straits. The route journeys via wild beaches, peat bogs, native forest, and waddling penguins to reach the cape's huge iron cross – some semblance of salvation in this hostile place.

255

EL CAMINO REAL

California, United States

The Spanish started making serious forays into what is now California in 1769. As these prospectors and Catholic missionaries blazed about the state, however, they were probably using trails laid down by Native American peoples many centuries before. The Spaniards' route became known as El Camino Real, or 'the Royal Road'. Today, it is an unofficial, unmarked footpath, based on a map from 1812. It traces an 800-mile (1,285km) trail south from the Mission San Francisco Solano, in the city of Sonoma, to Mission San Diego, just shy of the Mexican border. The route travels via Pacific cliffs, rolling hills, army bases, and San Francisco's Golden Gate Bridge, mixing timeless natural splendour with twenty-first-century urban sprawl.

RIGHT: Split Apple Rock is just one of the landmarks of
Abel Tasman National Park.

ABEL TASMAN COAST TRACK

South Island, New Zealand

{ Trace a spectacular shore where Maori tribes and New World navigators once roamed. }

By the seventeenth century, the Maori had been foraging on the north coast of New Zealand's South Island for around 400 years. However, the honour of this region's name now belongs to Abel Tasman, the Dutch seafarer who sailed by in December 1642 and became the first European to see New Zealand – and what an honour. Abel Tasman National Park is a knockout. There are golden beaches, marble and granite cliffs, glassy streams, and sparkling turquoise seas. Bellbirds and tui sing amid the forest, little penguins swim offshore, and fur seals loll on the rocks.

The Abel Tasman Coast Track, a 32-mile (51km) shoreside tramp north from the tiny settlement of Marahau to Wainui Bay, showcases the park's best parts. The trail ducks into stands of beech, manuka, and kanuka trees, wends between mossy gullies, and negotiates estuaries. It scrambles over boulders, bounces across suspension bridges, strides along white sand, and tops lofty ridges.

There are also worthwhile add-ons. For instance, nip out to Pitt Head to look down on the honeyed crescent of Te Pukatea Bay and visit an old Maori *pa* (fort) site. Or duck inland from Torrent Bay to splash in the cascades of Falls River.

Either way, the track is simple to follow, easy underfoot, and spectacular at every turn. Abel Tasman would be proud.

Need to know
- *Point in time: 1642 (Abel Tasman first landed on South Island)*
- *Length: 32 miles (51km); 3–5 days*
- *Difficulty: Easy – well marked; mostly gentle*
- *Best months: Oct–Apr*
- *Top tip: Check tide tables for estuary crossings*

257
Methye Portage Trail

Saskatchewan, Canada

In 1778 explorer Peter Pond unlocked the first overland trade route to Canada's northwest. With the help of First Nations guides, he used this 13-mile (20.5km) trail from Lac La Loche.

SYDNEY GREAT COASTAL WALK

New South Wales, Australia

{ Discover what attracted Captain Cook to the wonderful, wave-smashed shores of eastern Australia. }

Need to know
- *Point in time: 1770 (Captain Cook landed in Botany Bay)*
- *Length: 58 miles (94km); 7–8 days*
- *Difficulty: Easy/ moderate – good facilities; undulating*
- *Best months: Oct–Apr*
- *Top tip: A good public transport network, including ferries, serves many points on the route*

Botany Bay and its surrounds have changed a bit since 1770, when Captain James Cook dropped anchor here. Then, it was a coastal wilderness and home to groups of Gayamaygal people. Today this stretch of coast is home to Sydney, Australia's most populous city. The area is still an absolute beauty, only now the rocky headlands and sunny beaches come with lifeguards, hip cafés, and easy access to downtown Sydney, with its iconic harbour and air of cool.

The Sydney Coastal Walk doesn't skip a single part of this magnificent urbanised waterfront. It runs for 58 miles (94km) between Barrenjoey Beach in the north to the golden sands of Cronulla, passing right through the city centre via the famed Sydney Harbour Bridge. En route lie beaches to suit all preferences: empty ones, like Bilgola and Bungan; long ones, like Narrabeen and Collaroy; family-friendly Bronte; surfing paradise Bondi; and peaceful Malabar, where two shipwrecks lie offshore. The walk passes wind-whipped lookouts, rippling dunes, and ancient Gayamaygal carvings. It also takes in Circular Quay (now home to the Sydney Opera House), where the first colony was founded in 1788.

The southernmost few miles offer the biggest historical hit. Just north of Cronulla, Kamay Botany Bay National Park contains a monument marking Cook's Landing Place as well as more than thirty Aboriginal sites. Here, Australia's indigenous and colonial heritage sit side by side.

LEFT: The Sydney Great Coastal Walk is a wonderful way to explore the history and natural beauty of Sydney and the surrounding area.

259
LANTAU TRAIL

Hong Kong, China

The Portuguese established trading posts on mountainous Lantau Island in the early sixteenth century. However, over time, the many parties interested in the region – including the British, Dutch, French, and Chinese – mostly moved on, travelling to other outposts in the Pearl River Delta. While Hong Kong Island, just 6 miles (10km) east, is a skyscrapered megalopolis, Lantau Island remains relatively quiet and undeveloped. This provides the unexpected opportunity for some wild hiking. The 44-mile (70km) circular Lantau Trail loops along the island's south coast and across its rugged spine. It tops out at 935m (3,065ft) Lantau Peak, and then runs via ancient fishing villages, tucked-away beaches, and the giant Buddha of Po Lin Monastery. There are also stone circles thought to be thousands of years old.

260
Les Loups Trail

Québec, Canada

This 7-mile (11km) out-and-back trail leads to a viewpoint over the Laurentian Mountains in Canada's Jacques-Cartier National Park. It is named for the Frenchman who arrived here in 1534.

261
Mutrah Trail

Muscat, Oman

The Portuguese seized Mutrah (now part of Muscat) in 1515. This 1.5-mile (2.5km) section of the former trade route over the Hajar Mountains was once the only land access to the Arabian port.

262
Queen Charlotte Track

South Island, New Zealand

This 44-mile (70km) hike amid the Marlborough Sounds starts at Ship Cove. This is where British explorer Captain James Cook had his first significant encounter with the Maori people, in the 1770s.

263
James Cook Heritage Trails

Queensland, Australia

Cooktown was named for Captain Cook, who landed here in 1770. Trails, totalling 9 miles (14.5km), link his statue in the town centre to the rainforest of Mount Cook National Park.

FREEDOM TRAIL

Boston, United States

{ Follow the red line to explore Boston and the most dynamic period of early American history. }

Need to know
- Point in time: 1775–83 (American Revolution)
- Length: 2.5 miles (4km); 2–3 hours
- Difficulty: Easy – short; gentle
- Best months: Apr–Oct
- Top tip: Follow the trail independently using a map (from the visitor centre) or on a guided tour

265
Alexander Mackenzie Heritage Trail

British Columbia, Canada

Named for Alexander Mackenzie, the first European to trek across North America in 1793, this 280-mile (450km) trail runs from the Blackwater River near Quesnel into the Bella Coola Valley.

The American Revolution, fought between American colonial residents and their British overlords, lasted from 1775 to 1783. Discontent had been bubbling long before that, however, and much of the bubbling occurred on the streets of Boston. The Massachusetts metropolis, founded by English Puritans in 1630, is one of the oldest cities in the United States, and historically one of its most rebellious. It was here that politician Sam Adams rallied support for the patriot cause in the mid-eighteenth century. It was also here that key events stoked the revolutionary fire. This includes the 1770 Boston Massacre (during which British forces killed five colonists) and the 1773 Boston Tea Party (a protest against British taxes).

The short-but-sweet Freedom Trail links sixteen locations relating to this game-changing period of American history. A red line marks the route, leading for 2.5 miles (4km) from the great green expanse of Boston Common, through downtown and Italian-influenced North End, and over the Charles River to the USS *Constitution*. Maps can be picked up from the visitor information centre in Boston Common, the United States' oldest park. From the city's earliest days, settlers grazed cattle here. Since then, the land has seen everything from parties to public hangings. It was from Boston Common that British redcoats set off for Lexington and Concord in 1775, unknowingly bound for the battle that started the revolution.

The Freedom Trail dissects the park's north corner, emerging at the golden-domed Old State House. This was built on Beacon Hill for the newly independent state's representatives in 1798. The rotunda was originally gilded

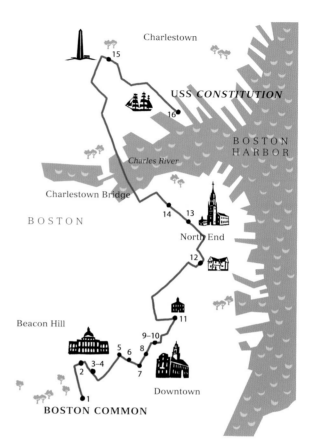

1. Boston Common
2. State House
3. Park Street Church
4. Granary Burying Ground
5. King's Chapel
6. Boston Latin School
7. Old Corner Bookstore
8. Old South Meeting House
9. Old State House
10. Boston Massacre site
11. Faneuil Hall Marketplace
12. Paul Revere's House
13. Old North Church
14. Copp's Hill Burying Ground
15. Bunker Hill Monument
16. USS *Constitution*

by coppersmith Paul Revere. From here, the trail passes Park Street Church to reach the Granary Burying Ground. This is the final resting place of Sam Adams and Paul Revere. There's also a marker for the victims of the Boston Massacre. Next is the glorious Georgian-style King's Chapel and its adjacent burying ground.

The trail then passes the Boston Latin School (the country's oldest public school), attended by five signers of the Declaration of Independence, including Benjamin Franklin, whose statue stands outside. The Old Corner Bookstore, built in 1718 and once the seat of Boston's esteemed literary scene, is currently a fast-food restaurant. No such fate has befallen the Old South Meeting House. You can head inside to see where 5,000 colonists (including Sam Adams) debated the fate of a certain shipment of tea in 1773. Grander still is the Old State House. Built in 1713 to house the colony's government, it became the epicentre of

events that triggered the revolution. In 1776 the Declaration of Independence was proclaimed from its balcony – and still is, every 4 July.

ABOVE: Boston's Old State House is one of the oldest public buildings in the United States.

Up Congress Street, via the site of the Boston Massacre, lies Faneuil Hall. Built as a place of commerce in 1741 – and now fronting Faneuil Hall Marketplace, where commerce continues – this historic gathering place is dubbed the 'Cradle of Liberty'. From Faneuil, the locations thin out a little. It's a longer walk, crossing the Rose Kennedy Greenway and passing the cannoli and pizza purveyors of North End, to reach Paul Revere's House. This is the oldest building in downtown Boston, and has been preserved as a museum.

Around the corner sits the Old North Church. Here, from the 58m (191ft) steeple, two lanterns were hung on 18 April 1775 (the night of Paul Revere's ride), to signal that British troops were advancing by sea. Copp's Hill Burying Ground is the final port of call before the Freedom Trail crosses the river over the Charlestown Bridge. It heads to Bunker Hill, where an obelisk marks the American Revolution's first big battle. The USS *Constitution*, launched in 1797, missed this conflict, but played its part in the War of 1812. It still sails into Boston Harbor every 4 July to join the independence celebrations.

266
Troy–Windsor
Trail

Jamaica

This 6-mile (10km) trail was blazed by the British Army during the eighteenth-century Maroon Wars (fought against escaped slaves). It is the quickest way across cave-riddled Cockpit Country.

GR20

Corsica, France

{ Head to the Mediterranean to tackle this tough but breathtaking island hike. }

Need to know
- *Point in time: 1755–69 (Corsica briefly independent)*
- *Length: 105 miles (170km); 10–12 days*
- *Difficulty: Strenuous – steep ups and downs*
- *Best months: June–Oct*
- *Top tip: Calenzana is 9 miles (15km) south of Calvi, which has an airport*

RIGHT: The GR20 is one of Europe's toughest hikes, but worth it for the challenge – and for the mountain views.

Brace yourself. The Grande Randonnée 20 (GR20), which cuts across the Mediterranean isle of Corsica, is often billed as Europe's toughest hike. This is largely because Corsica is so very hilly and rumpled, making the GR20 a relentless series of ups and downs. In total, the 105-mile (170km) trail involves around 19,000m (63,225ft) of ascent and descent. The fact that this trail masters all this mountainous terrain, however, is what makes it so magnificent. The GR20 enables mere hikers to reach extremes usually reserved for crampon-wearing climbers.

Central Corsica's seeming inaccessibility has long attracted people. Corsicans have a phrase, '*Prendre le maquis*', which means to hide away in the shrub-clogged interior. This is exactly what Corsican guerrillas did in the eighteenth century, when fighting the Genoese for independence. They gained independence in 1755, only to be reconquered by the French in 1769.

The GR20 truly does get lost in the hills. It follows old seasonal transhumance livestock paths and precipitous ridges in a northwest–southeast diagonal from the olive-growing village of Calenzana – site of a nationalist uprising in 1732 – to the village of Conca. The trail, which tops out at 2,225m (6,300ft) Brèche de Capitello, is split into sixteen stages, with basic refuges en route. These have communal kitchens and sell expensive provisions, but the views over glacial lakes, ice-crusted peaks, and glimpses of rare *mouflon* (mountain sheep) are worth every penny.

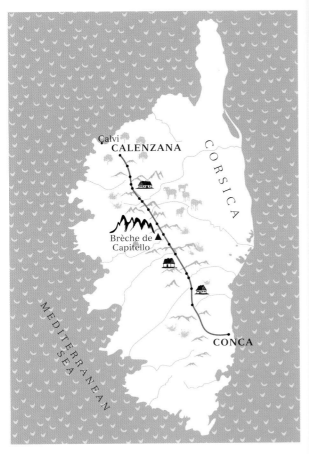

268
FORT TRAILS

Maharashtra, India

Was Chhatrapati Shivaji Maharaj a mountain bandit or a proto-nationalist Hindu hero? Opinion is divided on this warrior king. He founded India's Maratha Empire in 1674, and ruled from Raigad Hill Fort in Maharashtra. Indeed, Shivaji (as he is commonly known) was fond of forts. During his reign, he captured many existing strongholds and built some new ones. Eventually, he was in command of more than 350 fortresses. Some of these lie in the Western Ghats range, close to the city of Mumbai. Treks to them are possible with local guides. For instance, hike from the orchard-filled village of Prabalmachi up to the remains of Prabalgad. These abandoned ruins, now only inhabited by monkeys and birds, perch on top of a dramatic pinnacle, amid flat-topped mountains.

UPPER MUSTANG TREK

Mustang, Himalayas, Nepal

Seek permission to traverse
a timeless mountain 'kingdom'
untouched by the modern world.

Need to know
- *Point in time: 1790
  (Mustang annexed
  by Nepal)*
- *Length: 10 days*
- *Difficulty: Moderate/
  strenuous – remote;
  high altitude*
- *Best months: Mar–
  May; Sept–Nov*
- *Top tip: Permits
  are required to
  trek in Mustang*

Mustang is a land of near-mythical status. For a start, it's wonderfully remote, occupying a far-flung enclave of the Nepalese Himalayas entirely encircled by Tibet. Then there's its intriguing history as a once-powerful independent kingdom. There's the fact that foreigners were not allowed to visit the region until 1992. And there's the strong traditional Tibetan-influenced culture, still surviving here thanks to the region's lengthy period of isolation. All this makes Mustang (specifically Upper Mustang) irresistible to trekkers on the hunt for a real Shangri-la.

People have long walked here. Mustang once provided one of the easiest trade routes across the Himalayas between India and central Asia. The region subsequently prospered from the passage of salt, yak wool, grains, and spices. However, as trade routes changed, Mustang's fortunes faded. In 1790 the autonomous kingdom was annexed by Nepal. Shielded by mountains from both the European colonialists impacting the southern subcontinent and the Chinese assimilating the north, Mustang virtually fell off the map.

The fact that Mustang was so long ignored is a major plus point for today's hikers. Or, at least, those who secure one of the limited number of permits required to trek here. These lucky few get to enter a rarefied world that is untroubled by modernity. They also get to glimpse landscapes that are wonderfully strange. Mustang is an otherworldly rumple of red, yellow, brown, and blue fossiliferous sedimentary rocks carved into canyons by

ABOVE: A trip to remote Lo Manthang, one of the last bastions of Tibetan culture, is a truly unique experience.

the mighty Kali Gandaki river. It is raw, inhospitable, and utterly compelling.

The gateway to Upper Mustang is the village of Kagbeni, a two-hour walk north of regional hub Jomsom, which has an airport. Kagbeni is a cluster of mud houses, Buddhist *chortens* (shrines), and incongruously green terraces tucked away at 2,840m (9,320ft). It is also as far north as you can go without a permit. At the edge of Kagbeni, a 'Restricted Area' checkpoint, where documents will be inspected, marks the start of a loop up to the village of Lo Manthang and back, using the same trails as those ancient traders.

The trekking is dramatic, in parts following the Kali Gandaki Gorge itself, or traversing side furrows that lead off the main river. Rock walls striped in unlikely colours rear up on all sides, while the snow-capped Annapurna Range and 8,167m (26,795ft) Mount Dhaulagiri loom beyond. There are plenty of signs of human habitation too. Passes are strewn with prayer flags. *Chortens* painted white, red, and black, typical of the region, dot the plains. The honey-hued cliffs are pocked with mysterious, man-made cave dwellings that may be thousands of years old. Villages of tightly packed alleys perch in unlikely places, offering tea shops and warm welcomes. The houses are brightly painted, and many are adorned with sheep's horns

and hung with *zor* – thread-and-twig crosses supposed to catch evil spirits.

There are numerous architectural treasures, such as the vast *dzong* (fortress) of Tsarang and the old monastery of Dhi. However, Lo Manthang is the real prize. The town was developed as the capital of Mustang's Lo Kingdom in 1380. It thrived between the fifteenth and seventeenth centuries, when the kingdom was at its most powerful. Today, a 750m (2,460ft) long whitewashed wall still rings Lo Manthang's huddle of tiny lanes, vibrant houses, and four temples, the oldest dating to the 1440s. There's also the domineering Raja's Palace, former home of the kings of Mustang, a title that ceased to exist when Nepal became a republic in 2008. However, this democratic shift might just be the only thing that's changed in Upper Mustang for several centuries.

272
PAINTER'S WAY

Elbe Sandstone Mountains, Germany

Southeast Germany's Elbe highlands are, quite literally, 'as pretty as a picture'. Erosion has been especially creative here, sculpting the soft rock into aesthetically appealing cliffs, canyons, pillars, and ravines. These formations have inspired artists of all genres. First to popularise the place was landscapist Johann Alexander Thiele (1685 to 1752). The painter Canaletto, composer Richard Wagner, and writer Mary Shelley were also drawn here. The 70-mile (112km) Painter's Way reveals what attracted them. It runs from the Liebethaler Grund valley to the old town of Pirna, via Königstein Fortress, jagged Schrammsteine ridge, and the Bastei rocks. Pack a camera – or an easel.

273
VALLÉE DE MAI

Praslin, Seychelles

The idyllic Indian Ocean archipelago of the Seychelles is a paradise of dazzling sands and azure seas. It is also home to the fabled coco de mer tree, a kind of palm that produces nuts resembling a lady's buttocks and thighs. These risqué kernels used to wash up on distant shores, offering no hint as to where they had come from. The mystery was solved in 1768, when French explorer Marion du Fresne discovered coco de mer trees growing on the Seychellois island of Praslin. Today, these palms are extremely rare. However, a three-hour hike through the Eden-like forest of the Vallée de Mai provides a saucy glimpse.

MACCHABEE TRAIL

Black River Gorges National Park, Mauritius

{ Cut through the tropical forests of this Indian Ocean island to find its rarest birds – just not the dodo. }

Need to know

- *Point in time: 1662 (last widely accepted sighting of a dodo)*
- *Length: 6 miles (10km); 3 hours*
- *Difficulty: Easy – steep in parts*
- *Best months: May–Nov*
- *Top tip: While May to November is the driest period, the best time for blooming flowers is from September to January*

The Indian Ocean island of Mauritius is considered by some people to be the birthplace of wildlife conservation. Its endemic dodo, a large flightless bird related to the pigeon, fared badly after the Dutch settled here in 1598. It was easy to catch, and therefore was hunted by hungry mariners and the animals that they brought with them. Dodos are thought to have been wiped out by 1662. Centuries later, they were cited as one of the first examples of a species whose extinction was hastened by the acts of humans.

While you won't see any dodos along the island's 6-mile (10km) Macchabee Trail, you might spot a few other birds. The Black River Gorges National Park, through which this hike wends, is an untainted tranche of tropical forest. It is home to nine types of birds unique to Mauritius. This includes the rare pink pigeon, which was almost declared extinct in 1991 but is happily making a comeback.

The trail runs between the two main park entrances. Black River is close to the coast, while Le Petrin is in the hinterland. From Le Petrin, the trail follows a lush, flat forest track, passing a selection of the park's native trees and 300 species of flowering plants. At around the halfway mark, it opens up at a magnificent viewpoint where the Grande Rivière Noire Valley, the ocean, and green-fuzzed hills ripple off in all directions. From here it's a steep, slippery descent to the trail's end.

RIGHT: Look out for nine species of endemic birds on the Macchabee Trail. Sadly, this doesn't include the dodo.

HEKLA

Southern Iceland

With a reputation for explosive
and devastating eruptions, it's
little wonder that 1,488m (4,882ft)
Mount Hekla – one of Iceland's
most active volcanoes – was long
believed to be a 'gateway to hell'.
As such, no one dared to go near
it. That was until Icelandic
biologist Eggert Ólafsson risked
a summit attempt in 1750. An
entrance to the underworld was,
thankfully, not found. However,
the hike up Hekla (meaning
'hooded') remains a little hellish.
Starting around 100 miles (160km)
from Reykjavík, the eight-hour
return trip climbs barren slopes,
scored with spooky black lava
fields. The walk's final destination
is the mountain's ice-crusted,
sulphur-steaming craters, which
could blow at any second.

276
Bialowieza Forest

Eastern Poland

Long a royal hunting ground, Bialowieza Forest has been protected since an official decree in 1538. Today, it is Europe's last primeval forest. Various trails reveal wandering bison and ancient trees.

RIGHT: Spectacular views of western Europe's highest peak are guaranteed on the circular Tour du Mont Blanc.

TOUR DU MONT BLANC

France, Italy, and Switzerland

{ Circuit the highest mountain in the Alps in the footsteps of the earliest mountaineers. }

A hike through three countries, circumnavigating western Europe's highest peak, in the birthplace of mountaineering . . . simply, the Tour du Mont Blanc is an Alpine classic.

It was in 1767 that Swiss scientist Horace-Bénédict de Saussure first walked a circuit around the then-unclimbed 4,810m (15,781ft) Mont Blanc, searching for a route to the top. He was beaten to the summit – Mont Blanc was first conquered by Jacques Balmat and Michel-Gabriel Paccard in 1786. But for many, Saussure's stroll beneath the mountain sounds far more appealing. This way, hikers – not just technical climbers – can enjoy all the spectacular views, valleys, villages, glaciers, and meadows in its shadow.

Most trekkers begin the circular 105-mile (170km) Tour du Mont Blanc in Les Houches, at the southern end of France's Chamonix Valley, and walk anticlockwise. From here, the trail heads south to pretty Les Chapieux, then veers northeast into Italy, passing the lively town of Courmayeur. Crossing into Switzerland, the trail curves around via the chocolate-box village of Champex and the rocky 2,665m (8,745ft) Fenêtre d'Arpette, the circuit's highest point. It then heads south back into France, scaling the 2,368m (7,770ft) Col du Brevent, from where there are matchless views of Mont Blanc. Finally, you'll descend into the spirited Alpine town of Chamonix, where you can celebrate a walk well done.

Need to know
- *Point in time: 1767 (Horace-Bénédict de Saussure first circumnavigated Mont Blanc)*
- *Length: 105 miles (170km); 10–12 days*
- *Difficulty: Moderate/ strenuous – steep sections; good facilities*
- *Best months: June– Sept*
- *Top tip: There is plentiful and varied accommodation en route, including huts and hotels*

LOIRE ON FOOT TRAIL

Loire River, France

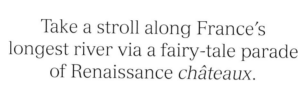

Take a stroll along France's
longest river via a fairy-tale parade
of Renaissance *châteaux*.

Need to know
- *Point in time: 1500–1800 (Renaissance period)*
- *Length: 775 miles (1,250km); 60–65 days*
- *Difficulty: Easy – minimal gradients; easy to follow*
- *Best months: Apr–June; Sept*
- *Top tip: Loire châteaux vary – some are fully open, some are open for garden visits, some remain in private hands*

Navigation is seldom an issue along France's oldest hiking path. The 'Loire on Foot Trail', otherwise known as the Grande Randonnée 3 (GR3), sticks to the valley of the Loire River for 775 miles (1,250km). It follows the flow from its source at Mont Gerbier-de-Jonc, a curious volcanic bump in the Massif Central, to its mouth at the Atlantic seaside resort of La Baule. It's a right angle of a route. First, it runs virtually due north through France's middle to the city of Orléans. It then turns west to the Bay of Biscay.

This is not a wilderness hike. The Loire is the longest river in France and has been an important trade route since the Iron Age. Subsequently, it is dotted with settlements, including the towns of Blois, Chinon, Saumur, and Tours. It also travels via hunting forests and rolling vineyards.

The Loire's most striking characteristic is its profusion of castles, or *châteaux*. The waterway served as the border between England and France during the Hundred Years' War (1337–1453). Due to the valley's frontier status, many estates and homesteads here were expanded to become huge medieval fortresses. Then, following the end of hostilities, conflict was replaced by culture as the flamboyant King François I came to power in 1515. The ideas of the Renaissance, a time of artistic, political, and philosophical reawakening, flourished along the riverbank. This was helped by the invention of the printing press, which could mass-produce books full of design inspiration. Many of the Loire's castles were rebuilt or prettified into fairy-tale

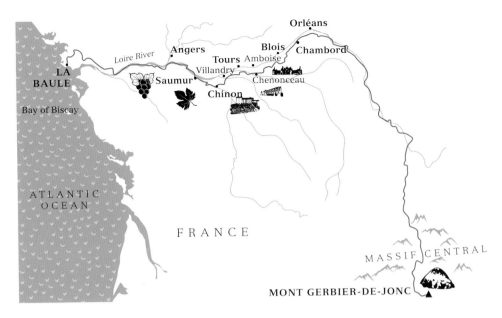

pleasure palaces, with romantic turrets, soaring spires, elaborate arches, crenellations, pilasters, and perfectly pruned gardens. Despite the anti-nobility ravages of the French Revolution (1789–99), when some of these regal residences were razed or ransacked, many of the Loire *châteaux* survive today.

Walking the whole GR3 takes a while, but you can pick a more manageable section. Opt for the stretch between Sully-sur-Loire (just east of the city of Orléans) and Chalonnes (west of the city of Angers). This particular 175-mile (280km) run of river is a World Heritage Site, on account of it being an 'outstanding cultural landscape'. Indeed, the countryside here is a bucolic confection of rolling hills, sweeping floodplains, rich farmland, and distant woods. It is glorious and green.

The river running through it is split into channels by many tiny islands. It is also hemmed in by embankments, built from the twelfth century in an effort to curb the Loire's overflowing tendencies. The river remains untamed, however. The region's typical low tufa and limestone cliffs have also been employed to great effect, providing both troglodyte cave dwellings and the stone used in the construction of *châteaux*.

French Renaissance–style Chambord, the biggest of the Loire Valley *châteaux*, is moated and turreted. It was commissioned by the aforementioned King François I in the early sixteenth century as a hunting lodge. It contains more than 400 rooms and eighty-four staircases.

The slightly less grand Chenonceau was a small riverside fortress when nobleman Thomas Bohier acquired it in 1512. Over successive decades, it was transformed into a glorious Gothic-Renaissance mansion. It boasts fountains in the grounds, and an impressive arched gallery that spans the lazy Cher River. During the First World War, this gallery was used as a hospital.

Other *châteaux* worth noting include Villandry, built around 1536 and renowned for its exquisite gardens; island-sited Azay-le-Rideau, the sixteenth-century reimagining of an earlier medieval bastion; and imperious Amboise, a medieval fortress that was converted by France's King Charles VIII into a luxurious retreat. He died here in 1498, after hitting his head on a door lintel.

With regal splendour at virtually every meander of the Loire, this is a very grand Grande Randonnée indeed.

279
Ankarana Reserve

Madagascar

Hike through strange *tsingy* (sharp limestone pinnacles) and learn about the indigenous Antankarana peoples, whose roots here can be traced back to the sixteenth century.

280

PIETERPAD

Netherlands

The 288-mile (464km) Pieterpad is the path to pick if you don't like hills. This trail runs right across the Netherlands, which first became recognised as an independent nation in 1648. Although it finishes with an ascent of Mount St Pieter (the route's highest point), the 'mount' is only 110m (360ft) high. Starting at coastal Pieterburen, the Pieterpad gives a comprehensive overview of Dutch landscapes. From the vast, dyke-humped northern flats, it wiggles south through farmland and lonely forests (where you'll find the former sites of Nazi transportation camps). It then nips briefly into Germany, passes castles, and finishes amid the 'hill country' around cosmopolitan Maastricht, right on the Belgian border.

281
Keukenhof Garden Trails

Lisse, Netherlands

In the 1630s, tulips were traded for huge amounts of money, until the Tulip Crash of 1637. Appreciate their appeal at Keukenhof, which has 9 miles (14km) of footpaths and 7 million flowering bulbs to enjoy.

282
Golden Age Canals

Amsterdam, Netherlands

Relive the seventeenth-century Dutch Golden Age by tracing three of the period's finest canals through the capital: the Herengracht (Gentlemen's Canal), Keizersgracht (Emperor's Canal), and Prinsengracht (Prince's Canal).

283
The Constitutional

Philadelphia, United States

Take a 3-mile (5km) stroll in 'America's Birthplace'. Independence Hall, where the Declaration of Independence was signed in 1776, is one of its thirty historic sites.

284
Gardens of Versailles

France

Versailles became France's political nucleus when King Louis XIV moved here in 1682. It also became an ostentatious pleasure palace. Take a 6-mile (10km) promenade around its glorious, fountain-glittered grounds.

285
WALL WALK

Cartagena, Colombia

There's a good reason why the Caribbean coastal port of Cartagena is enclosed within such formidable ramparts. The city, founded by the Spanish in 1533, was a literal treasure chest, used to store Inca gold on its way to Europe. The initial ramparts were bolstered over subsequent centuries, safeguarding the multicoloured, flower-draped Old Town within the most extensive fortifications in South America. It is now World Heritage–listed. The old *murallas* (walls) stand in four sections and the Wall Walk is a not-quite-continuous loop of all four, taking about ninety minutes. Start a circuit from the bastion of San Francisco Javier (built in 1617) in the late afternoon to look down on both the sea and the city under a golden sunset glow.

ICON TRAIL

San Valley, Poland

{ Amble through the church-scattered
hills of Poland's southeast for
a lesson in the region's iconic art. }

Need to know

- *Point in time: 1510–1659 (wooden Orthodox church built in Ulucz)*
- *Length: 44 miles (70km); 3–4 days*
- *Difficulty: Easy/ moderate – not well marked; gentle walking*
- *Best months: May–Oct*
- *Top tip: Trains connect Sanok to Krakow, which is 124 miles (200km) to the northwest*

The Szlak Ikon, or 'Icon Trail', that runs through the San Valley in the wooded foothills of the Bieszczady Mountains is a walk through the history of iconic art. The area is scattered with villages that retain their old Orthodox and Uniat (Eastern-rite Catholic) churches, many of which are decorated with ancient icons. These are sacral images painted on wood, mostly dating from between the fifteenth and seventeenth centuries.

The 44-mile (70km) Icon Trail starts in the town of Sanok, where a visit to the Historical Museum provides a good grounding in such treasures. Located in Sanok's old sixteenth-century castle, the museum contains Poland's most important collection of religious art. It also displays liturgical objects, including antique books and bishops' medallions. From Sanok, the route follows the San River amid tree-cloaked slopes, looping through a series of villages, each with an elegant, onion-domed house of worship. In Tyrawa Solna you can see the wooden Orthodox church of John the Baptist (built in 1837), which is now a Roman Catholic church. Dobra Szlachecka has a unique seventeenth-century log-hewn gatehouse as well as an elegant church with a fine iconostasis (decorated screen).

It is the village of Ulucz, however, that is home to one of the oldest wooden Orthodox churches in Poland. It was originally thought to have been built in 1510, but recent dendrochronological analysis (dating by the rings of wood) suggests that 1659 is more likely. Either way, perched on a steep hill, overlooking the river, it is as pretty as a picture.

RIGHT: Pretty villages, ancient iconic art, and the San River are all highlights of the Icon Trail.

Ulucz

Dobra Szlachecka

POLAND

Tyrawa Solna

San River

SANOK

SAN VALLEY

BIESZCZADY MOUNTAINS

TAJ NATURE WALK

Agra, India

Historical sites don't get any more romantic than the Taj Mahal. Built at the behest of Mughal emperor Shah Jahan to house the tomb of his favourite wife, Mumtaz Mahal, the Taj was completed in 1653. It is a mausoleum of matchless craftsmanship, with domes of white marble, *pietra dura* (mosaic work using precious stones), and exquisite calligraphy. These days, the Taj Mahal is generally heaving with tourists. But the 6-mile (9.5km) Taj Nature Walk, which leads from the Eastern Gate into a nearby reserve, offers an opportunity for some peace and reflection in the monument's shadow. Walk amid the trees, flowers, and birds, and climb the raised watchtowers for views back to the Taj Mahal itself.

288
MALTA COASTAL WALK

Malta

The small yet strategic Mediterranean isle of Malta has been safeguarded from invasion by coastal lookouts since the Middle Ages. But it was the crusading Catholic Knights Hospitaller (later to become known as the Knights of Malta) who built an extensive network of watchtowers. Largely constructed during the seventeenth century, the fortifications crowded the shore, each one in sight of the next. A 100-mile (160km) circumnavigation of the island takes in today's remaining towers. These include striking-red St Agatha's Tower, and Triq il-Wiesg, now paired with a First World War pillbox. Aged Wignacourt, completed in 1610, is the oldest tower still standing.

289
REVOLUTION WALK

Paris, France

Take a 3-mile (5km) walk in eighteenth-century Paris, strolling through the Age of Enlightenment and the rage of the French Revolution. Start at the Panthéon mausoleum. It was commissioned by King Louis XV, and now houses works by Voltaire, Rousseau, and other key figures of the Enlightenment. Next, head west into the Jardin du Luxembourg. Then go gradually northeast, via Café Le Procope (where Voltaire used to drink), and the former Palais Bourbon (repurposed as the seat of the democratic National Assembly in 1795). Crossing the Seine, finish in Place de la Concorde where, during the French Revolution, more than 1,000 people – including Marie Antoinette and King Louis XVI – met their end under the blade of the guillotine.

290
PORTICO OF 666 ARCHES

Bologna, Italy

Privileged were the pilgrims traipsing to the sacred icon (allegedly painted by St Luke) inside Bologna's hilltop Sanctuary of the Madonna of San Luca. There would be no exposure to the elements for them. Between 1674 and 1793, a covered portico of almost 2.5 miles (3.8km) – the world's longest of its kind – was built. The portico leads from the Saragozza Gate in the old city walls up to the sacred basilica, keeping the faithful nice and dry. It is supported by 666 arches, while fifteen prayer stops punctuate the upper section. From the top, there are views over the terracotta-hued medieval city and the green Po Valley beyond.

292
Paseo del Morro

San Juan, Puerto Rico

Walk the 2-mile (3km) Paseo del Morro trail alongside the sturdy walls, built to protect the port of Old San Juan in the 1630s.

291
QUÉBEC CITY WALLS

Québec, Canada

Capital of French Canada for most of the seventeenth and eighteenth centuries, and strategically sited on the St Lawrence River, Québec City was deemed well worth protecting. Between 1690 and 1745, a great grey enceinte, measuring almost 3 miles (4.6km) and strengthened by redoubts, guard posts, and cannons, was built around this far-flung outpost of France. It was built mainly to keep the British at bay – which didn't entirely work. Now Québec City is the only remaining fortified city in North America. Follow the walls' perimeter, negotiate the gates, peer through the embrasures, and look over the alleys of Old Québec huddled inside.

293
Douro Valley

Portugal

Take a 10-mile (16km) circular walk in the vineyard-striped Pinhão Valley, in the heart of the Douro. This region was designated as a protected port wine–producing appellation in 1756.

ROB ROY WAY

Southwest Scotland, United Kingdom

Follow a legendary Scottish outlaw across grand glens, lovely lochs, and wild highlands.

Need to know
- *Point in time: 1671–1734 (lifetime of Rob Roy)*
- *Length: 77 miles (124km); 7 days*
- *Difficulty: Moderate – undulating; boggy; exposed in places*
- *Best months: May–Sept*
- *Top tip: Buses run to Drymen from Glasgow and to Pitlochry from Edinburgh; Pitlochry also has a railway station*

Rob Roy MacGregor is Scotland's most notorious fugitive. Born at Glengyle on Loch Katrine in 1671, red-haired Rob was a tough, gutsy 'boy of the hills'. In 1689 he fought against the English at Killiecrankie, a key battle of the first Jacobite uprising that saw many Scottish Highlanders fight to restore the Catholic King James II to the thrones of England and Scotland. Rob went on to become a clan leader, and made money by cattle rustling, and then safeguarding cattle from other rustlers.

Things went wrong in 1713. Rob defaulted on a loan and was declared an outlaw. He returned to rustling, rallied the MacGregors against the English, was tried for treason, and lived on the run. Twice he was caught, but twice he escaped. In 1725 he gave himself up, received a royal pardon, and died quietly in 1734. However, by this stage Rob was already a legend. The 1723 tome *The Highland Rogue* embedded him in Scottish folklore. Later, renowned romanticiser Sir Walter Scott immortalised him in his 1817 book *Rob Roy*. Hero or not, this infamous cattleman, idealised as a dashing, raffish, ginger-curled bandit, came to symbolise a vanishing way of life.

Happily, the Rob Roy Way, which follows tracks and byways used by clansmen, drovers, and Jacobites, offers a suitably romantic introduction to the Scottish countryside. The 77-mile (124km) trail runs northeast from the village of Drymen, in Stirling, to the Victorian resort town of Pitlochry, in Perthshire. It begins by plunging through the Trossachs, a region of wooded lochs and

ABOVE: Visit the places where outlaw Rob Roy hid and was sheltered.

glens. Rob drove cattle through Drymen, just east of Loch Lomond, into the safety of the oak and Caledonian pine forests here. A cave where Rob hid and schemed is nestled alongside Loch Ard, just off the trail. You could also detour west to his birthplace, now replaced by Glengyle House. In the village of Aberfoyle, one of the main hubs of the Trossachs, Rob Roy legends (and namesake businesses) abound.

Between Aberfoyle and the small town of Callander, the Rob Roy Way heads into the Menteith Hills and to Loch Venachar, offering spectacular views. The route then follows the River Teith upstream, passing the Falls of Leny to reach the tiny district of Strathyre. Nearby is the beautiful glen of Balquhidder, where Rob settled after his pardon. He is buried (with his wife) in the church. Next stop, via rugged ridges and sparkling Loch Earn, is Killin. This village is home to the Falls of Dochart and ruined Finlarig Castle, where Rob reputedly sheltered when he was on the run.

From Killin the route climbs to its highest point (565m / 1,855ft), with exposed moorland and the southern shores of Loch Tay leading to Ardtalnaig. This is truly remote walking. Indeed, the scenery is straight from a Walter Scott novel all the way to Aberfeldy. If you want to add an extra challenge, there's an alternative, wilder route from Ardtalnaig, via Glen Almond, Amulree, and

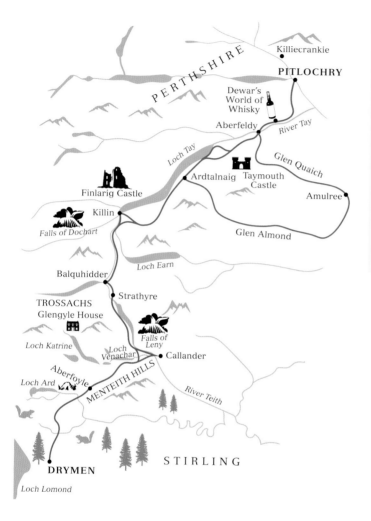

**295
Mediterranean
Steps and
Douglas Path**

Gibraltar

The British claimed
Gibraltar, a rock off
the coast of southern
Spain, in 1713. This
4.5-mile (7km) hike
via wildflowers and
Barbary apes
leads to their old
fortification.

Glen Quaich. This longer trail extends the hike to 94 miles
(151km).

The final leg from Aberfeldy crosses moors and follows
the River Tay to finish in a small memorial garden in
Pitlochry. The battle site of Killiecrankie is just to the
north, if you fancy another Rob detour. Or simply relax
in Pitlochry, a genteel Highland resort, to raise a glass
of whisky to the MacGregor clan's main man.

296
Mount Vernon Trail

Virginia, United States

This 18-mile (29km) route runs along the Potomac River, from George Washington's Mount Vernon estate (which he owned from 1761 until his death) to Theodore Roosevelt Island, via the Pentagon and skyline views of Washington DC.

297
The Narrow Road

Honshu, Japan

In 1689 Japanese poet Matsuo Basho began a 1,490-mile (2,400km) journey north from Tokyo. He recorded it in his book *The Narrow Road*. Sections can still be followed.

298
Goethe Trail

Harz Mountains, Germany

This 10-mile (16km) ascent from the village of Torfhaus up the Brocken (the highest peak of the Harz Mountains) was taken by the author Goethe in December 1777. It was said to have cured his writer's block.

299
Christian's Cave Climb

Pitcairn Island

Make the forty-minute hike from Adamstown – capital of Pitcairn Island in the South Pacific – to the cave where Fletcher Christian purportedly used to look out to sea after mutinying on the *Bounty* in 1789.

300
TUDOR TRAIL

Southern England, United Kingdom

No monarch looms as large in British history as King Henry VIII – husband to six wives, and creator of the Church of England. The 53-mile (85km) Tudor Trail links sites connected to this sixteenth-century king. It starts at Penshurst Place, once owned by the powerful Duke of Buckingham, who Henry beheaded in 1521. Running south across the bucolic Weald, the trail travels via Hever Castle (family seat of Anne Boleyn, wife number two). It then visits Ashdown Forest (where Henry enjoyed a hunt), Lewes Priory (razed in 1537 when Henry dissolved the monasteries), and Thomas Cromwell's manor (given to Anne of Cleves, wife number four, after Henry executed Cromwell in 1540).

301
SULTAN'S TRAIL

Austria to Turkey

{ March from Vienna to Istanbul
in the style of a 'magnificent'
Ottoman emperor. }

Need to know
- *Point in time: 1520–1566 (rule of Süleyman the Magnificent)*
- *Length: 1,326 miles (2,133km); 4 months*
- *Difficulty: Moderate – long; varied terrain*
- *Best months: May–Oct*
- *Top tip: Lodging options vary along the route; in some areas a tent may be required*

The ruler of the Ottoman Empire from 1520 to 1566 was known as Süleyman the Magnificent. He was considered a paragon of Islamic leadership, a just and astute politician, a patron of art and architecture, and an accomplished poet. He was also a bold military strategist, which in 1529 led him to muster an army, march west, and lay siege to Vienna. It was one of the greatest Muslim incursions on Christian Europe. However, despite his brilliance, Süleyman was defeated, and forced to troop back to Constantinople (now Istanbul).

The Sultan's Trail retraces this retreat. It is a suitably magnificent 1,326-mile (2,133km) hike through what was

LEFT: Retrace the retreat of Süleyman the Magnificent from Austria to Turkey, passing through Transylvania.

the western Ottoman Empire. Today, this area comprises much of Austria, Slovakia, Hungary, Croatia, Serbia, Romania, Bulgaria, Greece, and Turkey. The route starts at St Stephen's Cathedral in Vienna (the bells of which are made from melted Ottoman cannons), and ends at Istanbul's Süleymaniye Mosque. This is the city's biggest mosque, and home to the sultan's tomb.

There's so much to see en route. Depending on which trail you follow, this includes the Danube River at Bratislava, the fortress of Belgrade, Transylvania's castles, the capital cities of Bucharest and Sofia, ruin-ridden Greek Macedonia and Thrace, and the onetime Ottoman capital city of Edirne. By the time you hit Istanbul and the shores of the Bosphorus Straits, Asia lies just across the water.

302

EVLIYA ÇELEBI WAY

Turkey

Evliya Çelebi was a man who liked to wander. This Ottoman Turk spent forty years travelling and writing about his adventures. In 1671 he set off on a hajj (pilgrimage) to Mecca. The 205-mile (330km) Evliya Çelebi Way follows a fraction of that journey, from near Yalova, on the Izmit Gulf (a ferry ride from Istanbul), to Simav, in the Aegean region. The trail meanders – Çelebi rarely chose the quickest route. It follows riverside paths, goat tracks, and Roman roads, via varied Turkish scenes. This includes tiny villages, Ottoman relics, mountain slopes, fertile valleys, innumerable *kahvehane* (coffeehouses), and the walled city of Iznik. It also visits tile-producing Kütahya, Çelebi's ancestral home.

303

PUNAKHA WINTER TREK

Western Bhutan

In Bhutan, there are flying phalluses everywhere. They are painted on walls, and carved wooden versions dangle from eaves. Do not be shocked. They are simply the symbol of Lama Drukpa Kunley (1455–1529), Bhutan's favorite saint. Also known as the 'Divine Madman', Kunley used wit and outrageousness to spread Buddhism across the country. The easy three-day Punakha Winter Trek follows an old footpath from near riverside Dechencholing Palace (near the capital of Thimphu) to Zomlingthang, in the Punakha Valley. It visits Chorten Ningpo, an ancient stone monument linked to the saint. You can camp here overnight. The trek also takes in the 3,400m (11,155ft) Sinchula Pass, pristine forests, traditional villages, and plenty of phalluses too.

304

SHAKESPEARE'S WAY

Southern England, United Kingdom

William Shakespeare was born in a half-timbered house in Stratford-upon-Avon in 1564. He grew up to be the world's greatest wordsmith. While Shakespeare loved his hometown, during his most prolific period of writing he lived in London. The 146-mile (235km) Shakespeare's Way links Stratford-upon-Avon and London, following a route the Bard might have taken on his journeys between the two. The countryside has changed a little since the sixteenth century, but still offers treats. This includes Cotswold villages built with honey-coloured stone, grandiose Blenheim Palace (birthplace of Winston Churchill), Oxford's dreaming spires, and the banks of the Thames. The trail ends at Shakespeare's Globe Theatre, a riverside reconstruction of the 1599 original.

305

GRIMMSTEIG

Central Germany

There's an air of magic along the 52-mile (84km) Grimmsteig. The wooded thickets of the Kaufungen Forest and the Meissner Mountains seem to harbour fairies and frog kings, Snow White, Cinderella, and golden geese. That's because this is 'Grimm country'. The famed Brothers Grimm, masters of the fairy tale, spent a large part of their lives compiling and editing stories in the grand city of Kassel (home to a Brothers Grimm Museum). The Grimmsteig route, named in their honour, makes a loop to the east of Kassel. It veers through medieval villages and bewitching countryside that must have provided rich inspiration for their stories. Highlights en route include the half-timbered huddle of Oberkaufungen and the romantic ruins of Reichenbach Castle.

CAMINO REAL

Panama

{ Walk between the Caribbean Sea and the Pacific Ocean on the trail of the Spanish conquistadores and their convoys of gold. }

Need to know
- *Point in time: 1513 (Vasco Núñez de Balboa first crossed the Isthmus of Panama)*
- *Length: 50 miles (80km); 5 days*
- *Difficulty: Strenuous – humid; wet; remote*
- *Best months: Dec–Apr*
- *Top tip: Hiking poles, insect repellent, binoculars, and bathing suit all recommended*

As you hack your way along this steamy jungle trail carrying only a backpack, be grateful that your load is a lot lighter than those hefted by the Spanish conquistadores some five centuries before. For a while, the wild, 50-mile (80km) Camino Real, or 'Royal Road', was the most crucial route in the Spanish Main. It was used by the colonialists to cart Incan gold and gems overland, from ports on the west coast of Central America to ports on the east. These treasures were then sailed across the Atlantic Ocean back to Spain.

Of course, the Spaniards weren't the first to hike this way. This shortcut across the Isthmus of Panama – the skinny strip of land separating the Pacific Ocean from the Caribbean Sea – was long known to the indigenous Embera people. However, the conquistadores only found out about it in 1513, just after Spanish explorer Vasco Núñez de Balboa became the first European to see the Pacific Ocean. Balboa made a tortuous, twenty-five-day trek across the wider Darien Province to glimpse the world's biggest ocean. He soon learned from the Embera people that, if he'd set off further to the north, he could have done the journey in just five days. Armed with this new knowledge, a superhighway of riches was born.

The importance of the Camino Real was fairly brief. British privateers quickly arrived on the scene and, during the following century, crushed the Spaniards' transportation of treasures. The cobblestones of the Royal Road were subsumed by Mother Nature's tropical

RIGHT: Follow the Camino Real all the way to the Caribbean and the impressive military remains in Portobelo.

abundance and all but forgotten. Until now. With a knowledgeable guide and a sense of adventure, it is possible to retrace this gilded route.

The Camino Real originally began in Panamá Viejo, where Latin loot would be unloaded. Founded in 1519 and now a suburb of Panama City, Viejo is the oldest European settlement on the Americas' Pacific coast. Its World Heritage–listed remains include sixteenth-century houses and churches. However, to avoid tramping through the modern conurbation, today's explorers should start in the traditional Embera village of San Juan de Pequeni, a two-hour drive inland.

Ahead lies four or five days of challenging jungle hiking in Chagres National Park. It includes wading thigh-deep in rivers, squelching through mud, and keeping a lookout for fer-de-lance snakes and the paw-prints of jaguars. Indeed, there's lots you might see. The Panamanian jungle is one of the most biodiverse places on the planet. In all, the country is home to more than 10,400 species of plants, 255 species of mammals, and 972 species of birds. It's worth scanning around for anything shiny, too. It is alleged that all sorts of gems, jewels, and ingots were lost in transit. Some lucky people have even found gold flakes in the rivers and bullion off the coast. Some continue to search, looking for the fabled 'Viper Pits', into which cartloads of Spanish bounty reputedly fell and were never retrieved, for fear of the snakes slithering within.

The maintained trail makes it possible to traverse this otherwise untamed jungle, albeit by negotiating slippery rocks, splashing through creeks, and climbing up rocks. However, the forest all around is an impenetrable abyss. This is illustrated by an old railway nearby, which was only abandoned in the mid-twentieth century. It has already been eaten up by the forest.

The Camino Real finally hits the Caribbean at Portobelo, now a sleepy fishing village but once the embarkation point for all that lovely loot. The crumbling remains of impressive military forts serve as a reminder of those conquistadores' golden days.

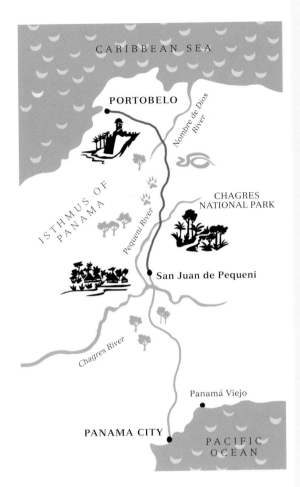

CARIBBEAN SEA

PORTOBELO

Nombre de Dios River

ISTHMUS OF PANAMA

Pequeni River

CHAGRES NATIONAL PARK

San Juan de Pequeni

Chagres River

Panamá Viejo

PANAMA CITY

PACIFIC OCEAN

309
MONARCH'S WAY

Southern England, United Kingdom

In the mid-seventeenth century, England was embroiled in a bitter internal conflict. The English Civil War ended in 1651 when King Charles II was beaten by Oliver Cromwell's Parliamentarian forces. The country became a republic and the king was forced to flee. The 615-mile (990km) Monarch's Way traces King Charles's escape from Worcester, in the West Midlands, to the English Channel at Shoreham, from where he sailed to France. It's a circuitous route across the Cotswolds, the Mendips, and the South Downs. As Charles was chased, he made diversions, which are mimicked by this route. Highlights include his hiding spots at Boscobel's Royal Oak and Moseley Old Hall's priest hole. The route also visits the towns of Bristol, Charmouth, Salisbury, and Arundel.

307
Rembrandt Trail

Leiden, Netherlands

The Dutch painter Rembrandt was born in Leiden in 1606. A short city trail links places of note, from his birthplace to the studio where he learned his craft.

308
Brine Trail

Salzkammergut, Austria

This 25-mile (40km) trail follows the world's oldest pipeline. It was created in 1607 to transport brine from Lake Hallstatt to Ebensee, through the Salzkammergut region's pretty peaks.

GOLD TRAIL

Costa Verde, Brazil

{ Follow a cobblestone path through the rainforest, built by slaves to transport eighteenth-century gold. }

Need to know

- *Point in time: 1696 (gold found in Minas Gerais)*
- *Length: 60 miles (100km); 4–5 days*
- *Difficulty: Moderate – hot; wet*
- *Best months: Apr–Oct*
- *Top tip: Serra da Bocaina has limited facilities – a guide is essential*

311
El Camino Real de Tierra Adentro

Mexico and United States

'The Royal Road of the Interior Land' was a 1,600-mile (2,560km) trade route between Mexico City and San Juan Pueblo, New Mexico, from 1598 to 1882. Segments can still be walked.

Southern Brazil's Costa Verde, meaning the 'Green Coast', hides a 'golden' hiking trail. The route begins in the coastal town of Paraty, which was once a more important Brazilian hub than Rio de Janeiro. It was founded in 1597, and formally established as a town in 1667 by Portuguese colonisers. However, the area was already populated by the indigenous Guaianás people, who called the whole region Paraty, meaning 'River of Fish'.

In 1696 large gold deposits were discovered by *bandeirantes* (seventeenth-century Portuguese fortune hunters) in the nearby inland state of Minas Gerais. A road was subsequently built to link the mining town of Ouro Prêto, in Minas Gerais, with Paraty. From the latter, gold bullion could be loaded onto boats, and sent across the Atlantic Ocean to the Portuguese motherland.

This transportation road – quite literally a gold trail – was built in the early eighteeenth century by African slaves. They were forced to hack back the jungle and haul stones from the river to create a cobblestone pathway for riches that they would never possess. The road they built ran for a total length of around 745 miles (1,200km). Today's Trilha de Ouro, or 'Gold Trail', is a 60-mile (100km) segment of this route, travelling over the Serra do Mar mountain range to the coast at Mambucaba. It cuts through Serra da Bocaina National Park and explores short, mossy sections of the old road.

RIGHT: You can still explore short sections of the old 'Gold Trail', built by African slaves in the early eighteenth century.

312
RIBEIRA DA JANELA LEVADA

Madeira, Portugal

Mountainous Madeira was not the easiest place to cultivate. The Atlantic island's extreme gradients and uneven water distribution posed a challenge to the colonising Portuguese. However, from the sixteenth century onward, the settlers set about constructing *levadas* (channels) to move water from the wet northwest to the drier, more habitable southeast. Along the way, they also created a network of excellent footpaths. Madeira is now riddled with trails alongside levadas. The 7.5-mile (12km) out-and-back trail along the Ribeira da Janela Levada is a good example. It follows a well-preserved channel from the water house at Lamaceiros, via cascades, apple orchards, hydrangeas, and dark tunnels. At the end is a lookout over the steep-sided valley and the sea.

313
NAKASENDO WAY

Honshu, Japan

{ Hike from Kyoto to Tokyo, following the original old stones of a historic highway. }

Need to know
- *Point in time: 1603–1868 (Edo period)*
- *Length: 330 miles (533km); 18–20 days*
- *Difficulty: Easy/ moderate – some climbs; good infrastructure*
- *Best months: Apr–Oct*
- *Top tip: Shinkansen bullet trains link Kyoto with Tokyo in 2.5 hours*

314
Tokaido Trail

Honshu, Japan

Linking Kyoto with Tokyo via the coast, the 305-mile (492km) Tokaido Road was an alternative to the Nakasendo Way – though less of this seventeenth-century highway still exists.

When Tokugawa Ieyasu became shogun of Japan in 1603 – marking the start of the country's Edo period – he wanted roads. Roads, he reckoned, enabled greater control over the people. So, as military commander-in-chief (considered even more powerful than the emperor), he set about the construction of five major highways, all leading to his political headquarters – Edo. This is now known as Tokyo.

This wasn't a brand-new idea. Japan had a transportation network from at least the eighth century. It was inaugurated so that tax payments could be moved around more easily. However, as time passed, greedy officials and wayside bandits made it increasingly difficult and dangerous to travel. What Tokugawa and his successors did, from the 1600s, was utilise these existing thoroughfares and bring them into the seventeenth century.

The Nakasendo, meaning 'the Road through the Mountains', was one of the period's main highways. It linked major destinations on Honshu, Japan's largest and main island. This included Kyoto, Japan's capital at the time, the ever-expanding Edo, and parts of the island's interior. The Tokaido route, a bigger and busier alternative, also connected Kyoto with Edo, but via Honshu's Pacific coast. Today, a larger amount of the Nakasendo remains intact, while the Tokaido has been mostly built over.

The Nakasendo once stretched for 330 miles (533km). From Kyoto, it skirted Lake Biwa and rose over the mountains at the town of Sekigahara. It then traversed the plains near the southern Japanese Alps, headed along the

ABOVE: Step back 400 years by walking on part of the ancient Nakasendo road.

Kiso Valley, and veered south over the Kanto Plain to Edo. It was dotted with sixty-seven post towns. These were evenly spaced rest stops where travellers could find food, drink, and lodgings, and from which the shogun could control who was using the road. Initially the network was supposed to cater to *daimyo* (lords), *samurai* (high-class military men), and government officials. However, pilgrims, merchants, and pleasure seekers quickly began using the roads too.

A walk along the whole Nakasendo is not really viable. Too much has been lost. But there are plenty of preserved fragments that offer a taste of life in Edo-era Japan. Kyoto makes a fine beginning. Here you can visit Zen gardens and Shinto shrines, glimpse geisha skittering through the alleys of Gion district, and walk across the now-concrete Sanjo-ohashi bridge. This is the Nakasendo's official beginning.

From Kyoto, follow the Nakasendo Way farther east, to trace a 54-mile (87km) section of the old road from Sekigahara to Lake Nojiri. Sekigahara was the site of a decisive battle in 1600 that ended decades of civil war and ushered in the Tokugawa shogunate. The route leaves the strategic town via a few *namiki* (the Nakasendo's original trees). It uses patches of old stone road and travels past wayside shrines on a rolling route to the post town of Hosokute. Here, you can stay in a seventeenth-century inn.

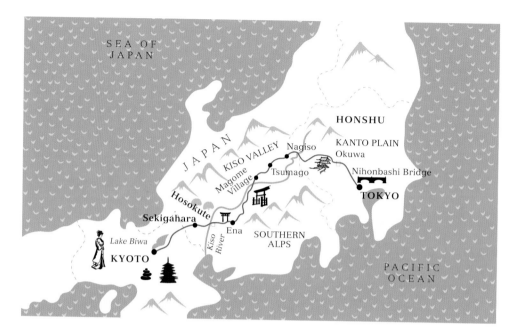

From Hosokute, the trail continues to the post town of Ena, treading a segment of *ishidatami* (original paving), hidden by forest and believed to be the country's longest continuous old pavement. However, the real heart of the Nakasendo is in the Kiso Valley, reached after the steep hike up to Magome (Horse Basket) Pass. This, and Magome village, get their name from the time when travellers had to abandon their horses here in order to tackle the mountainous terrain ahead.

Tsumago, the best-preserved post town on the route, is just beyond. There are no telephone poles or vending machines on the main street. Instead, there are traditional Edo-era houses, one of which is now a museum. From Tsumago, the old highway heads to the town of Nagiso, through a sylvan idyl of farms and hamlets. It crosses the Kiso River via an old wooden bridge, before finishing at Okuwa (formerly Nojiri).

The Nakasendo's true finale, however, is at central Tokyo's Nihonbashi, or 'Japan Bridge'. It was – and still is – the mile-zero marker for the country's national highway network. The bridge is now made of stone, but you can stand on a replica of the wooden original in the city's Edo-Tokyo Museum – and pretend you've stepped back 400 years.

315
Vikos Gorge

Pindus Mountains, Greece

Hike over Ottoman-era mule trails and stone roads, and visit remote Zagori villages in and around the dramatic 12.5-mile (20km) Vikos Gorge in northern Greece.

316
SILVER TRAIL

Copper Canyon, Mexico

This gaping ravine in northwestern Mexico is longer and deeper than Arizona's Grand Canyon. Although it is called Copper Canyon, it is famed for its silver. Spanish explorers discovered rich deposits of silver here in the seventeenth century. They built mines, then hacked paths to transport the stuff out. Now these routes are used only by indigenous Tarahumara Indians (renowned for their running skills) and intrepid trekkers. The 100-mile (160km) Silver Trail runs from the town of Carachic, where Spanish mule trains once unloaded their bounty, to the town of Batopilas, deep within the canyon system. En route there are pools, springs, cave houses, pine forests, towering mesas, and the villages of the Tarahumara people.

317
CANAL DU MIDI

Southern France

The Canal du Midi, constructed between 1666 and 1681, links the Mediterranean Sea to the Garonne River (and, ultimately, the Atlantic Ocean) via an ingenious succession of locks, aqueducts, bridges, and tunnels. It is brilliantly practical, but also designed to blend beautifully with its surroundings. The hike along the canal towpath from Toulouse to Beziers is 150 miles (240km) long. The walking is fine, flat, and filled with magic moments. Eat bean *cassoulet* in the town of Castelnaudary (the dish's spiritual home). Explore the fortified medieval city of Carcassonne. Watch the sunlight stream through the canal-side plane trees. And wave at colourful barges as they quietly glide by.

318

GRIBOEDOV CANAL

St Petersburg, Russia

Founded in 1703 by Peter the Great, St Petersburg soon expanded across a scatter of islands in the Neva River Delta. Riddled with creeks and canals, it is a city on, and of, water. Peter saw it as his 'Venice of the North'. Griboedov is the grandest canal, developed from 1739. It is flanked by St Petersburg's finest architecture, and crossed by twenty-plus bridges. This includes Bank Bridge, whose four gilded griffins are a symbol of the city. Follow Griboedov's embankment for 3 miles (5km), and you'll pass the Church of the Savior on Spilled Blood (built where Alexander II was assassinated in 1881), huge Kazan Cathedral, and the Art Nouveau Singer Building (now a bookshop).

319

PRAGUE–VIENNA GREENWAYS

Austria and Czech Republic

Vienna and Prague are two of Europe's greatest capitals, and the 250–350-mile (400–560km) web of greenway trails between them packs in lots of historic sites. This includes 2,000-year-old Slavic fortifications and Iron Curtain relics. Particularly appealing is the section that passes the fine Renaissance centres of Telc and Slavonice. These cities grew rich in the fifteenth and sixteenth centuries, thanks to their location on the main Vienna–Prague road. Architectural highlights from that era include Telc's wonderfully well preserved Moravian Renaissance chateau, completed in 1580, as well as Slavonice's elegant town houses, adorned with decorative *sgraffito* (scratched-away) plasterwork.

320
WEST COAST TRAIL

Vancouver Island, Canada

{ Go back to nature on a wild, Pacific-side walk that's redolent with First Nations spirit. }

Need to know
- *Point in time: 1778 (Captain Cook arrived on Canada's Pacific Northwest coast)*
- *Length: 47 miles (75km); 5–7 days*
- *Difficulty: Strenuous – no facilities; rugged terrain*
- *Best months: May–Sept*
- *Top tip: Permits are required – advance booking is essential*

Before British explorer Captain James Cook first arrived at Canada's Pacific Northwest in 1778, the First Nations Nuu-chah-nulth people were happily coexisting with Vancouver Island's rugged wilderness. They were perfectly in tune with its fluctuating tides, tumultuous seas, and thick forests. Diseases and strife brought by Europeans decimated their numbers. However, the spirit of the Nuu-chah-nulth people's lifestyle lives on in the West Coast Trail.

This is one of Canada's most famous – and most arduous – hikes. It runs along the country's Pacific coast

Trace the wild Vancouver Island shore on the West Coast Trail.

for 47 miles (75km), between Pachena Bay and the Gordon River. It is a trail that requires all who tackle it to be completely self-reliant.

There are no coffee shops, motels, or roads. Hikers who choose to follow the West Coast Trail must carry everything they need, except water. This can be collected from streams (then purified). Hikers must also be able to handle slippery rocks, river crossings, treacherous tides, and notoriously unreliable weather.

However, the rewards of this privation are manifold. This is some of the most inspiring terrain on the planet. It is a splendid spread of old-growth forest harbouring enormous trees. It boasts wild beaches strewn with driftwood and shipwrecks. It offers hidden coves and pools. Plus, there is rock art by First Nations peoples. Best of all, the West Coast Trail is not crowded – at least not with people. A maximum of fifty hikers are allowed to start the trail each day. However, there is no limit to the number of black bears, wolves, seals, and eagles that might be spotted en route.

321
Sentier du Sel

Vaud, Switzerland

The 8-mile (12.5km) Sentier du Sel (Salt Trail) follows an old wooden pipeline through forests and meadows. It travels from Plambuit sur Ollon to the seventeenth-century salt mine at Bex.

322
ROUTEBURN TRACK

South Island, New Zealand

The Maori first ventured to the Routeburn area, deep in South Island's Fiordland, in around 1500. They were looking for *pounamu* (greenstone), which they used to craft much-prized treasures. The Routeburn Valley wasn't a fruitful source. It did, however, provide a conduit between the Dart Valley and the Arahura River, both major repositories of greenstone. Today, the 24-mile (39km) Routeburn Track feels little changed since those sixteenth-century treasure hunters trooped by – aside from the four comfortable hikers' huts. The trail is a great introduction to alpine New Zealand, lined with mossy forest, flower-flecked pastures, lakes, waterfalls, and kea (a type of parrot). The route peaks at 1,255m (4,020ft) Harris Saddle for marvellous mountain views.

323
BANDIAGARA ESCARPMENT

Central Mali

The Dogon people weren't the first humans to seek refuge in the long sandstone ridge of the Bandiagara Escarpment. There are cliff-hewn tombs and settlements here dating back to 200 BC. But it is the Dogon people who call it home now. According to oral tradition, they came here in around AD 1500, escaping invaders and drought. Exploring Bandiagara is a real adventure, and a local guide is essential. You will need one to lead you between the traditional villages, and to help you negotiate the cultural etiquette involved when meeting *hogons* (spiritual leaders). Highlights include watching an exuberant Dogon masked dance. Check travel advice before you go.

324
Kennet and Avon Canal

Southern England, United Kingdom

The 87-mile (140km) Kennet and Avon Canal, linking Bristol with Reading, was built between 1794 and 1801. A towpath walk passes the city of Bath and 105 canal locks.

WAITUKUBULI NATIONAL TRAIL

Dominica

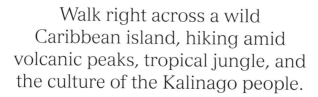

{ Walk right across a wild Caribbean island, hiking amid volcanic peaks, tropical jungle, and the culture of the Kalinago people. }

Need to know
- *Point in time: 1660–1773 (Dominica resisted colonisation)*
- *Length: 115 miles (185km); 10–14 days*
- *Difficulty: Moderate – poor waymarking; undulating*
- *Best months: Dec–Apr*
- *Top tip: Trail passes are required; fees vary dependent on pass duration*

Welcome to the Caribbean's first long-distance hiking trail. In this paradisiacal region usually renowned for hot beaches rather than hiking boots, the island of Dominica is an anomaly. For a start, it doesn't do stereotypically splendid white sand – most of the beaches here are volcanic black. This footpath on Dominica also largely abandons the coast. Instead, it favours the wild and untamed interior.

The indigenous Kalinago people, known for their boatbuilding and weaving, call the island Waitukubuli, which translates as 'Tall Is Her Body'. This references Dominica's towering, mountainous spine. Christopher Columbus was the first European to spot the island, one weekend in 1493. He subsequently christened it Dominica, from the Latin word for 'Sunday'. Subsequent attempts by the British and French to colonise were fiercely resisted by the Kalinago people and, in 1660, both the British and the French decided Dominica should be left alone. This accord didn't last. In 1763 the island was claimed by the British. It only fully gained its independence in 1978.

The Waitukubuli National Trail manages to squeeze 115 miles (185km) of hiking into an island just 30 miles (47km) from top to bottom. The trail starts in the south, by the Scotts Head Peninsula, which is crowned by eighteenth-century Fort Cachacrou. It finishes in the northwest, at Fort Shirley in Cabrits. In between, waterfalls splatter, hummingbirds purr, and plants – including heliconias, bromeliads, buttressed chataignier trees, *bwa kanno* (trumpet trees), umbelliferous giant ferns, and vivid orchids – are the

stars of the show. There are also scattered plantations, ripe with cocoa, mango, banana, and breadfruit. There are hundreds of species of birds, amphibians, and reptiles (none of them poisonous). Plus, there are gnarled peaks that soar over 1,370m (4,500ft) high.

The trail is split into fourteen segments, which can be hiked continuously, in batches, or on their own (you will need to arrange trailhead transport). Segment 4, for example, runs from Wotten Waven (known as the hot spring capital of Dominica) to Pont Cassé. It dissects the bird-filled forest of Morne Trois Pitons National Park, and includes glorious mountain views. An optional detour takes in the island's headline site, Boiling Lake, a 63m (207ft) wide natural cauldron of gurgling grey-blue water and steam.

Alternatively, try Segment 6, from the village of Castle Bruce to Hatton Garden. This leads along the roiling Atlantic coast, through the heartland of Dominica's Kalinago people. Segment 8 is perfect for energetic trekkers. From First Camp to Petite Macoucherie, this is a tough trek that tops the highest ridges and plunges into verdant valleys. Walkers of this section may be serenaded by sisserou and jaco parrots along the way. Film-lovers will prefer Segment 12, which wends through the foothills of 860m (2,824ft) Morne aux Diables to Vieille Case, a location used during the filming of *Pirates of the Caribbean: Dead Man's Chest*.

326
Rif Mountains

Northern Morocco

After the Moors were ousted from Spain, they retreated to Morocco's Rif Mountains, founding the blue-washed city of Chefchaouen in 1471. It thrived in the 1500s, and is the base for forays into the mountains.

While the wilderness is alluring, the walk also has a strong cultural appeal. One motivation behind the Waitukubuli National Trail is to bring business to villages that seldom see visitors. Cafés, shops, and guest houses are accessible from the trail, providing both respite and local interaction. This is an essentially human route, largely following time-worn paths. These include the hunting trails of the Kalinago people, the tracks of old plantations, and escape routes once used by Maroons (runaway slaves).

The way is marked – by yellow and blue posts – but maps or, better, guides are required: this is a wonderfully little-walked route, great for getting away from the crowds but all too likely to be reclaimed by Mother Nature.

327
WITCH TRAIL

Massachusetts, United States

Danvers was a scary place to be in 1692. In that year, witch mania overcame this small Massachusetts town, resulting in the Salem Witch Trials and the hanging of nineteen allegedly evil souls. The 10-mile (16km) Witch Trail from Danvers to Salem passes sites central to this hysterical era. This includes Ingersoll House, where many of the accused were questioned; the homestead and memorial of Rebecca Nurse, one of the executed 'witches'; and the ruined Salem Village Parsonage, where Reverend Parris lived with his slave Tituba. One of the first accused, Tituba's confession led to the accusations of many others.

329
Magose Pass

Honshu, Japan

The 7-mile (11.5km) Aiga to Osoneura hike is a scenic remainder of Japan's Iseji Kumano pilgrimage. Here, a seventeenth-century stone path leads through the bamboo.

328
BREWERIES PATH

Bavaria, Germany

It was in Bavaria, in 1516, that the Reinheitsgebot (purity law) was first enacted, limiting the ingredients of beer to just water, hops, and barley. Today, North Bavaria, known as Franconian Switzerland, is home to more than seventy beer houses. The village of Aufsess alone has more breweries per capita than anywhere else in the world. This makes the looping 8-mile (13km) Brauereienweg (Breweries Path) less a walk than a stagger. It starts in Aufsess, which is also home to a 900-year-old castle. From here the trail visits breweries in Sachsendorf, Hochstahl, and Heckenhof. It finishes back in Aufsess, for one final drink.

330

LUTHER TRAIL

Central Germany

{ Walk between the churches, castles, and countryside connected to the man who transformed Western religion. }

Need to know

- *Point in time: 1517 (Martin Luther published his Ninety-five Theses)*
- *Length: 1,240 miles (2,000km); 3–4 months*
- *Difficulty: Moderate – varied terrain*
- *Best months: May–Sept*
- *Top tip: The trail is split into four routes; walking shorter sections is straightforward*

When German friar Martin Luther pinned a letter known as the *Ninety-five Theses* to the door of Wittenberg Cathedral in 1517, he essentially started the Protestant Reformation. Luther had become increasingly disillusioned with the Catholic Church. He was especially critical of its corrupt practice of selling 'indulgences' to absolve sin, and spelled out this viewpoint in his revolutionary letter. Refusing to recant his writings, he was excommunicated by the pope. However, he continued to spread the word, and ultimately revolutionised Western religion.

The Lutherweg, or 'Luther Trail', was created to celebrate 500 years since Martin Luther's dissertation. It comprises four trails, one in each of the German states of Saxony, Saxony-Anhalt, Thuringia, and Bavaria. Together, these trails total around 1,240 miles (2,000km), and link sites key to the Protestant Reformation and Martin Luther himself.

For instance, the Thuringian section of the Luther Trail (around 600 miles / 1,000km long) passes Glasbachgrund, where the friar was taken into protective custody. It then visits the medieval cliff-perched castle of Wartburg in the town of Eisenach, where Luther translated the Bible's New Testament into German. Next, it travels to the city of Erfurt, Luther's spiritual home. He lived in the Augustine Monastery here and, in 1507, became a priest at Erfurt Cathedral.

For the best insight, follow the Saxony-Anhalt section (255 miles / 410km long). It runs between the town of Eisleben – where Luther was born, raised, and died – and the city of Wittenberg, where he ultimately changed the world.

RIGHT: The Luther Trail visits the old castle of Wartburg.

KUMANO KODO

Honshu, Japan

The cobblestones of Japan's Kumano Kodo trail have carried myriad pilgrims since the seventeenth century. The Kumano area, on Honshu's Kii Peninsula, has been considered sacred since prehistoric times. However, the improved roads laid down in the 1600s encouraged many more devotees to visit. The Kumano Kodo isn't one trail but a network of them, weaving through the forested Kii Mountains. The Nakahechi, or 'Imperial Route', was one of the most popular pilgrimage trails during the Edo period (1603–1868). Today, you can follow a 25-mile (40km) section of it, from Takijiri-oji (a secondary temple) to ridgetop Kumano Hongu Taisha, one of Kumano's three big shrines. The latter is also home to the largest *torii* (traditional Japanese gate) in the world.

Hike the 24-mile (39km) Routeburn Track for a spectacular introduction to alpine New Zealand including mossy forest, flower-flecked pastures, huge valleys, and breathtaking mountain views. Soak up the view at Lake Mackenzie, one of the walk's most dramatic vistas (p. 255).

CHAPTER FIVE
19TH CENTURY

{ Take a hike into the 1800s, when empires rose and fell, science and invention flourished, and architecture reached new heights. }

CHILKOOT TRAIL

United States and Canada

{ Hike a once-treacherous trail from Alaska towards the Yukon, in the boot-prints of gold rush stampeders. }

Need to know
- Point in time: 1897–98 (Klondike gold rush)
- Length: 33 miles (53km); 3–5 days
- Difficulty: Moderate/ strenuous – steep climbs; variable weather
- Best months: May–Oct
- Top tip: This is bear country; hikers must store supplies correctly at campsites

One word: 'Gold!' That was all it took to create the Chilkoot Trail. When prospectors Skookum Jim Mason, Dawson Charlie, and George Washington Carmack found gold in a tributary of the Klondike River in Canada's Yukon in August 1896, they triggered one of the world's greatest gold rushes. Between 1897 and 1898, more than 100,000 stampeders set off for the Klondike, though fewer than 30,000 made it to the actual gold fields. By the time most arrived, the decent stakes had already been claimed. Rather than yellow treasure, they found hardship, cold, and misery.

Chief among those hardships was the overland journey required to get from Skagway, Alaska (where many stampeders arrived by boat) to the gold fields near the Yukon's Dawson City. This tough 33-mile (53km) journey, now known as the Chilkoot Trail, even required the crossing of the United States–Canada border. It had long been used as a trade passage by the Tlingit people. Now it was being trodden by thousands of prospectors. Worse, the stampeders were heavily laden with supplies. In order for them to enter Canada, the Canadian government required them to carry their 'grubstake', a year's worth of provisions. As such, many stampeders walked the Chilkoot dozens of times, gradually hoicking their wares over the treacherous terrain.

Yes, treacherous. The Chilkoot was, and still is, a challenge, though modern hikers need carry far less weight in their packs. Also, it's become far less crowded. While thousands trudged across the international border in the 1890s, now just fifty people are permitted to do so each day.

The trailhead is at Dyea on Taiya Inlet, 9 miles (14.5km) from Skagway. A former boom town, built to serve the gold-seeking arrivals, Dyea is now abandoned. A few metal scraps and lonely cemeteries are all that nod to its former status. The only inhabitants are bears that come to feed in salmon season.

From sea level, the trail starts gently, wending through spruce and cottonwood, and climbing bluffs above the Taiya River to reach Finnegan's Camp. Then it gets more taxing, leading via creek crossings, bare granite, and many ups and downs to reach Sheep Camp. Now swallowed by forest, this camp was once a 'city', with hotels, laundries, and saloons. Next, the trail breaks the tree line and the landscape becomes more inhospitable (and prone to avalanches). It's a stiff haul up to the Scales, which was once the final weighing station before the push up to 1,067m (3,500ft) Chilkoot Pass itself. Many stampeders, faced with the impossible-looking climb, simply gave up here, leaving their grubstake behind. Artifacts can still be seen.

The toil up the often snow-covered pass became known as the Golden Staircase. In winter, workers carved steps into the ice, and a single-file procession of weary souls paid a toll to troop up. It's still a tough ascent, subject to wild weather. The top is dramatic, desolate, and exposed.

LAKE BENNETT

Bare Loon Lake

Lindeman Camp

Deep Lake

Happy Camp

Stone Crib

Chilkoot Pass

Scales

Taiya River

Sheep Camp

Pleasant Camp

Canyon City

Finnegan's Camp

DYEA

Taiya Inlet

BRITISH COLUMBIA

ALASKA

333
Livingstonia Trail

Malawi

This wild three-day hike runs from Chelinda, on the wildlife-rich Nyika Plateau, to the Livingstonia Mission overlooking Lake Malawi. The explorer David Livingstone travelled to these parts in the 1850s.

It's a far gentler onward hike, via a succession of lakes, to Happy Camp. Then it's mostly downhill to Lindeman Camp, where old tent terraces and a small cemetery still stand. One last uphill lies between Lindeman and Bare Loon Lake, before the trail dips through boreal forest to its finish at Lake Bennett. It's hard to believe that, briefly, this isolated spot was one of the most important settlements around. Now there are rusting metal oddments and a small Presbyterian church (the Chilkoot's only gold rush-era building still standing). The boot-prints of old prospectors have been replaced by the tracks of caribou and moose.

334
OVERLAND TRACK

Tasmania, Australia

Cradle Mountain–Lake St Clair National Park is used to people. Indigenous Australians had lived in the area for 10,000 years before explorers and trappers turned up in the 1820s. Today, most visitors are hikers. The park's 40-mile (65km) Overland Track is Tasmania's most popular trek, showcasing a glorious gamut of glacial valleys, moorland, and forests of eucalyptus, King Billy pine, and beech. It starts at Ronny Creek, beneath Cradle Mountain, and ends at Narcissus Hut, by Lake St Clair. Here, catch the ferry. Alternatively, carry on, taking a final 11-mile (17.5km) stroll around the lake.

335
BAKER HISTORICAL TRAIL

South Sudan and Uganda

In the 1860s, the British explorer, hunter, and abolitionist Sir Samuel White Baker and his wife Lady Florence Baker (a former white slave) set off on a central African adventure. The aim was to discover the source of the Nile. They didn't. But they did travel extensively through what is now South Sudan and Uganda. The 500-mile (805km) Baker Historical Trail commemorates their journey. The route runs from Gondokoro (near Juba, South Sudan's capital) to Baker's View, a lookout in western Uganda. This is where Sir Baker became the first European to see Lake Albert, which he named in honour of Queen Victoria's prince consort. This walk is an insight into the Bakers' epic endeavours. Just check that the region is safe before traveling.

LEWIS AND CLARK NATIONAL HISTORIC TRAIL

Montana, United States

{ Hike a small part of a huge journey, mastering Montana's mountains in the wake of the area's earliest explorers. }

Need to know

- *Point in time: 1804–6 (Lewis and Clark expedition)*
- *Length: 14 miles (22.5km); 6–7 hours*
- *Difficulty: Moderate – steep sections*
- *Best months: June– Sept*
- *Top tip: The trail runs near US Highway 12; there is limited parking near the trailheads*

In the two and a half years that it took Meriwether Lewis and William Clark to travel from their camp near St. Louis to the Pacific Ocean, and back again, they covered more than 8,000 miles (12,875km). They had been commissioned by President Thomas Jefferson to find out what lay in America's west, and set off from Missouri in May 1804. What they encountered was a lot of testing terrain. It was a dangerous, daring adventure that gathered scientific, cultural, and topographical data, as well as inspiring many more pioneers to follow. The trip laid much of the groundwork for the westward expansion of the United States.

These days, parts of Lewis and Clark's route can be traced, but largely by car or boat. However, one of the expedition's most infamous stretches, which saw them master the Continental Divide, is fit for hikers. The 14-mile (22.5km) Lewis and Clark National Historic Trail (L&CNHT) in Montana runs from Grave Creek, west of Lolo, to 1,595m (5,233ft) Lolo Pass. After a tip from the Native American Shoshone people, this was the party's chosen route across the Bitterroot Mountains. In his journal, on 12 September 1805, Clark described it as a 'verry [sic] bad passing'.

The L&CNHT negotiates the steep, slippy north side of Lolo Creek, passing Lolo Hot Springs and finishing near the pass. This is a tiny taste of Lewis and Clark's 'Wild West'.

337
Eagle Walk

Tyrol, Austria

The 257-mile (413km) 'Adlerweg' – a route resembling an eagle's spread wings – links the Kaiser Mountains with the Arlberg range. It includes the heights of the Tyrol, and celebrates the nineteenth century's climbing pioneers.

ABOVE: Retrace the footsteps of Meriwether Lewis and William Clark across Montana's Bitterroot Mountains.

HUME AND HOVELL WALKING TRACK

New South Wales, Australia

> Follow in the intrepid footsteps of Hamilton Hume and William Hovell on a journey through the bush of southeastern Australia.

Need to know

- *Point in time: 1824 (Hume and Hovell expedition)*
- *Length: 273 miles (440km); 20–24 days*
- *Difficulty: Moderate/ strenuous – remote; changeable weather*
- *Best months: Mar– June; Sept–Oct*
- *Top tip: There are seventeen campsites en route; in places, towns with lodgings are accessible via short detours*

Explorers Hamilton Hume and William Hovell had a simple plan when, on 3 October 1824, they set off into the uncharted Australian bush. The plan was to keep bearing to the southwest. At the behest of Sir Thomas Brisbane, governor of New South Wales, the duo's goal was to find new grazing land for the expanding colony. The east coast settlers knew what lay inland as far as Lake George (near the modern city of Canberra), and they knew of distant Western Port on the country's south coast (near the modern city of Melbourne). But they knew nothing of the vastness between. By setting their compasses in a single direction, Hume and Hovell hoped to cut a diagonal from one to the other, documenting what they found en route.

Australian-born Hume was a keen explorer and a knowledgeable bushman. Hovell was a former ship's captain from England who moved to Australia in 1813. They had a few fallings-out during their expedition (and continued to argue until their deaths). However, despite this, and despite traversing challenging terrain, they made it to the south coast by 16 December 1824. Due to depleted supplies, they had to set off on the return journey almost immediately, and arrived back by Lake George on 18 January 1825.

Hume and Hovell didn't actually trek to Western Port. Rather, they hit the Southern Ocean at Port Phillip (now the city of Geelong), a few clicks west. However, that was immaterial. In only sixteen weeks, they had hiked over

ABOVE: Traverse wild
Kosciuszko National Park
on the Hume and Hovell
Walking Track.

1,180 miles (1,900km) and discovered some of the richest agricultural land on the continent.

The Hume and Hovell Walking Track doesn't make it to Western Port either, nor even to Port Phillip. This 273-mile (440km) track traces only the New South Wales portion of the route, from Yass to Albury. However, this doesn't make it any less spectacular.

The track starts in the town of Yass, at Cooma Cottage. This is the former home of Hume, now decked out in nineteenth-century paraphernalia, and open to visitors. After a short trudge in earshot of the Hume Highway – the main road between the cities of Sydney and Melbourne – the trail hits quiet backcountry. The landscape is dotted with farmsteads, gum trees, and flocks of cockatoos and galahs all the way to Lake Burrinjuck. Created by a dam on the Murrumbidgee River, the lake has no ferry service, so hikers must be as resourceful as pioneers and organise their own transportation across. Although perhaps not quite like Hume and Hovell – when they were faced with the rain-swollen Murrumbidgee River, they crossed it by converting one of their carts into a boat.

From the town of Wee Jasper, on the other side of Lake Burrinjuck, the trail undulates through Buccleuch Forest and Micalong Swamp, alongside the Blowering Reservoir (good for swimming and fishing). It then travels up to alpine

plateaus of snow gums to enter Kosciuszko National Park. Here stands 2,200m (7,310ft) Mount Kosciuszko, Australia's highest peak. West of the national park, at Big Hill (near the town of Tumbarumba), Hume and Hovell became the first Europeans to sight the Australian Alps. Hovell was impressed, writing: 'A prospect came into view the most magnificent, an immense high mountain covered nearly one fourth of the way down with snow.'

Beyond this, more magnificent forest and trickling creeks line the way, as well as remnants of old gold and tin mines. The track passes sun-dappled eucalyptus forest, cow-grazed pasture, high ridgetops, and the rolling woodland of Woomargama National Park. This is home to kangaroos, wallabies, wombats, and echidnas (spiny anteaters).

Hume and Hovell were initially flummoxed at what is now the town of Albury. They spent three days debating how to cross the Murray River here, eventually cobbling together a tarpaulin raft. For today's hikers, however, this is the end of the track. The trail officially finishes at the Hovell Tree, a river gum marked by Hovell in 1824.

339
Teton Crest Trail

Wyoming, United States

Hike in this peaked frontierland of fur trappers and nineteenth-century pioneers. This trail is a 40-mile (64km) backcountry adventure from Teton Pass to String Lake.

340
BERLIN HIGH TRAIL

Zillertal Alps, Austria

The Berliner Hütte, a large mountain hut encircled by high peaks, was opened by the Berlin branch of Austria's Alpine Club in 1879. At first it simply provided food and shelter for hikers. However, by the turn of the twentieth century, it housed a shoemaker's workshop, post office, and photographers' darkroom. The Berliner Hütte is just one stop on the 45-mile (73km) Berlin High Trail, inaugurated in 1889. The trail loops between Kasseler Hut (near the town of Mayrhofen) and Gams Hut (near the town of Finkenberg) via the best of the Zillertal Alps, an ocean of soaring summits.

341
BURCHELL TRAIL

Victoria, Australia

During the 1850s Brisbane Ranges gold rush, the town of Steiglitz was noisy with diggers, quartz-crushers, church bells, and a population of 1,500 people. Today, its population totals about eight people. The prospectors might be gone, but the Court House (now a historic monument) provides an interesting trailhead for the 24-mile (38km) Burchell Trail. This delves into the ranges from whence the gold came, finishing at the Boar Gully Camping Area. En route lie eastern grey kangaroos, groves of grass trees, golden wattles, ridge climbs with big views, pretty Little River Gorge, and evidence of the area's former mining days – from old shafts to deep pits.

342
HAUTE ROUTE

Valais, Switzerland

{ Make the ultimate Alpine traverse, first blazed by pleasure-seeking mountaineers in the nineteenth century. }

Need to know

- *Point in time: 1861 (Haute Route first hiked)*
- *Length: 110 miles (180km); 10–14 days*
- *Difficulty: Strenuous – high climbs; snow possible on passes year-round*
- *Best months: June–Sept*
- *Top tip: German or French language skills are useful for booking accommodation; alternatively, travel on an organised trip*

The beginnings and finales of treks don't come much more dramatic than this. Switzerland's high-level Haute Route links two high-altitude monsters: Mont Blanc and the Matterhorn. This classic 110-mile (180km) trail begins just over the French border in the resort town of Chamonix, in the shadow of 4,810m (15,781ft) Mont Blanc, or 'White Mountain'. It traverses some of the finest paths in all of the Alps to reach the resort of Zermatt, which sits under the 4,478m (14,692ft) Matterhorn's forbidding gaze.

Utilising trade routes trodden since medieval times, the Haute Route was first blazed for pleasure by the British Alpine Club in 1861. A book published in 1871 referred to the Alps as 'the Playground of Europe'. These mountains have not lost their appeal in the years since.

Today's Haute Route hikers still encounter magnificent passes, squeaking marmots, and an abundance of big and beautiful peaks – including the twelve highest mountains in the Alps. There are also icy lakes and streams, hill-scampering chamois, cow-grazed pastures, charming hamlets, and creaking glaciers dangling in valleys – though many of these glaciers have receded somewhat since the 1860s.

The trail is well-served by villages and mountain huts that offer creature comforts, great food, and hiker camaraderie. The Haute Route is a tough challenge, with potentially hazardous weather and 12,000m (39,370ft) of elevation gain. Successfully completing it, however, delivers the ultimate Alpine high.

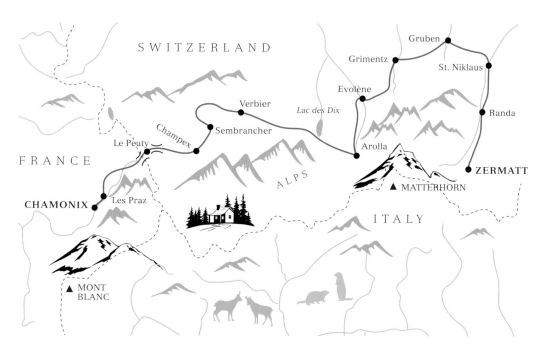

SWITZERLAND

FRANCE

ALPS

ITALY

Gruben

Grimentz

St. Niklaus

Evolène

Randa

Verbier

Lac des Dix

Champex

Sembrancher

Le Peuty

Arolla

CHAMONIX

Les Praz

▲ MATTERHORN

ZERMATT

▲ MONT
   BLANC

LEFT: Gaze down at Alpine lakes as you trek the Haute Route in Switzerland.

343
Giles Track

Northern Territory, Australia

The first European to venture into what is now Watarrka National Park was George Gill in 1872. This 14-mile (22km) bush walk from Kings Canyon to Kathleen Springs bears his name.

344
Chinaman's Walk

*Northern Territory,
Australia*

This short path links
the site of Darwin's
old railway yards
with its big banyan
tree. Its name refers
to the many Chinese
immigrants who
disembarked in
Darwin in the 1880s,
and made this walk.

345
Le Morne Brabant

Mauritius

In the early
nineteenth century,
the 556m (1,824ft)
basaltic monolith of
Le Morne Brabant
was a refuge for
runaway slaves.
Now it is a three-
hour climb, with
views over the
turquoise sea.

346
St James Walkway

*South Island,
New Zealand*

This 41-mile (66km)
subalpine tramp
begins at Lewis Pass,
first discovered by
Europeans in 1860.
It leads through
beech forest and the
old St James sheep
station to reach the
village of Boyle.

347
Australian Alps
Walking Track

Southeast Australia

This 404-mile
(650km) trail
runs through
southeastern
Australia's high
country, from the
town of Walhalla
(Victoria) to the
village of Tharwa
(near Canberra).
This region proved
irresistible to gold
prospectors in the
nineteenth century.

348
FAMINE TRACK

Connemara, Ireland

A million people died during
Ireland's Great Famine (1846 to
1852). Potato blight ravaged the
main crop of an island already
strained by socio-economic
problems. Public works schemes,
such as building unnecessary
roads, gave desperate people
something to do, in return for a
small stipend and a bowl of soup.
One such road was what is now
known as the Famine Track, in
wild Connemara county. This area
saw its population fall by two-
thirds during the 'Hunger'.
A 6-mile (10km) trail traces
this melancholy path through
magnificent countryside. It leads
along the shore of Killary Harbour
to the fishing hamlet of Rosroe and
the ruined famine village of Foher.
It also passes 'lazy beds' – grassy
ridges where those blighted
potatoes were once grown.

349
FUGITIVE'S TRAIL

KwaZulu–Natal, South Africa

{ Beat a retreat across the sunbaked savannah, in the wake of fleeing soldiers and Zulu warriors. }

It all looks so peaceful. The swaying blond grasses, the earthy plains pocked with scrubby bushes, cacti, and thorn trees. There are hills rolling away into the heat haze, and a curious rock monolith, known as Isandlwana, standing sentinel over the landscape. It is peaceful now, but that was not the case on 22 January 1879.

The inland northwestern region of South Africa's KwaZulu-Natal state was, in the nineteenth century, the heartland of the Zulu people. This Nguni ethnic group rose to prominence under the rule of fearsome warrior Shaka Zulu (1787–1828), who organised the disparate clans of the area into a single, formidable force. This increased Zulu brawn was felt first by the Dutch Voortrekkers, who emigrated from the Western Cape into Natal to get away from the British. The Dutch ended up fighting the Zulu at the Battle of Blood River in 1838.

Then the Zulus took on the expansion-hungry British colonialists. The Anglo-Zulu War was brief but brutal. It lasted for just under six months, from January to July 1879, and was ultimately won by the British. However, it also involved the worst defeat on African soil in Britain's colonial history.

This defeat happened in the shadow of the sphinx-like Isandlwana. The British had set up camp on the plain here, under the command of Lord Chelmsford, who gravely underestimated the Zulu threat. He decided to set off with two-thirds of his 5,000-strong force to thwart a supposed assault from the southeast. Meanwhile, around 20,000 Zulu were amassing to the northeast, just 5 miles (8km) from the depleted, vulnerable camp. After a British scout stumbled on

Need to know
- *Point in time: 1879 (Battle of Isandlwana)*
- *Length: 5 miles (8km); 3 hours*
- *Difficulty: Moderate – rugged; steep sections*
- *Best months: Mar–June; Sept–Oct*
- *Top tip: An expert guide is recommended, to bring the battlefield's history to life*

ABOVE: Walk among white cairns beneath Isandlwana – site of a fierce Anglo-Zulu battle.

this huge *impi* (regiment), the spear-wielding Zulu attacked, employing their *izimpondo zankomo* (horns of the buffalo) encirclement tactic. The result was utter carnage. Many of the 1,750 remaining British soldiers and auxiliaries were killed near Isandlwana. Many others were picked off as they fled the camp, running towards the Buffalo River, then the boundary between Zululand and 'safe' Natal, with the Zulus following in hot pursuit. The 5-mile (8km) Fugitive's Trail follows this escape route, and is now dotted with whitewashed stone cairns marking where the soldiers died. Many Zulus died here too.

The trail starts among the graves at Isandlwana. Looking out from the rock's saddle, the densest clusters of cairns illustrate where the fighting was fiercest. There are also views to Rorke's Drift, some 8 miles (13km) away. Here, also on 22 January 1879, 140 British soldiers successfully defended their post against 3,000 Zulus.

Heading down through the rough and rugged savannah, the trail passes more cairns, scattered amid the grass and acacias. Nestled at the bottom of a gully, the clear, burbling Manzinyama stream seems idyllic now. It is a perfect place for trekkers to cool their toes. However, it must have been hellish in 1879 for British soldiers fleeing the plain near Isandlwana. They would have had to splash through, and then climb up steep Mpete Hill on the other side. Only those on horseback really stood a chance.

The trail continues by negotiating hilltop rocks before descending through prickly thickets, obstructive boulders, and loose shale. At an unexpected cliff edge, the view of Fugitives' Drift opens up. Here, flanked by scrubby hills, is the rapid-running Buffalo River. Those soldiers who had made it this far had to wade through more water, swollen by recent rains that day, to get to the relative safety of the opposing bank. And there was more fighting to come. Some British survivors regrouped, holding off the Zulus who crossed the river. Lieutenants Melvill and Coghill, who tried to go back to rescue the Queen's Colour (their regimental flag), were slaughtered here. Both were posthumously awarded the Victoria Cross medal. The trail ends at the pair's hillside tombstone, which sits in splendid isolation amid the rocks, the trees, and the grazing antelopes – a chilling reminder under the warm African sun.

350
Windjana Gorge Walk

Kimberley, Western Australia

Long sacred to the Bunuba people, Windjana Gorge was the hideout of their leader Jandamarra, who waged war against the Europeans in 1894. A 2-mile (3.5km) gorge walk here reveals fine rocks and basking crocodiles.

351
ELLIOT'S PASS

Ascension Island, British Overseas Territory

When Napoleon Bonaparte was exiled to St Helena in 1815, the British set up a naval garrison on the nearby South Atlantic island of Ascension. This was so it couldn't be used as an escape route for the erstwhile French emperor. Ascension long remained a military outpost of the United Kingdom, a base for policing the illegal slave trade. In 1840 its defences were bolstered by a new lookout. A pathway, arches, and tunnels were hacked into the volcanic rock, leading up 732m (2,400ft) Green Mountain, the island's highest point. A 90-minute trail circles the peak, via the abandoned 1830s barracks, small observation caves, and a fringe of native ferns.

352

BATONGGUAN TRAIL

Yushan National Park, Taiwan

{ Cross the island's lofty mountains along trails laid by two separate imperialist powers. }

Need to know
- *Point in time: 1875–1921 (Batongguan trails built)*
- *Length: 56 miles (90km); 7 days*
- *Difficulty: Moderate/ strenuous – steep climbs; cliff drop-offs*
- *Best months: Oct–Dec; May–June*
- *Top tip: Permits are required to hike in Yushan National Park*

The Chinese Qing dynasty annexed Taiwan in 1683. In 1875 they built the Batongguan Trail, a cross-island highway, ostensibly to control the Bunun people, the Tsou people, and other ethnic groups. After losing the first Sino-Japanese War, China ceded Taiwan to the Japanese in 1895. In 1921 the Japanese constructed a second Batongguan Trail to facilitate communications and also to keep the aboriginal people in check. This overlapped with the Chinese highway at the hot spring village of Dongpu.

   The Qing-era Batongguan road ran for 95 miles (152km) from Linyipu to Yuli, via Dongpu and Batongguan (Jade Mountain). It travelled along a high,

282   *19th Century*

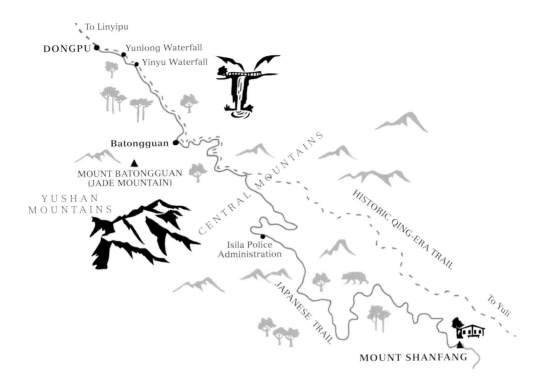

To Linyipu

DONGPU

Yunlong Waterfall

Yinyu Waterfall

Batongguan

MOUNT BATONGGUAN
(JADE MOUNTAIN)

YUSHAN
MOUNTAINS

CENTRAL MOUNTAINS

HISTORIC QING-ERA TRAIL

Isila Police
Administration

JAPANESE TRAIL

To Yuli

MOUNT SHANFANG

LEFT: Follow part of one of
Taiwan's oldest roads on the
Batongguan Trail.

tough route. Some of its stone steps remain, but it is
overgrown and hard to follow. The 56-mile (90km)
Japanese route, however, which begins in Dongpu and
traverses the Central Mountains to Mount Shanfang,
is in much better condition.

The latter trek involves negotiating narrow cliffside
paths, with sheer drops to churning rivers. Walkers
also need to hold onto ropes to inch around landslides.
It is worth the challenge for the forests laced with old
man's beard (and roamed by black bears) and meadows
blooming with azaleas. There are also various remains
from Japanese days. These include ruined police stations,
steles (commemorative stones), and an old suspension
bridge. Above it all sit the misty Yushan Mountains,
the enduring rulers of this untamed land.

353
CITADELLE LAFERRIÈRE TRAIL

Northern Haiti

{ Walk up to the big, bold fortress
in Haiti, the Caribbean's first
independent country. }

Need to know
- *Point in time: 1805–20 (Citadelle Laferrière built)*
- *Length: 7 miles (11km); 2–3 hours*
- *Difficulty: Moderate – uphill; hot and humid*
- *Best months: Dec–Apr*
- *Top tip: An entrance fee must be paid to visit the Citadelle*

In 1791 Haiti's slave population revolted against its French overlords. Even the 34,000-strong French army dispatched by the Emperor Napoleon couldn't quell the rebellion. In 1804 Haiti declared itself independent, becoming the first ever black-led republic.

Into this brave new world stepped Henri Christophe, a former slave and revolutionary leader who became president (and, later, self-proclaimed king) of Haiti's north. To demonstrate the authority of the newly founded nation, and to keep it safe from future French assaults, Christophe constructed a huge fortress known as Citadelle Laferrière. It was built on the top of 910m (3,000ft) Bonnet à l'Evèque, a few miles inland from the coast. It took around 20,000 men, working from 1805 to 1820, to build this enormous, angular fortress. It was fitted with 365 cannons, but was never attacked and remains remarkably intact.

The 7-mile (11km) trail up to the Citadelle Laferrière begins in Milot, at Sans-Souci (Carefree) Palace. This was one of nine palaces that King Christophe built for himself. It was once known as the 'Versailles of the Caribbean', but now stands in ruins. Much of it was destroyed by an earthquake in 1842. From here, the paved trail leads up, via hawkers selling coconut juice and views of tumbling hills. The Citadelle appears ahead, poking up from the mountain like the prow of a battleship. Inside the fortress lie dark dungeons, munition stores, and stone steps leading up to the battlements. Here, there are excellent views over the seas and valleys, from which invasion never came.

RIGHT: Walk up to the Citadelle Laferrière, on Haiti's Bonnet à l'Evèque mountain.

VICTORIA LINES

Northern Malta

The Victoria Lines is a series of walls and watchtowers built by the British across Malta, running east to west along the Great Fault escarpment. It was built to protect the Grand Harbour to the south. Spanning 7.5 miles (12km), the fortifications were largely completed by 1897, in time for British Queen Victoria's Diamond Jubilee. Never tested militarily, the defences now provide walkers with a high and historic vantage. A full traverse links Kuncizzjoni (on the west coast) and Madliena Heights (on the east). En route lie forts and tunnels, wildflowers, ancient cart ruts, gun emplacements, trenches, dramatic dry river valleys slicing through folds of limestone, and sweeping views of the sea.

JOHN MUIR TRAIL

California, United States

{ Pay your respects to John Muir, one of the godfathers of conservation, as you hike through his favourite place. }

Need to know
- *Point in time: 1838– 1914 (John Muir's life)*
- *Length: 211 miles (340km); 20–24 days*
- *Difficulty: Moderate/ strenuous – self- sufficiency required*
- *Best months: July– Sept*
- *Top tip: A wilderness permit is required; apply up to 24 weeks in advance*

Scottish-American writer, naturalist, and nomad John Muir might just be the most important man in this book – at least in the context of hiking through nature. Without this unconventional pioneer, there might be fewer wildernesses left to walk through.

Muir became one of the earliest advocates of safekeeping the environment. Born in Scotland in 1838, he emigrated to Wisconsin with his family when he was eleven. Following a factory accident that almost left him blind, he turned his back on the industrial world to focus on the natural one. He spent years walking across backcountry America, living off the land, being at one with the mountains, the prairies, the woods, and the waterways. He wrote impassioned treatises about landscape preservation, and helped to secure protection for the United States' wild places.

His true love was Yosemite, the great, grey granite valley in California's Sierra Nevada. Yosemite was, Muir wrote to a friend in 1869, 'by far the grandest of all the special temples of Nature I was ever permitted to enter.' Muir revelled in its flower-flecked alpine meadows, its spattering waterfalls, its crystal-clear rippling rivers, and the hooded hulk of Half Dome glaring down on it all. This was his playground. More important, he felt Yosemite should be *everyone's* playground.

Having moved to the area in 1869, and having witnessed the detrimental effects of logging and grazing, Muir wanted Yosemite to be declared a national park. He managed to gain

ABOVE: Commune with
nature on the John Muir Trail
around the Sierra Nevada.

a wide audience for his views by getting the editor of the influential *Century Magazine* on his side. His wish was eventually granted. In 1890 Yosemite became one of the United States' – and indeed the world's – first national parks.

It seems appropriate, then, that this tough, 211-mile (340km), wilderness-immersing tramp around Muir's precious Sierra Nevada was called the John Muir Trail (JMT). It leads south from the trailhead in Yosemite Valley to the top of 4,421m (14,505ft) Mount Whitney, the highest peak in the contiguous United States.

The JMT is not to be taken lightly. There's a lot of undulation. Walk the full route, north to south – the most popular direction – and the total height gain is about 12,800m (42,000ft). Walk south to north, and the height gain is almost 14,434m (47,000ft). You can also add on a vertiginous ascent of Half Dome, if you're keen. The Half Dome Trail is a 7-mile (12km) detour from Little Yosemite Valley, which is itself traversed on day one of the JMT.

The biggest challenge on the JMT, however, is carrying your pack. There are no hotels and few places to resupply en route, so trekkers must carry their tent, associated kit, and most of their provisions. Food becomes the main topic of conversation around the campfire.

It's well worth struggling under the weight of three weeks' worth of dried noodles and oats, though. The JMT's

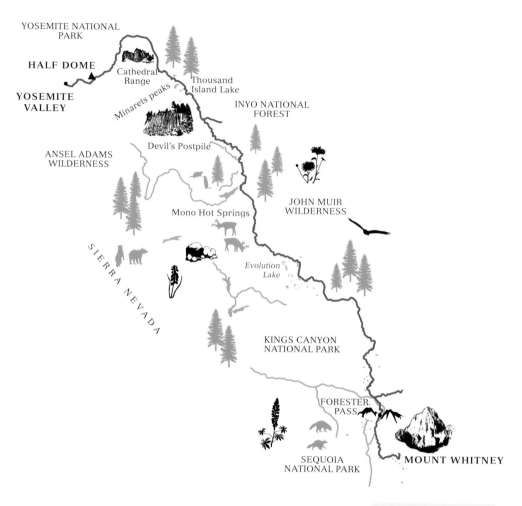

YOSEMITE NATIONAL
PARK

HALF DOME

Cathedral
Range

Thousand
Island Lake

**YOSEMITE
VALLEY**

Minarets peaks

INYO NATIONAL
FOREST

Devil's Postpile

ANSEL ADAMS
WILDERNESS

JOHN MUIR
WILDERNESS

Mono Hot Springs

S I E R R A   N E V A D A

Evolution
Lake

KINGS CANYON
NATIONAL PARK

FORESTER
PASS

SEQUOIA
NATIONAL PARK

MOUNT WHITNEY

pay offs are manifold. Enjoy golden sunrises over Thousand Island Lake, the jagged Minarets peaks reflected in its glassy sheen. Get close up with the bizarre columnar basalt of the Devil's Postpile. Wander along the shores of Evolution Lake, among lupins, coyote mint, mountain violet, and mariposa lilies. Encounter mule deer, marmots, raccoons, and black bears. And drink in the magnificent views from 4,009m (13,153ft) Forester, the JMT's highest pass. At the trail end, there is Mount Whitney. From there, you can survey all the wonderful wilderness you've managed to cross. As John Muir said: 'In every walk with Nature one receives far more than he seeks.'

**356
Great Ocean Walk**

Victoria, Australia

Take the Great Ocean Walk for 65 miles (104km) from Apollo Bay to the Glenample homestead. It travels via the fossils, cliffs, shipwrecks, and koalas of Australia's south coast.

357
WALDEN POND LOOP

Massachusetts, United States

'I went to the woods because I wished to live deliberately . . . I wanted to live deep and suck out all the marrow of life.' So said the great American naturalist Henry David Thoreau, who turned his back on the world in 1854 to live by Walden Pond. He wrote about the experience in his classic book, *Walden*. The pond, near the town of Concord, isn't the wilderness it once was. An expressway now rumbles nearby. Walking the 1.7-mile (3km) loop around the forested water's edge, however, will make you hanker for a simpler life too. Crunch over pine needles, spy on chipmunks and chickadees, and pause at the site of Thoreau's old cabin (marked with posts) on the way through.

358
BOH TEA ESTATE TRAIL

Cameron Highlands, Malaysia

In 1885 colonial surveyor William Cameron set off on a mapping expedition of the Titiwangsa Range, in what was then British Malaya. He soon spied a lofty plateau to the southeast, but failed to note its location. It wasn't until the 1920s that his find, subsequently named the Cameron Highlands, was rediscovered. Its cool, alpine-esque environment proved the perfect place for planting tea. Now a range of short treks wends amid the jungle here. Trail 9A (also known as the Boh Tea Estate Trail) is easy and takes about 90 minutes. It links Robinson Falls with the leafy Boh Tea Estate. Here, you can take a free tour and sip a cup of black-leaf tea while looking out on the rippled hillsides where it was grown.

SIERRA NEGRA VOLCANO

Galápagos Islands, Ecuador

{
Take a hike on the archipelago that, thanks to its flutter of finches, inspired Charles Darwin's theory of evolution.
}

Need to know
- *Point in time: 1835 (Darwin visited Galápagos Islands)*
- *Length: 9 miles (15km); 4–6 hours*
- *Difficulty: Easy/ moderate – uneven terrain; gentle climb*
- *Best months: Feb–May*
- *Top tip: The Galápagos are reached via flights from mainland Ecuador; a park entrance fee must be paid on arrival*

British naturalist Charles Darwin disembarked on Isabela Island in September 1835. This is the largest of the remote, Pacific-strewn Galápagos Islands. It was just one stop on the HMS *Beagle*'s map-charting voyage to South America, but it was among the most important. For it was on Darwin's visits to this volcanic archipelago that he observed the islands' unusual species, most notably its finches. From these observations he developed his idea of evolution by natural selection.

The *Beagle* dropped anchor at Tagus Cove, on Isabela Island's northwest coast, and Darwin spent four days collecting specimens. Today, tourist boats visit here, and it's possible to make a short, steep hike via palo santo trees to

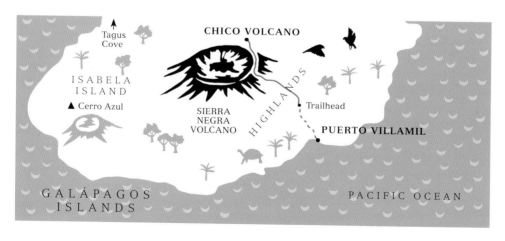

a lookout with views over Darwin Lake and Darwin Volcano. The trees are full of the famed finches.

However, the best hike on Isabela Island is to 1,124m (3,688ft) Sierra Negra, one of the archipelago's most active volcanoes. From the town of Puerto Villamil, it's a short drive to the trailhead in the highlands. From here, a 9-mile (15km) route climbs gradually uphill, through fern-frilled trees to the crater rim. This is where Sierra Negra Volcano's vast caldera (one of the world's biggest) comes into view. The trail follows the caldera's rim and drops to Chico Volcano. It then crosses a scorch-marked, lunar-like landscape of lava fields, sulphur splotches, steaming vents, and fumaroles. Keep a lookout: several of 'Darwin's finches' might be seen.

ABOVE: Walk over the lava fields of the Sierra Negra volcano.

360
MOUNT FUJI

Honshu, Japan

{ Ascend the country's highest peak, a symbol of the nation and muse to artistic genius Katsushika Hokusai. }

Need to know
- *Point in time: 1820s (Katsushika Hokusai depicted Mount Fuji)*
- *Length: 3–5 miles (5–8km); 4.5–7.5 hours*
- *Difficulty: Moderate – steep; good facilities; crowded*
- *Best months: July– Sept*
- *Top tip: There are more than forty huts on Fuji; overnight stays must be booked in advance*

The perfect cone of Mount Fuji is one of Japan's most recognisable icons. At 3,776m (12,388ft), it's also the country's highest peak. Fuji has long been considered sacred but grew in popularity during the Edo period, when the power balance shifted east and Tokyo (then known as Edo) became the de facto Japanese capital. On a clear day, you can see Fuji's snowy summit from the city.

No individual did as much for the mountain as artist Katsushika Hokusai who, in the 1820s, began a series of woodblock prints called *Thirty-six Views of Mount Fuji*. These turned Fuji into an artistic muse. The mountain's image was everywhere.

Climbing Mount Fuji is a rite of passage, and the slopes are crowded during climbing season (between July and early September). This makes an ascent as much of an insight into the local psyche as it is a good hike.

Four routes, ranging from 3 to 5 miles (5 to 8km) one-way, lead to the summit. These are: Yoshida, the busiest route; Fujinomiya, the shortest; Gotemba, the longest; and Subashiri, the most forested. Many people hike up Mount Fuji's ashen slopes at night in order to summit for sunrise. Alternatively, set off midafternoon and overnight in one of the highest huts to be well placed for the magical *goraiko* (arrival of light) the next morning.

MOUNT FUJI

Fujinomiya Trail

Ninth Station ▲

Eighth Station ▲

Yoshida Trail

Gotemba Trail

Seventh Station ▲

▲ Sixth Station

Subashiri Trail

Komitake Shrine

SUBASHIRI   Fifth Station   MOUNT KOFUJI

361
John Muir Way

*Scotland,
United Kingdom*

The famed conservationist John Muir was born in Scotland in 1838. This 134-mile (215km) trail runs from the west-coast town of Helensburgh to the east-coast town of Dunbar, Muir's birthplace.

LEFT: Snow-capped Mount Fuji, sacred mountain and nineteenth-century muse.

362
KEMERI AND CENA BOG WALKS

Kemeri National Park, Latvia

In the nineteenth century, people suffering ailments of the nerves, joints, bones, or muscles would head to the Baltic Sea resort of Kemeri. The discovery of its therapeutic mud baths and sulphur springs, which were first scientifically analysed in 1818, led to an influx of patients keen to be cured. Now the lagoons, bogs, mires, and forests here are protected within the Kemeri National Park (25 miles / 40km from Riga). Combining short walks to the Kemeri Bog and Cena Bog reveals the diversity of this landscape. It is splashed with vivid lichens, spongy mosses, bog spurge (a flowering plant), and butterfly orchids. It also shelters a range of wildlife, from sea eagles and elk to wolves and wild boar.

363
KING LUDWIG'S WAY

Bavaria, Germany

Ludwig II, king of Bavaria from 1864 to 1886, wasn't your standard monarch. He was a reclusive fantasist, definitely eccentric, and possibly mad. His overactive imagination, however, did inspire Neuschwanstein Castle, one of the most fairy-tale-like castles in the world. This is almost the end point for the scenic 60-mile (100km) King Ludwig's Way. The trail starts at Lake Starnberg. Here in 1886 Ludwig and the psychiatrist who had just certified him insane both died in unexplained circumstances. The trail passes Andechs Abbey (famous for its brewery), Lake Ammersee, 994m (3,261ft) Hoher Peißenberg, dense forest, Pöllat Gorge, and the magical hilltop turrets of Neuschwanstein. It ends in the town of Füssen, nestled at the foot of the Alps.

RIGHT: Follow King Ludwig's Way past the fairy-tale turrets of Neuschwanstein Castle.

364
Faulhornweg

Bernese Alps, Switzerland

Arguably the best day-walk in the Alps, this 16-mile (26km) ridge hike above Interlaken was made easier in 1893. It was then that the cog railway to the Schynige Platte trailhead opened.

365
Creek Walk

Dubai, United Arab Emirates

The city of Dubai became a tax-free port in 1894, helping it morph from a pearl-fishing outpost into a skyscrapered powerhouse. The 2-mile (3km) Creek Walk is a glimpse of old Dubai.

ROBERT LOUIS STEVENSON TRACK

Cévennes, France

{ Follow in the footsteps of the Scottish writer through the villages, gorges, and fascinating history of south-central France. }

Need to know

- *Point in time: 1878 (Robert Louis Stevenson walked through southeast France)*
- *Length: 165 miles (265km); 10–12 days*
- *Difficulty: Moderate – hills; regular villages*
- *Best months: Apr– June; Sept*
- *Top tip: The trailhead towns of Le Puy-en-Velay and Alès have train stations*

'That fine intoxication that comes from much motion in the open air . . . begins in a sort of dazzle and sluggishness in the brain, and ends in a peace that passes comprehension.' So wrote Robert Louis Stevenson, a firm believer in the benefits of a long walk. In 1878, aged twenty-seven, the yet-to-be-successful Scottish author travelled to south-central France and hiked across its sparsely inhabited countryside. He walked for twelve days, with a donkey named Modestine. He wrote about this amble, and his tale was published as *Travels with a Donkey in the Cévennes*, in 1879. It was one of Stevenson's earliest works, paving the way for a lauded literary career that would include *Treasure Island* and *Kidnapped*. Sadly, Stevenson died in 1894, aged just forty-four years old.

As beloved as those later novels are, Stevenson's travelogue about his journey in the Cévennes was arguably more groundbreaking. Here was a man walking for walking's sake, sleeping outside in a specially made sleeping bag (an early prototype), and then writing about the adventure of it all. The book was a trailblazer for much modern travel writing. And because Stevenson wrote such a detailed account, it's easy to follow in his footsteps.

The Robert Louis Stevenson Track, also known as the GR70, roughly follows Stevenson's route. It runs from the medieval village of Le Puy-en-Velay (in the Haute-Loire region) – renowned for its rock-perched chapel and its

ABOVE: Retrace Robert Louis Stevenson's steps through the Cévennes.

type of lentil – to the town of Alès, in the region of Languedoc-Roussillon. It covers 165 miles (265km), slightly longer than Stevenson's original 120-mile (193km) journey.

Stevenson chose this mountainous, impoverished region to walk in because it was one of the only parts of France where Protestantism was still the dominant faith. He was intrigued by stories of the Camisards – he saw similarities between the suppression of these French Protestants during the sixteenth-century Wars of Religion and the Highland Clearances in Scotland. He also reasoned that his readers were middle-class Scottish Protestants who would rather learn about the landscapes of their spiritual kinsmen than those that were dominated by Catholics.

Today's hikers might choose the GR70 less on the basis of faith and more for a sense of escapism. The terrain it passes remains some of France's least populated. The trail often follows old bridleways, transhumance routes used by herders moving livestock between pastures, and pilgrimage roads. It offers long stretches of walking immersed in wild hills, slopes of sweet chestnut, and deep river gorges. The settlements that lie along the way are often ancient villages, resonant with reminders of the Wars of Religion.

From Le Puy-en-Velay (where Stevenson had his sleeping bag made), the trail leads along the volcanic plateaus of the Velay via twisted pines and the Loire. It visits the village of Le Monastier, where Stevenson began his own travels. It then journeys to the old town of Pradelles, attacked during the Wars of Religion in 1588. The town was saved by a girl who dropped a rock on the invading leader's head.

Next, the GR70 crosses the Allier River into the Gévaudan region, allegedly home to a man-eating wolf that stalks the heather and pine. The trail traverses wildflower fields and rolling uplands, following a small stretch of the Lot River. It then heads up 1,699m (5,574ft) Mount Lozère, the highest peak in Cévennes National Park. This is untamed country, gouged by gorges. It is scattered with prehistoric megaliths, ruined castles, and churches that have been here since the Middle Ages.

The path eventually climbs to Saint-Pierre Pass, where Stevenson and Modestine shared their last meal, before descending into St Jean du Gard, former headquarters of the Camisard resistance. Stevenson finished here, but the GR70 extends on to Alès. As Stevenson said, 'I travel not to go anywhere, but to go. I travel for travel's sake. The great affair is to move.'

LE PUY-EN-VELAY

HAUTE-LOIRE

VELAY
MOUNTAINS

Le Monastier

Allier River

Loire River

Pradelles

GÉVAUDAN

Lot River

▲ MOUNT
LOZÈRE

CÉVENNES NATIONAL PARK

Saint-Pierre Pass ▲

ALÈS

St Jean du Gard

LANGUEDOC-ROUSSILLON

367
Stevenson's Grave

Mount Vaea, Samoa

Hike to the tomb of writer Robert Louis Stevenson, who died in the South Pacific in 1894. A steep 2-mile (3km) trail, known as the 'Road of Loving Hearts', goes from his former villa to his grave.

368
Brontë Way

West Yorkshire and Lancashire, United Kingdom

This 43-mile (69km) trail pays homage to the literary Brontë sisters, Charlotte (1816–55), Emily (1818–48), and Anne (1820–49). Visit their home at Haworth and the countryside that inspired Emily Brontë's novel *Wuthering Heights*.

369
EMPEROR'S TREK

Southeast Brazil

The Brazilian monarchy was short-lived. It lasted from 1815, when Portugal granted kingdom status to its colony, to 1889, when Brazil (having gained independence in 1822) became a republic. During that time, however, the royals established summer homes at both the city of Petrópolis (named for Emperor Pedro II), and the city of Teresópolis (named for Emperor Pedro's wife, Dona Teresa). The 26-mile (42km) hike between these two cool alpine towns reveals both imperial prowess and natural drama. From Petrópolis's bygone streets and 'Pink Palace', it is a short transfer to the trailhead in Correas. Hikers head into the Serra dos Órgãos mountain range, and trek via caves, valleys, the Atlantic rainforest, and 2,263m (7,425ft) Pedra do Sino, before finishing in Teresópolis.

370
PICO DUARTE

Dominican Republic

Pico Duarte is the Dominican Republic's highest point. In fact, it is the highest point in the whole Caribbean. It is named after Juan-Pablo Duarte, who was instrumental in securing the Dominican Republic's independence from Haitian rule in 1844. Duarte's role is honoured on this 3,098m (10,164ft) summit, topped by his bust. The 29-mile (46km) Ciénaga route is the easiest way up and down Pico Duarte. It leads through the Cibao Valley and rises via the Cordillera Central's northern slopes. Spend a night at a refuge near the top of Pico Duarte, and get up early to see the sun rise over the whole Caribbean.

371

GR21

Normandy, France

Strolling along the Normandy coast on the GR21 is like walking through a work of Impressionist art. The trail runs for 107 miles (172km), from the town of Le Tréport to the port of Le Havre. The section along the Alabaster Coast is particularly artistically significant. In the city of Dieppe's St Jacques Church you can see a series of artworks by Pissarro. In the town of Étretat you can visit the rock arches that Monet painted many times. The resort town of Sainte-Adresse has an 'Impressionists' Promenade', where replica works sit in the precise spots on which the originals were created. Finally, it was in the port of Le Havre in 1872 that Monet painted the famous *Impression, Sunrise*. It was this blurry painting that gave the movement its name.

372
William Wordsworth Way

Cumbria, United Kingdom

Wander lonely as the Romantic poet William Wordsworth (1770–1850). This 168-mile (270km) hike starts and ends at his birthplace in Cockermouth, and ambles amid the Lake District that so inspired him.

373
Constable Country

Suffolk, United Kingdom

Take a 4-mile (6.5km) stroll through the bucolic Stour Valley and Dedham Vale to stand where the Romantic landscapist John Constable painted his famous *The Hay Wain* in 1821.

374
Heidi Trail

Maienfeld, Switzerland

Make a 4-mile (6.5km) circuit inspired by fictional mountain girl Heidi, made famous in the 1881 book by Johanna Spyri.

375
Snæfellsjökull

Western Iceland

Snæfellsjökull is the 'snow mountain' in the French novelist Jules Verne's 1864 book *Journey to the Center of the Earth*. In six hours, you can hike up it using crampons.

WATERLOO
Lion's Mound
Wellington
Museum
(Auberge
Bodenghien)

WATERLOO
BATTLEFIELDS

Ligny

WALLONIA

Fleurus

Charleroi

Ham-sur-Heure

BEAUMONT

376
Hans Christian Andersen Trail

Odense, Denmark

The children's author Han Christian
Andersen was born in Odense in
1805. This 2-mile (3km) stroll visits
many Andersen sites, from his
birthplace to where his mother
worked as a washerwoman.

RIGHT: The Napoleon Trail finishes at
the Waterloo battlefields, where you'll find
Lion's Mound.

NAPOLEON TRAIL

Wallonia, Belgium

{ Relive the last battle of the 'Little General' on a walk through the Belgian countryside. }

Napoleon Bonaparte, who became emperor of France in 1804, is considered one of the greatest military strategists in history. However, in 1814, following a calamitous invasion of Russia – and other defeats – he was exiled to the Mediterranean isle of Elba. He escaped and, in February 1815, he marched back to Paris. In the following 'Hundred Days of Napoleon', between 20 March and 8 July 1815, he reinstated himself as leader, and staged further military campaigns. He was defeated again, this time by the Duke of Wellington at Waterloo. He was exiled once more, this time to the remote island of St Helena in the Atlantic Ocean.

The Napoleon Trail, in Belgium's French-speaking region of Wallonia, is the route taken by Napoleon on four days out of his famous hundred – specifically 15 June to 18 June 1815. The trail starts in the town of Beaumont, where Napoleon's troops camped by the eleventh-century tower. It finishes in the village of Waterloo, at the Auberge Bodenghien, where Napoleon set up his headquarters; this is now the Wellington Museum. Along the way lies the hamlet of Ham-sur-Heure, where Napoleon watched his troops parade. You can also visit the town of Fleurus, where he set up a hospital.

The 58-mile (94km) Napoleon Trail is aimed at drivers and cyclists, but hikers can follow it too. Detours are also possible, including a 5-mile (8km) loop around the village of Ligny. This is the site of Napoleon's last victory. You can also stroll through the Waterloo battlefields, 6,200 acres (25km²) of hills, valleys, and grassland. These are best surveyed from Lion's Mound, an artificial hill built in 1820 to commemorate the battle.

Need to know
- Point in time: 1815 (Battle of Waterloo)
- Length: 58 miles (94km); 5 days
- Difficulty: Easy – gentle terrain
- Best months: Apr–Oct
- Top tip: Waterloo is around 12.5 miles (20km) south of the Belgian capital of Brussels

378
Sainte-Victoire Mountain

Provence, France

The artist Paul Cezanne (1839–1906) was born near 1,011m (3,317ft) Sainte-Victoire Mountain, and painted it often. Hike up it to see the world through his eyes.

379
MOUNT RIGI MARK TWAIN TRAIL

Lake Lucerne, Switzerland

Climbing Mount Rigi was a rite of passage for well-to-do nineteenth-century 'Grand Tour' travellers. This was especially the case after Queen Victoria was hauled up it, in a sedan chair, in 1868. A railway to the 1,798m (5,899ft) summit opened in 1871. That didn't dissuade American writer Mark Twain from walking up Rigi when he visited in 1897, however. Don't let it stop you either. The 6-mile (10km) Mark Twain Trail from the resort town of Weggis, on Lake Lucerne, is an unrelenting climb. What you get in return is an uncrowded experience, exploring farmland, forest, and waterfalls looking out over mountain peaks rising above a sea of clouds.

380
KING PETAR'S FOOTSTEPS

Western Montenegro

The poet Petar II Petrovic-Njegos is considered to be the Shakespeare of the Slavic world. He was an acclaimed spiritual and political leader, as well as a writer, becoming ruler of Montenegro in 1831. The King Petar's Footsteps trail is a 65-mile (105km) hike from the town of Tivat, on the Bay of Kotor, to the town of Budva, on the Mediterranean coast farther south. It runs via cobbled Kotor Town, twisty old trade routes, the village of Njegusi (Petar's birthplace), and Centinje (Petar's old royal capital). It also passes Petar's mausoleum, which is perched up in the rocky heights of Lovcen National Park.

381

BYRON'S JOURNEY

Southern Albania

'Land of Albania! Let me bend mine eyes / On thee, thou rugged nurse of savage men!' These lines come from *Childe Harold's Pilgrimage,* the long poem that established its author, Lord Byron, as a literary great. Lord Byron was inspired to write the poem by his travels across Albania with his friend John Hobhouse, in 1809. Hobhouse kept a diary, and the 75-mile (120km) Byron Trail from Ioannina in Greece to Tepelena in southern Albania loosely follows their route. The Albanian section starts in the city of Glina, and follows old caravan trails via villages, monasteries, and mountains. It finishes at Tepelena Palace, where the vizier Ali Pasha once entertained the passing poet.

382

TSAR'S PATH

Yalta, Ukraine

This 4-mile (6.5km) trail, sandwiched between the Crimean Mountains and the Black Sea, is more of a therapeutic prescription than a hike. It was built in the 1860s on the orders of Tsar Alexander III's doctor, who believed the stroll would ease the tsar's tuberculosis. The path begins at the neo-Renaissance Livadia Palace. This was the summer retreat of the Russian imperial family of the time. It was also the venue for Stalin, Churchill, and Roosevelt's post-war Yalta conference in 1945. From there, the trail runs through forest to a breezy lookout in the town of Oreanda. It finishes at Swallow's Nest, a fairy-tale-like castle on top of the plummeting Cape Ai-Todor cliffs. One thing: do check the current security situation before travelling.

383
Jack the Ripper Walk

*London,
United Kingdom*

This three-hour walk, starting at Liverpool Street Rail Station in London's East End, visits sites where the notorious 1880s serial killer Jack the Ripper stalked his victims.

384
Ned Kelly Siege Site

Victoria, Australia

Infamous Australian outlaw Ned Kelly was finally captured in the small town of Glenrowan in 1880. This short trail visits sites that tell the story of Kelly's last stand.

385
The Raven's Trail

*Massachusetts,
United States*

This short loop walk is dedicated to the author Edgar Allan Poe, and explores Boston, where he was born in 1809. It starts at his statue in Edgar Allan Poe Square.

386
Royal Canal Way

Ireland

The canal linking the Irish capital of Dublin with the village of Cloondara, on the River Shannon, was completed in 1817. You can now walk for 89 miles (144km) along the restored towpath.

387
TELEGRAPH TRAIL

British Columbia, Canada

In the nineteenth century, the American communications giant Western Union wanted to lay down a telegraph line that would lead north from California, through Canada, under the Bering Sea, and across Russia to Moscow. They didn't succeed. However, between 1865 and 1867, they managed to build a sizable portion of it. This meant engineers traveling through the wilderness of British Columbia, from the city of New Westminster to the city of Quesnel, and up to the village of Hazelton. They used First Nations pathways and tackled thick forests and unruly rivers en route. The Telegraph Trail is a 60-mile (100km) section of their journey, from near Quesnel to the Blackwater River.

SOUTH WEST COAST PATH

Southern England, United Kingdom

{ Walk amid smuggling history, basking sharks, craggy cliffs, and fishing villages, always in sight of the sea. }

Need to know
- *Point in time: 1809 (Preventative Water Guard founded)*
- *Length: 630 miles (1,014km); 6–8 weeks*
- *Difficulty: Moderate/ strenuous – varied; very undulating*
- *Best months: Apr– June; Sept–Oct*
- *Top tip: The trail frequently enters towns and villages; wide range of accommodation options available, from campsites to B&Bs*

Thank you, smugglers. For without your nefarious doings, this hike would not exist. The South West Coast Path (SWCP) wraps itself around the sea-facing edges of counties Somerset, Devon, Cornwall, and Dorset. And it owes its origins to the miscreants who once worked this shore, and the authorities' need to stop them.

The coast here is riddled with hidden coves and secret bays. As such, in the eighteenth and early nineteenth centuries, when import duties were high, smuggling was rife. Lace, brandy, rum, tobacco, tea, and more were illicitly moved. However, the founding of the Preventative Water Guard in 1809 was a blow to the bootleggers. Using clifftop patrol paths, sentries could better watch the action occurring offshore. Today, those same paths allow hikers access to the sea-salty splendour.

The South West Coast Path runs for 630 miles (1,014km) from Minehead in Somerset to Poole in Dorset. It is a lovely, long, twisty unravelling of fishing villages tucked into natural harbours, gorse-cloaked hills, golden sands, and rocky promontories that fling themselves out into the sea. Some spots en route are busy in summer, but the joy of the Coast Path is that, if you just walk on around the next headland, you leave all the tourists behind. Then it's just you, the scent of brine and bracken, chirruping birds, and the path snaking ahead. You might even see a seal or a basking shark playing in the waves.

Navigation from Minehead is simple: keep the sea on your right. From this holiday resort, the trail traverses Exmoor National Park, then climbs 318m (1,043ft) Great

Hangman, the SWCP's highest point. It might not sound high, but it's not absolute altitude that's the challenge on this trail – it's the relentless ups and downs. In total, the SWCP notches up 35,000m (114,800ft) of ascent.

The path passes whitewashed, tumbling Clovelly (the quintessential Devon fishing village), ruined Tintagel castle (steeped in Arthurian legend), and pretty Port Isaac. It runs to the world-class seafood restaurants of Padstow, the rock pools of the Bedruthan Steps, and the surf town of Newquay. The St Agnes area is rich in mining heritage, while the artistic town of St Ives is home to the Tate St Ives gallery. Land's End – England's westernmost point – is dramatic, though it is also home to a busy theme park.

From here the SWCP turns east. It passes the cliff-side Minack Theatre at Porthcurno and St Michael's Mount, a medieval chapel stranded on a tidal island. Prussia Cove, the Lizard Peninsula, and the Helford River are rich in

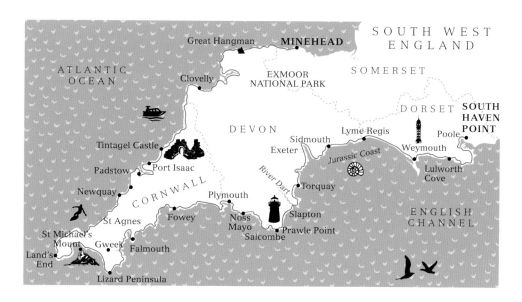

smuggling legends. Author Daphne du Maurier set stories in these parts, including *Frenchman's Creek*.

From the lively harbour of Falmouth the trail heads around the Roseland Peninsula. It continues to Fowey's yacht-filled harbour, Polperro (which has a Museum of Smuggling), and the lengthy sands of Whitsand Bay. The maritime city of Plymouth is a jolt back to civilisation, but is soon left behind for the hidden-away village of Noss Mayo and the sailing hub of Salcombe. The shingle beach at Slapton is the place to remember the hundreds of American troops who lost their lives here during rehearsals for the Second World War D-Day invasion of Normandy.

Sites linked to crime author Agatha Christie dot the Dart Estuary and the coast to Torquay. Then the trail hits its home straight, tracing Dorset's fossil-flecked Jurassic Coast. It runs via Lyme Regis harbour, the busy seaside town of Weymouth, rolling chalk cliffs, perfectly circular Lulworth Cove, and Old Harry Rocks. Finally, it negotiates a (nudist) beach to reach South Haven Point, and a sign that declares: 'Minehead 630 miles'.

LENÇÓIS

Cachoeira
da Fumaça

CAPÃO VALLEY

CHAPADA DIAMANTINA
NATIONAL PARK

PATI VALLEY

ANDARAI

Igatu

RIGHT: The sandstone mesas of Chapada
Diamantina National Park are among the
Grand Circuit trail's many highlights.

GRAND CIRCUIT

Chapada Diamantina National Park, Brazil

{ Hike through the mountains of Bahia, where diamonds were discovered in the nineteenth century. }

Chapada Diamantina National Park, a striking chunk of northeast Brazil's Bahia state, dazzles on multiple levels. For starters, it is visually resplendent. It is a *Lost World*–style tumble of flat-top sandstone mesas riven with secret ravines. It boasts pools, waterfalls, underground rivers, and explorable caves. Orchids, cacti, and bromeliads fill the forests and grasslands, and monkeys and hummingbirds swoop between the trees. In the mid-nineteenth century, however, it wasn't the landscape's aesthetics that drew people. It was its hidden treasure. In 1844 diamonds were discovered in the Mucugê River, bringing an influx of *garimpeiros* (prospectors) hoping to make it big.

These diamond-seeking hopefuls founded Lençóis as a base for explorations into the mountains. Today the town, with its bright nineteenth-century houses, is the starting point for hikes in Chapada Diamantina National Park. The 62-mile (100km) Grand Circuit is one of the best hikes, offering spectacular countryside and plenty of villages with characterful *pousadas* (inns) en route.

From Lençóis, the trail heads into the Capão Valley and over the plains to pretty Pati Valley. There is the chance to dip in pools and cascades, and hike up to sweeping viewpoints. Or you can detour from Lençóis to Cachoeira da Fumaça, one of Brazil's highest waterfalls. The trail also visits quartzite caves before heading to the neighbourhood of Andarai. Here, another detour runs to the ruins of Igatu. From Andarai, it's a two-day walk back to Lençóis.

Need to know
- *Point in time: 1844 (diamonds discovered in Bahia)*
- *Length: 62 miles (100km); 5–7 days*
- *Difficulty: Moderate – undulating; some steep climbs*
- *Best months: Mar–Oct*
- *Top tip: The trail starts in Lençóis, which is 270 miles (430km) from Salvador; buses connect the two*

390
CONFEDERATION TRAIL

Prince Edward Island, Canada

In 1871 construction began on a railway right across the British colony of Prince Edward Island, but it was an expensive undertaking. The Canadian confederation offered to foot the bill if Prince Edward Island joined them. It subsequently became a province of Canada in 1873. The railway lasted for just over one hundred years, closing in 1989. However, its tracks live on, cleared and resurfaced to create the easygoing 255-mile (410km) Confederation Trail. The main route runs from the westerly fishing community of Tignish to eastern Elmira, where there's a Railway Museum in the old station. En route lie rolling hills, fertile farmsteads, and pretty villages.

391
UNDERGROUND RAILROAD TRAIL

Maryland, United States

The Underground Railroad Trail in Maryland's Montgomery County is only 2 miles (3km) long. However, it gives a flavour of the much longer Underground Railroad, the system of routes used by slaves fleeing the southern United States for the north and Canada in the nineteenth century. The trail starts near the Quaker-founded community of Sandy Spring, at Woodlawn Manor, built in 1832 and purportedly a slave safe house. It ends at a 300-year-old ash tree. En route interpretive signs add detail describing the slaves' hiding spots in tree hollows and the creeks they had to cross.

392
CONVICT TRAIL

New South Wales, Australia

Australia's Great North Road was built to connect the city of Sydney with the fruitful Hunter Valley. It was also built as a statement. It was proof to those back in Britain that this new outpost on the other side of the globe could do things just as well. The road was constructed by convicts, 165,000 of whom were transported to Australia between 1787 and 1868. They provided the bulk of the road's labour force. From 1826 to 1832, these bonded men chiselled 150 miles (240km) of highway. Today, the 26-mile (42km) section between Wisemans Ferry and Mount Manning is known as the Convict Trail. It is closed to motorised traffic but can be walked, and reveals original walls, buttresses, culverts, and colonial graffiti. It also boasts the oldest bridge still in use in continental Australia.

393
High Line, New York

United States

The disused spur of New York's old West Side Line railway, built in the 1850s, has been triumphantly repurposed as a 1.5-mile (2.5km) linear park. It includes naturalised planting and views of the Hudson River.

394
Blue Mountain Peak

Jamaica

A 7-mile (12km) climb up Jamaica's 2,256m (7,402ft) Blue Mountain Peak passes a profusion of ferns, eucalyptus, and birds. It also takes in coffee plantations that were founded in the nineteenth century.

395
Pony Express

United States

Established in 1860, the Pony Express relay system could deliver mail across eight states in ten days. The 125-mile (200km) South Pass segment in Wyoming offers a tiny taster.

396
Olive Oil Greenway

Jaén, Spain

The 34-mile (55km) Olive Oil Greenway follows a disused nineteenth-century railway. It once transported olive oil through the grove-cloaked countryside, crossing old bridges and viaducts en route.

HILL TRIBE TREKS

Sapa, Vietnam

{ Head into the northern highlands
to hike amid colourful villages and
the lush mountains that so bewitched
the colonial French. }

Need to know
- *Point in time: 1891 (Sapa incorporated into French Indochina)*
- *Length: 1–5 days*
- *Difficulty: Moderate – bad weather possible; guide advised*
- *Best months: Mar–May; Sept–Nov*
- *Top tip: Sapa can get cold, especially at night – take warm clothes*

When the French colonised Indochina in the late nineteenth century, they called the people they encountered in the hills the Montagnards, meaning the 'mountaineers'. This name specifically applied to the ethnic Degar of Vietnam's jungly, isolated Central Highlands. However, the term has been co-opted to describe any Vietnamese indigenous peoples living at altitude. Today, many of them live around the small town of Sapa, in the country's hilly north.

Perched on the edge of a high plateau, and often swirled in mist, Sapa is lodged at 1,600m (5,250ft) among the Tonkinese Alps, just south of the border with China. There are unexplained petroglyphs in the area thought to date back to the fifteenth century. Sometime after that, the Hmong, Dao, Tay, Giay, and other hill tribes are thought to have settled here. The French arrived in the 1880s and incorporated Sapa into their colony of Vietnam in 1891. By 1922 it was a French resort town, replete with a church, hospital, and villas. However, a torrid period of wars and economic hardships followed. Sapa was virtually destroyed. The hill tribe peoples survived.

Now the area has been regenerated, and hikers head to Sapa's lush, rice-terraced surrounds to seek a better insight into its rich cultural mix. The best way to do this is to walk from Sapa to the outlying villages. There are no set routes. Treks tend to range from two to six hours a day, and amble amid tumbling green slopes that are cut with paddy fields and trampled by water buffalo. It can be

ABOVE: Hike past mesmerising rice terraces in Vietnam's mountainous north.

wet, slippery, and undulating, but the pace is generally slow, to allow time for human interaction. A guide is essential, to lead you to the most interesting settlements and introduce you to local customs. You can stay in Dao and Hmong homestays each night. You also have the chance to try traditional foods (or help to prepare the meals), lend a hand in the garden, or tend the pigs and chickens.

Sapa used to be tough to reach. These days it's easy to catch an overnight train from the Vietnamese capital of Hanoi to the northern hub of Lao Cai, from where it's a 24-mile (38km) journey to the hill station by bus or taxi. In the early days, visitors were transferred from Lao Cai to Sapa in sedan chairs.

Few of the buildings erected during the French colonial era remain. The white stone church is still there, but most old remnants have been replaced by less elegant modern hotels. Still, Sapa isn't about the architecture, it's about meeting the Montagnards.

You'll encounter many hill tribe peoples in Sapa itself, especially on market day (Saturday). The Black Hmong are most numerous, recognisable by their indigo aprons, leggings, and circular hats. The Red Dao sport crimson, turban-like headdresses drooping with tassels. The Giay wear black pants and bright shirts, with a band from

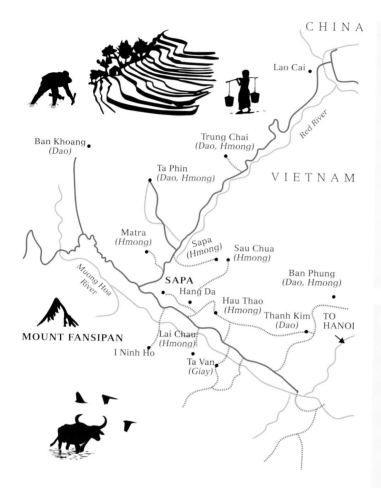

CHINA

Lao Cai

Red River

VIETNAM

Ban Khoang
(Dao)

Trung Chai
(Dao, Hmong)

Ta Phin
(Dao, Hmong)

Matra
(Hmong)

Sapa
(Hmong)

Sau Chua
(Hmong)

Muong Hoa River

SAPA

Ban Phung
(Dao, Hmong)

Hang Da

Hau Thao
(Hmong)

Thanh Kim
(Dao)

TO HANOI

MOUNT FANSIPAN

Lai Chau
(Hmong)

I Ninh Ho

Ta Van
(Giay)

collar to armpit. The overall result is a riot of colour
and decoration.

If, after a hill tribe trek, you hanker for greater heights,
consider 3,143m (10,311ft) Mount Fansipan, the 'Roof of
Indochina'. Sapa stares right at Vietnam's highest
mountain, and summit expeditions from the town take
three to five days. These hikes pass colourful villages
before entering a lush wilderness populated only by
monkeys and mountain goats. The weather can be grim,
but it's not a technical climb. And reaching the zenith of
this fascinating land will make you feel like an honorary
Montagnard yourself.

400
KALAUPAPA TRAIL

Molokai, Hawaii, United States

Hansen's disease (leprosy) arrived on the Hawaiian Islands in the early nineteenth century. From 1866 sufferers were exiled to the Kalaupapa Peninsula, an area of solidified lava surrounded by the Pacific Ocean on three sides and backed by sheer, 488m (1,600ft) cliffs. It is utterly cut off, with no chance of escape. A cure for leprosy was found in the 1940s, and isolation laws were lifted in 1969. Now guided tours make the steep, hairpin 3.5-mile (5km) descent to the site. Visit the old lava-rock church, gaze over the ocean from the magnificent cliffs, and learn about Kalaupapa's poignant past.

401
TRAIL OF TEARS NATIONAL HISTORIC TRAIL

Southeast United States

The Indian Removal Act of 1830 forced Native American peoples who lived in the southeast of the United States to move west from their ancestral lands to designated Indian Territory in what's now Oklahoma. This included members of the Cherokee, Muscogee, Seminole, Chickasaw, and Choctaw tribes. Many never made it. The Trail of Tears National Historic Trail, which encompasses thousands of miles of road, track, and river routes, commemorates their torturous journeys. Segments can still be walked. For instance, a 2.75-mile (4.5km) loop visits Kentucky's Mantle Rock, a natural sandstone bridge under which 1,766 Cherokee holed up for two weeks in the bitter winter of 1838–39 – only halfway through their 800-mile (1,288km) trudge.

HEADHUNTERS' TRAIL

Sarawak, Borneo, Malaysia

{ Trek through the primary rainforest
of Malaysian Borneo, where
headhunters once roamed. }

Need to know
- *Point in time: 1841
(headhunting
suppressed)*
- *Length: 12 miles
(19km); 2–3 days*
- *Difficulty: Easy –
humid; low gradient*
- *Best months: Mar–Oct*
- *Top tip: A park guide
and rental of a
longboat is required*

The Headhunters' Trail links Gunung Mulu National Park
with the river port of Limbang. It follows the route that
headhunting parties of Kayan people once took to launch
raids on neighbouring tribes. The warriors travelled up
Melinau Gorge, then hauled their canoes overland to the
Terikan River to reach their foes, sometimes decapitating
them and preserving their heads as grisly souvenirs.

Headhunting was rife in Borneo in the 1800s. In 1841,
however, the region's governor, James Brooke (later the
first 'White Rajah of Sarawak'), suppressed the practice.
Today, most visitors actively seek out interactions with the
local tribes. Back in the early nineteenth century, they
would have run a mile.

Gunung Mulu National Park is an adventurer's dream.
It is a den of mountains, limestone spikes, and primary
rainforest. It is home to some of the world's biggest caves,
and it is brimming with wildlife. Starting the trail requires a
longboat trip from Gunung Mulu National Park's
headquarters to Kuala Berar. It's then a 5-mile (8km) hike,
through dipterocarp and riparian forest to reach Camp 5,
at the end of the gorge. Here you can stay overnight, take
a dip in the Melinau River, or add on an extra day for a
tough climb up the razor-sharp Pinnacles (limestone karst
rock formations). From Camp 5, it's a 7-mile (11km) trek
to the settlement of Kuala Terikan, where you can pick up
a riverboat and ride to an Iban longhouse to hear tales of
headhunters past.

RIGHT: Visit the rainforest of
Gunung Mulu National Park.
Be glad that the headhunters
are no longer there.

To Limbang

B R U N E I

M A L A Y S I A

Terikan River

KUALA TERIKAN

GUNUNG MULU
NATIONAL PARK

Melinau Gorge

Camp 5

▲ **PINNACLES**

KUALA BERAR

Melinau River

Clearwater Cave

Lagang's Cave

Park HQ

403
Glasgow Lakes
Look-off Trail

Nova Scotia, Canada

Scottish immigrants
flooded to Canada's
Cape Breton in the
1800s. The 5.5-mile
(9km) Glasgow
Lakes Look-off Trail
is a highland trek
in 'New Scotland',
a nod to the
motherland.

404
Mormon Pioneer
Trail

Utah, United States

From 1846 to 1869,
70,000 Mormons
journeyed over
1,000 miles (1,609km)
across the United
States to flee religious
persecution. On the
10-mile (16km)
Mormon Flat to Big
Mountain hike, you
can still see the ruts
left by their carts.

405

LAURA SECORD LEGACY TRAIL

Ontario, Canada

Laura Secord, wife of the Loyalist James Secord, was a Canadian heroine of the War of 1812. On 22 June 1813, she hiked 20 miles (32km) through American-occupied territory to deliver a message that would warn British forces of an imminent attack by the Americans. Today her role in the subsequent victory – unlauded back then – is honoured by the Laura Secord Legacy Trail. It follows Laura's route from her historic homestead in Queenston, a town near Niagara Falls, to the ruins of DeCew House, at that time the headquarters of the British Army. En route lie vineyards and orchards, the 'haunted' Screaming Tunnel, a plaque to Captain Pierpoint (fellow War of 1812 hero), and the sweeping Niagara Escarpment.

406

CALHETA DE NESQUIM LOOP

Pico, Azores, Portugal

Stuck out in the mid-Atlantic, the Azores archipelago has long been a prime spot for anyone interested in whales. Today, ecotourists come to watch them. In the nineteenth century – and until a whaling ban was enforced in the Azores in 1984 – fishermen came to hunt them. This was especially true on the island of Pico, where the first whaling station opened at the town of Calheta de Nesquim in 1876. A circular 7.5-mile (12km) walk from the village provides an insight into the grisly industry. It begins in the church square, at the statue of Captain Anselmo (founder of whaling on Pico), and visits the island's first clifftop *vigia* (lookout station).

407
HAIFA TRAIL

Haifa, Israel

Baha'i is one of the world's youngest religions, a monotheistic, inclusivist faith propounding the spiritual unity of humankind. It was founded in Iran in 1863 by a man named Baha'u'llah, a self-proclaimed messenger of God. However, the twin Israeli cities of Haifa and Acre now represent the world centre of Baha'i, with the holy Shrine of the Bab gleaming from Haifa's Mount Carmel. The 44-mile (70km) Haifa Trail is similarly inclusive. It explores not only Baha'i sites but also reminders of the many cultures that have contributed to this cosmopolitan, coastal city over the centuries, from Arabian alleyways to Christian churches.

LEFT: Follow the Haifa Trail to the Baha'i Shrine and Gardens on the slopes of Israel's Mount Carmel.

PAMIR MOUNTAINS

Southeast Tajikistan

{ Trek into the high-altitude playing field of 'the Great Game' between Britain and Russia. }

Need to know
- *Point in time: 1813–1907 (the Great Game played out)*
- *Length: 4–14 days*
- *Difficulty: Strenuous – self-sufficiency required; high altitude; no waymarking*
- *Best months: July–Sept*
- *Top tip: A special permit is required to visit the Gorno-Badakhshan Autonomous Region*

The period of imperialist rivalry between Britain and Russia during the nineteenth century was called 'the Great Game'. But this was no friendly football match. Both superpowers wanted to expand into central Asia, and from 1813 spent decades vying for supremacy, on the brink of war. Of major concern were the strategically critical and incredibly high Pamir Mountains, located at the junction of the British, Russian, and Chinese empires. The range was virtually unknown, and both the British and the Russians made hurried explorations. In 1895 the two countries finally reached an accord. They fixed their territorial borders with the Wakhan Corridor (part of Afghanistan) forming a buffer zone between them.

The Pamirs, which rise to the Wakhan Corridor's north, and which are now part of Tajikistan, remain little known. These mountains, which reach over 7,620m (25,000ft), are still untamed and barely populated. Trekking here is a true adventure.

Khorog is the only real town in the Pamirs (and hub of the Gorno-Badakhshan Autonomous Region). The western Pamirs are more accessible, with vast pastures, dazzling lakes, windswept passes, and forbidding peaks. The eastern range, dubbed Bam-i-Dunya (Roof of the World), is even more formidable. It's in the remote Murghab valleys here that you might spot a snow leopard. Throughout the range, overwhelming Pamiri hospitality is guaranteed.

RIGHT: The snowy peaks of the Pamir Mountains are truly remote.

RINGSTRASSE

Vienna, Austria

If a perambulation around Vienna's Ring Road was good enough for Sigmund Freud, then it's good enough for anyone. The Austrian psychoanalyst walked here daily, probably delighting in its unrestrained grandeur. The Historicist-inspired buildings along this 3.5-mile (5km) thoroughfare (which opened in 1865 and circles Vienna's First District) even spawned its own architectural subgenre: Ringstrassenstil, meaning 'Ring Road Style'. Highlights of the walk include the neo-Renaissance State Opera, a glut of ostentatious palaces, the Flemish-Gothic City Hall, and many fine museums and galleries. The Ringstrasse is also home to the Landtmann, one of Vienna's most elegant cafés, where Freud used to stop for a drink.

SINGALILA RIDGE

West Bengal, India

{ Combine visits to tea plantations with views of the Himalayas on a hike from the colonial hill station of Darjeeling. }

Need to know
- *Point in time: 1828 (Darjeeling hill station founded)*
- *Length: 52 miles (83km); 5 days*
- *Difficulty: Easy/ moderate – some climbs; generally gentle*
- *Best months: May– June; Oct–Nov*
- *Top tip: Permits and a guide are mandatory*

The Singalila Ridge, forming a natural border between India and Nepal, is one of the most magnificent lookouts in the whole of the Himalayas. It is located high above the torpid, dusty plains, doused in fresh air and leafy green, and gazes across to the snow-sparkled summits of the world's highest peaks.

The ridge area was ruled by the *chogyals* (monarchs) of Sikkim until 1780, when it was seized by invading Nepalese Gurkhas. The colonising British then got involved, keen to secure this strategic frontierland. The Anglo-Nepalese War, between 1814 and 1816, resulted in Nepalese defeat, and the British reinstated Sikkimese power. When the East India Company – a behemothic trading body and agent of British imperialism – came exploring in 1828, they found a site that they thought would be perfect for a soldiers' sanatorium. The grateful *chogyal* leased them the land, and the hill station of Darjeeling was born.

Over the next few decades, this formerly uninhabited, overgrown eyrie, perched at an altitude of 2,042m (6,700ft), was transformed by the British raj. Mansions, churches, parks, and clubs were built, and the slopes were cleared and cultivated with tea bushes. The tea leaves grown here turned out to have a most distinctive flavour, and Darjeeling is now renowned for producing the 'Champagne of Teas'.

A hot brew is just what's needed on a crisp morning, when you're standing on the veranda of a nineteenth-century plantation house, looking at a backdrop of some of the world's highest mountains. However, it's even better to get

closer to those peaks via a trek along the Singalila Ridge. By way of inspiration, Sherpa Tenzing Norgay – the first man to summit Everest, along with New Zealander Edmund Hillary – lived in Darjeeling, and set up the Himalayan Mountaineering Institute here.

The Singalila Ridge arcs west of Darjeeling, and the classic five-day trek begins 16 miles (26km) from the hill station, in the town of Maneybhanjang. From here a trail follows the ridge northwest along the international India-Nepal border to the peak of Phalut (11,810ft / 3,600m). It then veers southeast along the West Bengal–Sikkim frontier, finishing at the village of Rimbik. The trek is 52 miles (83km) of Himalayan wonder.

The trail zigzags up from Maneybhanjang at the foot of the ridge, passing meadows and rhododendron forest to reach the trekkers' hut at the small settlement of Tonglu. There are views across to Kanchenjunga, the world's third-highest peak, all the way. The next day's hike passes a *mani* wall (its stones inscribed with Buddhist mantras) that leads into the village of Jaubari. This is a good place to stop for tea. The hike then continues to Kalpokhari (meaning 'Black Lake') and 3,636m (11,930ft) high Sandakphu. The views from here are breathtaking. Indeed, four of the world's five highest peaks – Everest, Kanchenjunga, Lhotse, and

411
Maria Island

Tasmania, Australia

In the nineteenth century, many British convicts were transported to Maria Island, off Tasmania. Today, it is hiking heaven. A luxury guided, four-day trail combines its colonial ruins and natural splendour.

412
Colonial History Trail

Fort Canning, Singapore

Take a 1.25-mile (2km) stroll around Fort Canning Hill in Singapore, where Malay rulers once built their palaces, and where the British constructed a fort in 1860.

Makalu – can be seen. In 1856, it was from this spot at Sandakphu that Surveyor-General George Everest figured out which one of these mountains was the tallest. He did this by noting that the rising sun kissed one particulur summit before gradually illuminating the lower peaks. This mountain was subsequently named Everest in his honour.

The most spectacular views of all line the way from Sandakphu to Phalut. Here, prayer flag–festooned Singalila Peak (3,695m / 12,122ft) provides an excellent vantage. The trail then descends to the valley town of Gorkhey, through a mossy, bird-filled forest of rhododendron, oak, chestnut, silver fir, and giant magnolia trees. The 'Lost Valley' village of Samadeen is tucked ahead, before a final stride via rich farmland, the Siri Khola River, and the monastery at Maneydhara. The trail finishes at the village of Rimbik, where you can drink a well-deserved cup of Darjeeling tea.

413

THE BUND

Shanghai, China

The Bund has changed a bit since the early nineteenth century. Back then it was a muddy towpath used for hauling rice barges along the west bank of China's Huangpu River. After Shanghai became a trading port in 1846, this mile-long piece of real estate was reinforced, paved, and utterly transformed. Now the Bund is lined with a flourish of Art Deco and neoclassical buildings, and has views over the water to Pudong's modern skyscraper glitz. A stroll here is a walk through 150-plus years of Chinese history. It is best done early, when local people gather to practice t'ai chi as the sun glints off the steel-and-glass buildings all around.

414

NC–GR1

New Caledonia, French Overseas Territory

The South Pacific archipelago of New Caledonia was colonised in 1853 by the French, who originally established it as a penal colony. However, it is far too beautiful a place for a prison, with paradisiacal beaches and the bluest lagoons. New Caledonia remains a territory of France today, so there's also good food – and a Grande Randonnée hiking trail. The 76-mile (123km) NC–GR1 trail on the main island of Grand Terre runs from the remains of the convict centre at Prony, on the south coast, to Dumbéa, on the west coast. It uses trails first blazed by the indigenous Kanak people to traverse the bird-filled scrubland and the rainforest of Blue River Provincial Park.

Gaze over the Pacific Ocean from the magnificent cliffs of the Kalaupapa Peninsula on Molokai Island, Hawaii. This area of solidified lava is so cut off by the surrounding ocean and its steep cliffs that it was used to isolate leprosy sufferers in the nineteenth century (p. 317).

CHAPTER SIX
20TH CENTURY

{ Trek to the present via technological innovation, nature conservation, and the dark shadows of the two world wars. }

LONG TRAIL

Vermont, United States

{ Take on the United States' oldest long-distance hiking trail to journey through mountains and flaming forest. }

Need to know
- *Point in time: 1910–30 (Long Trail built)*
- *Length: 272 miles (438km); 18–28 days*
- *Difficulty: Moderate/ strenuous – mountainous; muddy*
- *Best months: June– early Oct*
- *Top tip: Almost sixty simple shelters (some huts, some lean-tos) lie along the route*

In the early twentieth century, the glorious Green Mountains in the state of Vermont were not viewed with pride or wonder. They were dismissed by most as a cold, forbidding place, and a physical obstacle to Vermont's economic development. Then a visionary with notions ahead of his time came along and convinced people to think differently.

The teacher, James P. Taylor, championed 'ecotourism' long before the word existed. In 1909 he was holed up in his tent on the top of Stratton Mountain (the highest point of the southern Green Mountains), waiting for the mist to shift. While there, he conceived the idea of a long-distance hiking trail running along Vermont's rugged spine. He dreamed of a trail that would make 'the Vermont mountains play a larger part in the life of the people'. In 1910 Taylor founded the Green Mountain Club (GMC), and his idea began to turn into reality. It took twenty years to fully blaze the route, which stretches for 272 miles (438km) from the Massachusetts state line (near Williamstown) to the village of North Troy, near the Canadian border. When the Long Trail was completed in 1930, it became the first long-distance hiking path in the United States.

It also provided inspiration for the behemoth that is the Appalachian Trail (AT), which subsequently opened in 1937. That route 'borrows' one hundred miles of the Long Trail on its way through Vermont. Indeed, AT visionary and American conservationist Benton Mackaye was also sitting on Stratton Mountain when he had his own eureka moment: '[The GMC] has already built the Long Trail for 210 miles',

RIGHT: Sit on top of Stratton Mountain in fall for views over Vermont's flaming forest.

he wrote in an essay in 1921. 'What the Green Mountains are to Vermont, the Appalachians are to the eastern United States. What is suggested, therefore, is a "long trail" over the full length of the Appalachian skyline, from the highest peak in the north to the highest peak in the south . . . '

The game-changing Long Trail crests almost all of the Green Mountains' main peaks. There are fifty-three named summits en route, twenty-seven of which are in excess of 1,066m (3,500ft). Mount Mansfield, at 1,339m (4,393ft), is Vermont's highest point. Camel's Hump, at 1,244m (4,083ft), is the state's most iconic one. The area around is generally wooded, and the trail wends through forests of maple, birch, beech, hemlock, spruce, pine, and balsam fir trees.

The Long Trail has also been lovingly planned. In 1915 some GMC members became concerned that a chunk of the route followed a fairly boring fire prevention trail, away from the scenic summits and hard to navigate. Fortunately, a retired New Jersey professor, Will Monroe, showed up. He reinvigorated the movement and set about blazing a new, improved trail. The section known as the Monroe Skyline, which takes in three of Vermont's five highest peaks, is considered to be the most spectacular part of the hike.

On a less positive note, the Long Trail is notorious for its mud, which can make you slip, and even 'steal' your shoes if you're not careful. This brown gloop is why the GMC asks hikers to stay off the trail in 'mud season'. This is usually from 15 April to the Friday of Memorial Day weekend each year.

Hikers should also factor in additional obstacles, such as gnarled roots, slippery rocks, fallen trees, and stiff gradients. This is especially true for the wilder, more rugged northern end of the trail. The pay offs, however, are many. There are peaceful nights in backcountry shelters far away from the world. There are moments of solitude in a sea of trees, especially memorable if you hike in the fall when the leaves blaze with color. There are chances to spot bears, moose, porcupines, and peregrine falcons. Plus, you too might sit on 1,200m (3,940ft) Stratton Mountain and have your own eureka moment.

CANADA

VERMONT

NORTH TROY

Mount Mansfield

UNITED
STATES

Camel's Hump

GREEN MOUNTAINS
Monroe Skyline

Mount Ellen
Mount Abraham

Killington
Peak

NEW YORK

NEW
HAMPSHIRE

Stratton
Mountain

WILLIAMSTOWN

MASSACHUSETTS

416
Wadi Rum

Jordan

The desert 'moonscapes' of Wadi Rum are forever linked to British officer T.E. Lawrence, who passed through during the Arab Revolt (1916–18). Hire a guide to explore.

417
Pathet Laos Caves

Vieng Xai, Laos

From the 1950s, Communist revolutionaries camped out in these remote karst caves. They did this when fighting the French, and sheltering from bombs during the Vietnam War. Guided hikes are possible.

418
SHACKLETON TRAIL

South Georgia

There's no better tale of survival against the odds than Sir Ernest Shackleton's 1914–15 South Pole expedition. When his ship the *Endurance* sank beneath Antarctic ice, Shackleton and a team of five others sailed 920 miles (1,500km) across the wild Southern Ocean from Elephant Island in a tiny lifeboat to reach the island of South Georgia. They then trekked for thirty-six hours non-stop to raise the alarm. They hiked right across the island, from King Haakon Bay to Stromness whaling station. As a result, Shackleton's entire crew was rescued. Many Antarctic cruise ships enable passengers to follow the final leg of the full 25-mile (40km) Shackleton Trail. This short, 3.5-mile (6km) journey from Fortuna Bay to Stromness is a great reminder of the strength of the human spirit.

MOUNT MULANJE

Southern Malawi

{ Hike up and around this mist-swirled monolith, a beguiling mountain of majesty and tragedy. }

Need to know

- *Point in time: 1949 (Sir Laurens van der Post's expedition on Mount Mulanje)*
- *Length: 3–5 days*
- *Difficulty: Moderate – steep parts; basic huts*
- *Best months: May–Oct*
- *Top tip: There are six main access points at Mulanje's base, from which various trekking routes start*

Mount Mulanje is a stocky inselberg of igneous rock rising from the Malawian plains. Its lofty, wide plateau is riven by ravines, flecked with unique plants (including the Mulanje cedar), and pinched into twenty separate summits. The highest of these peaks is 3,002m (9,849ft) Sapitwa, meaning 'Unreachable'. However, the slopes of Mulanje are accessible by the hikers of today. The Mountain Club of Malawi maintains several huts on Mount Mulanje, while trails spider all over the mountain. This includes a trail up Sapitwa Peak itself. In short, it is a trekking delight.

Mist-prone Mount Mulanje isn't without its dangers, however. In 1949 South African explorer and author Sir Laurens van der Post was commissioned by the British to survey the mountain. During the expedition, one of the party, Fred France, drowned while trying to cross a raging, rain-swelled river. The incident was described in van der Post's controversial travelogue *Venture to the Interior*.

Today's hikers can visit the Ruo Gorge, where France died. They can even stay in France's Cottage, the hut where he lived, and where van der Post also stayed.

Route options on Mulanje are manifold. For instance, it's a four-hour climb from the village of Likhubula at the mountain's base to France's Cottage. From here, it's three hours to Chisepo Hut, and then an exhilarating five-hour cave-crawling scramble up Sapitwa Peak. Really, it's best to spend several days on the mountain, hiking between huts, summiting peaks, and feeling like a proper explorer.

RIGHT: Follow one of several trails up huge Mount Mulanje.

JEJU OLLE

Jeju Island, South Korea

Volcano-sculpted Jeju Island, floating south of the Korean Peninsula, has always been a land apart. But in 1948, after the Second World War had ended Japanese rule and it appeared that Korea might be split in two (as it subsequently was), the people of Jeju protested, favouring a unified nation. In retaliation, the authorities massacred 30,000 islanders. Today, Jeju is a relatively peaceful place. It boasts 262 miles (422km) of *olle* (walking trails), which wriggle right around the island. These showcase Jeju's Hawaii-like topography and interesting quirks. For instance, look out for traditional *batdam* (drystone walls) and mysterious *hareubang* (grandfather statues). There are also the remains of villages destroyed during the Jeju massacre.

CORDILLERA HUAYHUASH CIRCUIT

Andes, Peru

{ Take a tough trek in the Andes, site of one of the greatest mountain-survival miracles of the twentieth century. }

Need to know
- *Point in time: 1985 (Joe Simpson and Simon Yates's expedition)*
- *Length: 75 miles (120km); 12 days*
- *Difficulty: Strenuous – high altitudes; steep, tough terrain*
- *Best months: May–Aug*
- *Top tip: Huarez is the regional hub; roads run from here to the trailheads at Llámac and Cuartelwain*

In 1985 English mountaineers Joe Simpson and Simon Yates conquered Peru's fearsome 6,344m (20,813ft) mountain Siula Grande. On the descent, however, Simpson broke his leg. As Yates was painstakingly lowering him down, Simpson fell off a cliff, still attached to Yates above. Yates, not knowing if his friend was dead or alive, and in danger of falling himself, made a big decision: he cut the rope. Incredibly, Simpson survived the fall, crawled deeper into a crevasse, found a way out, dragged himself over a glacier, and reached camp just as Yates was about to leave.

Hiking the 75-mile (120km) Cordillera Huayhuash Circuit is not quite as dramatic as the events laid out in Simpson's book (and subsequent documentary) *Touching the Void*, but it isn't far off. This classic high Andes trek traverses the remotest valleys in Peru. It weaves along knife-edge ridges, crosses 5,000m (16,400ft) passes, skirts turquoise lakes, passes soaring condors, dips in hot springs, and soaks up the culture of the indigenous Quechua peoples. It also travels via some of the country's biggest peaks, including the needly spire of Jirishanca and the now-infamous Siula Grande.

It is possible to add on a hike to Yates and Simpson's Siula Grande base camp. Here, you can gaze up at the mountain's imposing west face and the crevasse-streaked glacier, which Simpson somehow hauled himself down.

RIGHT: Trek amid jagged peaks and turquoise lakes in the Cordillera Huayhuash.

422
BERLIN WALL TRAIL

Berlin, Germany

{ Walk the line of the Berlin Wall, the chilling barricade that divided a city and its people between 1961 and 1989. }

Need to know
- *Point in time: 1961–89 (Berlin Wall existed)*
- *Length: 100 miles (160km); 7–10 days*
- *Difficulty: Easy – mostly flat; well marked*
- *Best months: May–Oct*
- *Top tip: Public transport services many points on the route, making it easy to walk in sections*

In the aftermath of the Second World War, Germany was split in two – and so was its former capital. Berlin was now physically located in newly created communist East Germany. However, a portion of the city was affiliated to newly created democratic West Germany, 100 miles (160km) distant. That isolated portion, known as West Berlin, became an enclave adrift in a politically disparate land.

As the century rolled on, increasing numbers of disaffected East Germans began to leave. By August 1961, a sixth of East Germany's population had gone. The easiest way to escape the country was to cross into West Berlin. Consequently, the communist regime built a barricade of barbed wire and concrete right around the marooned city-state. They called it an 'anti-fascist protection rampart', although it was clearly built to prevent its citizens from leaving, rather than to keep Westerners out.

The wall measured around 100 miles (160km), starting as a simple divide but evolving into a more elaborate fortification of double ramparts, trenches, watchtowers, and fences backed by 'asparagus beds' (strips of steel spikes, planted sharp end up). This barrier sliced through the centre of the city, dividing streets and squares, sundering friends and families. It also looped into the outskirts, bisecting lakes, cutting through woodland, and turning peaceful suburban neighbourhoods into bloodstained 'death zones'. From the wall's erection in 1961 till its symbolic fall in 1989 (it wasn't completely demolished until 1992), it was responsible for the deaths of at least 136 people.

Little remains of the wall these days, but the Berliner Mauerweg, meaning 'Berlin Wall Trail', follows its old footprint. The trail starts in Potsdamer Platz, once Berlin's busiest thoroughfare. The square was wrecked by Second World War bombing. It was then split by the wall and fell into ruin. Looking at the shiny, big-brand skyscrapers here now, this seems hard to believe.

The wall era is easier to comprehend at the nearby streets of Niederkirchnerstrasse and Zimmerstrasse, where a 200m (655ft) section of concrete has been preserved. On Friedrichstrasse, there's a re-creation of Checkpoint Charlie, the infamous border crossing used by foreign nationals. It was near here that teenager Peter Fechter was shot by East German guards while trying to abscond on 17 August 1962. He lay bleeding to death for an hour before being moved. A memorial pillar now marks the spot.

There are many such memorials along this walk, even amid the city's pretty western outskirts. By the lakes of Griebnitzsee

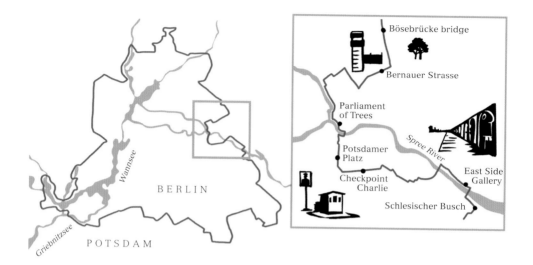

and Wannsee, markers commemorate the dead. This includes nineteen-year-old cadet Peter Böhme (killed while trying to escape), border guard Jörgen Schmidtchen (killed trying to prevent Peter from escaping), and Herbert Mende (not trying to escape, just in the wrong place at the wrong time). These were just a few of the wall's casualties.

The longest remaining chunk of wall is the 1,300m (4,265ft) East Side Gallery. Flanking the Spree River, it is slathered in slogans and street art. The wall remnant on Bernauer Strasse is the only section complete with its original 'death strip' fortifications. At a visitor centre here, you can listen to the recorded testimonies of residents who lived through this divided time.

However, the whole length of the Berlin Wall Trail is dotted with reminders, including: the information board on Ottostrasse, identifying where twenty-eight people successfully escaped via a tunnel in 1961; the 'Parliament of Trees' artwork, created from parts of old wall; the former watchtower at Schlesischer Busch; and the patrol road by the Bösebrücke bridge, now marked by cherry trees. From city-centre hubbub to residential suburb, from bucolic farmland to forest, every step of the trail tells a story. One thing doesn't change, however – the constant shadow of the wall that once severed it all.

423
Earl Grey Pass Trail

British Columbia, Canada

This 37-mile (61km) crossing of the Purcell Mountains was blazed by First Nations traders, and utilised by Kootenay silver miners. It was named for the governor-general of Canada, who built a cabin here by the trailhead in 1909.

424
ECHO CRATER WILDERNESS TRAIL

Idaho, United States

The phrase 'lunar landscape' is a bit of a descriptive cliché, but at Idaho's Craters of
the Moon Monument – a vast lava field dotted with cinder cones and sagebrush –
it couldn't be more true. It was here, in August 1969, that *Apollo 14* astronauts Alan
Shepard, Edgar Mitchell, Joe Engle, and Eugene Cernan came to learn the rudiments
of volcanic geology. They did this so that they could better identify rocks on the
surface of the Moon during their mission. The 8-mile (13km) Echo Crater Wilderness
Trail heads into the backcountry of the crater rim via 213m (700ft) Big Cinder Butte,
plus lava trees, billows, and caves.

425
SELMA TO MONTGOMERY TRAIL

Alabama, United States

'They told us we wouldn't get here. And there were those who said that we would
get here only over their dead bodies, but all the world today knows that we are here.'
So declared American Baptist minister and activist Dr Martin Luther King Jr, having
marched 54 miles (87km) from the Brown Chapel in the city of Selma to Montgomery,
the capital of Alabama. He did this on 21 March 1965, along with 25,000 other civil-
rights protestors. The Selma to Montgomery Trail retraces the steps of Dr King's
Selma–Montgomery march. It is not the most lovely route – it follows Highway 80.
However, it is one of the most important, paying homage to the fight to secure civil
rights for African Americans.

426
GALLIPOLI BATTLEFIELDS

Western Turkey

In just nine months in 1915, around 100,000 soldiers were killed and a further 400,000 wounded as Ottoman Empire and Allied forces fought for control of Turkey's Gallipoli peninsula. They were also fighting for the route up the Hellespont strait to Istanbul. The Ottoman Empire (allied with Germany) was triumphant, securing its greatest First World War victory. However, casualties were high on both sides. Now, the peninsula is a peaceful place of pine forest and brush, dotted with monuments. Trails riddle the rugged terrain, linking sites such as Lone Pine and Chunuk Bair cemeteries, and Anzac Cove, where the Allies landed on 25 April 1915. This date is now remembered each year as Anzac Day, when many Australians and New Zealanders come to commemorate their dead.

CARDAMOM MOUNTAINS CIRCUIT

Southwest Cambodia

{ Explore the last refuge of Cambodia's Khmer Rouge, in a beautiful biodiversity hotspot. }

The Khmer Rouge ruled Cambodia for only five years. During this time, however, Pol Pot's brutal communist organisation was responsible for the deaths of more than a million people. The Khmer Rouge regime was toppled in 1979 but continued to fight, fleeing to the almost inaccessible Cardamom Mountains in the country's southwest. For over a decade, these leafy, biodiverse hills remained a bloody battleground, with frequent clashes between Khmer Rouge guerrillas and local villagers.

Now that peace has been restored to the region, the communities devastated by years of war are looking to tourism to reverse their fortunes. Land mines have been cleared, trails and thatched shelters have been created, men who skirmished with the Khmer Rouge now work as guides, and the forest has been reclaimed.

Various treks are possible. Around 90 miles (145km) of paths have been cleared around the village of Chi Phat. One option is a 22-mile (36km) circuit that starts with a boat ride downstream. It spends two days looping back to Chi Pat, with a night spent camping in a jungle hut. The trail plunges into a forest of evergreens and mahogany trees, of giant ferns and enormous mushrooms. And the wildlife is rampant, if tricky to see – a wealth of species such as gibbons, sun bears, and clouded leopards are now the only beings hiding out in these hills.

Need to know
- *Point in time: 1979 (Khmer Rouge retreated to Cardamom Mountains)*
- *Length: 22 miles (36km); 2 days*
- *Difficulty: Moderate – humid; guide required*
- *Best months: Nov–Mar*
- *Top tip: Chi Phat is a three-hour drive, then a two-hour boat ride, from Phnom Penh*

LEFT: Camp out in the lush, rampant rainforest of the Cardamom Mountains.

428

PATH OF THE HEROES OF THE SLOVAK NATIONAL UPRISING

Slovakia

Between 1943 and 1945, Slovakia's isolated uplands were the hideouts of guerrilla fighters, who were battling German Nazis. Those guerrillas are the heroes of this 473-mile (762km) trail. The route travels northeast from Slovakia's capital of Bratislava to the Dukla Pass on the Slovak-Polish border. En route, the trail visits the Small Carpathians, Bradlo Hill (with its memorial to First World War commander General Stefánik), and rock-top Trenčín Castle. It also passes Dumbier (the Low Tatras' highest peak), the historic city of Košice, and Zborov castle. Finally, it heads to the Dukla Pass itself, site of a bloody tank skirmish in 1944 that claimed over 46,000 lives.

429

DEATH RAILWAY

Kanchanaburi Province, Thailand

The full Thailand–Burma Railway – also known as the 'Death Railway' – spanned 258 miles (415km). It was built by Japan between 1942 and 1943, using enforced Asian labourers and Allied prisoners of war (POWs). Today, you can trek a 3-mile (4.5km) section from Thailand's Hellfire Pass Museum towards Hintok River Camp. The path heads through Konyu Cutting, nicknamed 'Hellfire Pass'. This was the largest of a series of passages that the enforced labourers and POWs had to hack through solid rock, using just picks and shovels. By the time the cutting was finished, 70 per cent of the workers had died. Now this spot is peaceful and tree-lined. The trail leads on, via remnants of railway sleepers and trestle bridges, to Kwae Noi Valley Lookout.

430
PATH ALONG THE WIRE

Ljubljana, Slovenia

The Path Along the Wire is Slovenia's version of the Berlin Wall. When Slovenia's capital of Ljubljana was annexed by fascist Italy, and then by Nazi Germany, from 1942, the occupiers constructed a 20.5-mile (33km) barbed-wire fence around the capital. It was built to prevent resistance activists in the city and the surrounding countryside from communicating with each other. The loop is no longer manned by soldiers and police. Now it is a gravel path that runs through forests, meadows, and the city outskirts. It travels along Koseze Pond, up Golovec Hill, via the Renaissance Fužine Castle (now a design museum), and is dotted with memorial stones.

431
SABOTEURS' TRAIL

Telemark, Norway

The 5-mile (8km) hike from the Rjukan Fjellstue lodge (on the reindeer-grazed Hardangervidda plateau) to the village of Vemork is a spectacular walk through the steep gorges of the Telemark region. It's also a journey that tells of one of the Second World War's most effective acts of sabotage. After the Nazis invaded Norway in 1940, Allied forces wanted to keep the Vemork Hydroelectric Plant – capable of producing heavy water to make nuclear weapons – out of German hands. In February 1943, Norwegian resistance fighters clambered down icy ravines, crept up on the plant, and detonated enough explosives to render it useless. Plaques en route tell the story, as do exhibits at the old power station, now the Norwegian Industrial Workers' Museum.

KOKODA TRACK

Papua New Guinea

{
Hike through the hot, inhospitable tropics where Australian and Japanese soldiers once fought and died.
}

Need to know
- *Point in time: 1942 (Battle of Kokoda)*
- *Length: 60 miles (96km); 6–8 days*
- *Difficulty: Strenuous – hot and humid; tough terrain*
- *Best months: Apr–Nov*
- *Top tip: A guide and a permit are required*

It's tough to envisage a more hellish place to be than in the jungle of eastern Papua New Guinea in 1942. Just imagine it: a forest fortress, with roots snarled like tripwires; a profusion of scrub tangled like Mother Nature's barbed wire; the terrain rearing up and plunging down at terrifying gradients; relentless rain, sucking mud, sapping heat, unbearable humidity, voracious insects, and widespread dysentery. Worse, imagine an enemy army bearing down. This was the nightmarish reality of the Second World War's Battle of Kokoda.

In July 1942, Japanese forces landed on the north coast of Papua New Guinea. Their aim was to march south over the Owen Stanley Range to capture the capital of Port Moresby via the back door. The Australian forces, caught by surprise, quickly rallied to try to stop them. If Port Moresby fell, mainland Australia (a short hop across the Coral Sea) would be under serious threat.

The Japanese far outnumbered the Australians, and had soon progressed from the coast to the inland plateau village of Kokoda. The Kokoda Track, from Kokoda to Owers Corner, follows the route that the Australians and their Papuan allies took as the Japanese advanced. It was near Owers Corner, overlooking Port Moresby, that the Australians made their last stand. They eventually pushed the invaders back north along the very same route.

There are no enemy soldiers lurking amid the undergrowth now. However, this historic 60-mile (96km) hiking trail, which can be completed in either direction,

ABOVE: The Kokoda Track includes a tough climb up Mount Bellamy.

is still strenuous. Starting from the Port Moresby end, it's a short road transfer to the southern trailhead at Owers Corner. After wading across the Goldie River, the track climbs the punishing Imita Ridge. In 1942 the Australians dragged twenty-five-pounder guns up the 2,000 wooden steps of the 'Golden Staircase' here, enabling them to inflict decisive damage on the Japanese below. Now the stairs have rotted away, so trekkers must climb without them.

The route drops down, making multiple crossings of Ua-Ule Creek before climbing again to Ioribaiwa Ridge. This was the furthest south the Japanese reached before making their retreat. The sunsets can be spectacular. It's then a tough climb over the Maguli Range, via a succession of false summits, to Menari. Here, villagers grow crops on the fertile slopes and elders still recall past horrors. Beyond this lies Brigade Hill, a grassy summit looking across the Koiari Mountains, where more than seventy-five Australians were killed in an ambush. A plaque commemorates the event.

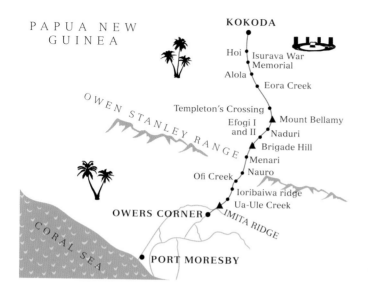

PAPUA NEW GUINEA

KOKODA

Hoi

Isurava War Memorial

Alola

Eora Creek

Templeton's Crossing

Efogi I and II

Mount Bellamy

Naduri

Brigade Hill

Menari

Ofi Creek

Nauro

Ioribaiwa ridge

Ua-Ule Creek

OWERS CORNER

IMITA RIDGE

OWEN STANLEY RANGE

CORAL SEA

PORT MORESBY

433
Guernsey Circumnavigation

United Kingdom and Channel Islands

Walk 24 miles (39km) around the edge of the bucolic island of Guernsey. It was occupied by Nazi forces between 1940 and 1945, and bunkers and forts dot the coast.

434
Berchtesgaden

Bavarian Alps, Germany

This alpine idyll is where Nazi leader Adolf Hitler liked to holiday. Trails here include the three-hour hike from Scharitzkehl to Eagle's Nest, the chalet given to Hitler in 1939.

The villages of Efogi I and Efogi II offer the chance to stock up on fresh produce as gardens here overflow with bananas, yams, and squash. The hiking is tough, with steep climbs and lack of shade. Ahead lies 2,190m (7,195ft) Mount Bellamy, the Kokoda Track's highest point. It's a challenging slog up through lichen-scabbed forest buzzing with birds. Next is the wilderness of dense jungle, fast-flowing streams, and steep gorges known as Templeton's Crossing. The withdrawing Japanese put up fierce resistance here, and many soldiers on both sides died. Further on is the Isurava Battlefield, the site where the two sides first clashed on the trail. It's now preserved as a memorial, and four pillars stand inscribed with the words 'Courage, Sacrifice, Mateship, Endurance'.

By the time hikers hit Kokoda village, exhaustion is inevitable, both physical and mental. To complete this track is to manage a week of sweat, slog, splendid mountains, tribal encounters, and the weight of one of the bloodiest campaigns in Australian and Papua New Guinean history.

435

RUTA GUERRA CIVIL

Madrid, Spain

Memories of the Spanish Civil War (1936 to 1939) are still raw in Spain. The conflict, which saw the left-leaning Republicans battle the ultimately victorious Nationalists of General Franco, was one of the bloodiest civil wars of the twentieth century. The Ruta Guerra Civil, meaning 'Civil War Trail', opened in 2013. It is the first government-established heritage route to commemorate the Spanish Civil War. The walk starts north of Madrid at Puentes Viejas reservoir, following the Frente del Agua (Water Frontline). This was the site of the battle for Madrid's water supply. The trail rolls through forests of holm oak and fir for around 2 miles (3km). En route lie trenches, gun posts, and concrete command centres gazing out across the now-peaceful hills.

436

SOMME FRONT LINE

Northern France

The Somme Front Line is a chilling place for a stroll. The spartan fields of northern France hold little scenic allure, and are overshadowed by the horrors of the First World War's bloodiest conflict – the Battle of the Somme. Between 1 July and 18 November 1916, more than a million soldiers (Allied and German) were killed or wounded here. This was trench warfare at its most devastating and futile. You can walk from Blighty Valley to Lonsdale Cemetery, the resting places of Commonwealth troops, many of whom were killed on the Somme's catastrophic first day. You can journey to the Leipzig Redoubt battleground, or Thiepval Memorial, dedicated to the unfound dead of the United Kingdom and South Africa. Or you can explore Beaumont-Hamel and Newfoundland Park, where wartime trenches and craters still pock the ground.

ALTA VIA 1

Dolomites, Northern Italy

{ Cross the jagged Dolomites range
for spectacular views and
First World War relics. }

Need to know
- *Point in time: 1915–18 (Italian Front battles)*
- *Length: 75 miles (120km); 10–12 days*
- *Difficulty: Moderate – some climbs; good facilities*
- *Best months: June– Sept*
- *Top tip: Rifugios (mountain huts) must be booked in advance*

During the First World War, the sublime pinnacles of the Dolomites became a bloody front line. Here, amid the jagged peaks, Italian soldiers (on the side of the Allies) fought the Austro-Hungarian/German forces for four years. They battled in the most testing of conditions, enduring freezing winters and breathtaking altitudes. To help them negotiate the mountains and observe the enemy, troops constructed *via ferrata* (iron roads), networks of fixed lines, ladders, rungs, and steps. Many of these iron roads are still there, and now people use them to traverse the Dolomites by choice rather than for battle.

The most popular hiking route is the 75-mile (120km) Alta Via 1. This 'High Trail' runs between forest-nestled Lago di Bráies and the town of Belluno, with its Renaissance-era old centre. The scenery is never short of breathtaking, with views of endless summits rippling away from numerous passes, reaching up to 2,752m (9,030ft). Also en route lie alpine meadows rife with wildflowers, dwarf pines, rhododendron forests, and chamois posing on outcrops. In parts, the trail follows First World War tracks and is dotted with poignant remnants. You can see gun ramparts, trenches and tunnels, old officers' quarters, bomb-shattered boulders, and sections of *via ferrata*. The Alta Via is also well-served by family-run *rifugios* (mountain huts), which deliver hearty food and a warm welcome.

RIGHT: Now trekkers rather than soldiers cross the Dolomites.

Lago di Bráies

Falzarego pass ▲

Giau pass ▲

Boite River

▲

Staulanza pass

ITALY

▲ Duran pass

Ardo River

Piave River

BELLUNO

MAGINOT LINE TRAIL

Alsace, France

After the devastation of the First World War, French thoughts turned to defence. In 1929 construction began on a line of fortifications along the country's border with Germany. The Maginot Line boasted fifty state-of-the-art *ouvrages* (large forts) and many smaller redoubts. However, when the Germans did attack in 1940, they simply went around this fortification line, invading *blitzkrieg* (lightning war) style, via Belgium. The 44-mile (71km) Maginot Line Trail follows this ineffectual barrier from the small town of Roeschwoog, near the Rhine, to the village of Dambach-Neunhoffen. It runs through Haguenau Forest and the Vosges foothills, passing many military remains. These include blockhouses, bastions, anti-tank ditches, and Ouvrage Schoenenbourg – barely damaged despite being heavily bombed.

439
GERMAN GREEN BELT

Germany

After the Second World War, the Soviet Union erected a physical barrier right across Europe, to isolate Soviet areas from the West. This 'Iron Curtain' stood for more than forty years, from 1945 to 1991. In Germany, the partition ran for 870 miles (1,400km) from the Baltic coast to the Czech border. It was a 'death zone' for people, but during this time plants and animals thrived. Now, it is a linear nature reserve. Walks in the Green Belt reveal fragments of Cold War history, such as old observation towers, plus 109 different wildlife habitats, from mountains to forests and streams.

441
Peter Habeler Route

Zillertal Alps, Austria

This route is a 35-mile (56km) circumnavigation of Peter Habeler's favorite peaks. The mountaineer from Mayrhofen was the first to conquer Everest without bottled oxygen, in 1978.

440
D-DAY BEACH WALK

Normandy, France

Sword, Juno, Gold, Omaha, and Utah are five pretty swathes of soft yellow sand backed by dunes. However, they are forever inseparable from the horrific events of 6 June 1944. These innocuous beaches were the site's of the Second World War's D-Day landings, when Allied forces invaded the Normandy coast. Around 100,000 men died. It seems impossible to imagine such carnage here now on this 50-mile (80km) stretch of seafront. Today, it's possible to walk along all five beaches via Café Gondrée (the first house in France to be liberated), Arromanches's floating Mulberry Harbour, the German battery of Longues-sur-Mer, and the rows of white crosses at Omaha's American Cemetery.

442
MOUNT ST HELENS

Washington, United States

On 18 May 1980, a powerful earthquake took place near the stratovolcano of Mount St Helens. It triggered the largest landslide ever recorded, and a volcanic eruption that spewed ash over a dozen states. The north face of the previously symmetrical summit of Mount St Helens simply collapsed. Fifty-seven people were killed. The landscape was forever altered, and can now be explored on a network of trails. The 8-mile (13km) Harry's Ridge Trail, for instance, runs from Johnston Ridge Observatory right to the crater mouth. The 10-mile (16km) Truman Trail–Pumice Plains route drops from Windy Ridge down into the blast zone, via a landscape of volcanic mud and rock that is gradually being reclaimed by nature.

443
Battlefields Hike

Falkland Islands, United Kingdom Overseas Territory

In 1982 Britain and Argentina began fighting for sovereignty of the isolated Falkland Islands in the South Atlantic. A hike in the hills west of the capital of Stanley and via Mount Kent and Goat Ridge crosses war-scarred terrain.

444
Main Sudeten Route

Poland

The Sudeten Mountains form the backbone of Sudetenland, the region Hitler annexed in 1938, pushing Europe to the brink of war. This 217-mile (350km) trail takes in the best of these mountains, with *bacówkas* (shepherd's cottages) en route.

445
Lord Curzon's Trail

Himalayas, India

Follow in the 1905 footsteps of Lord Curzon, then viceroy of India. This nine-day hike into India's Nanda Devi Sanctuary passes wildflower fields, remote settlements, dense forest, and snow-clad peaks, topping out at 3,650m (11,975ft) Kuari Pass.

446
Navvy Trail

Northern Norway

The Ofoten Railway stretches for 26 miles (42km), from the Norwegian town of Narvik to the Swedish border. This hike runs nearby, following the route used by 'navvies' (migrant workers) who built the tracks in 1902. Walk via valleys, mountains, and waterfalls.

BICENTENNIAL NATIONAL TRAIL

Eastern Australia

{ This huge hike celebrates the birthday of a nation, the hardy bushmen who crossed it, and the Australian Aborigines here before them. }

Need to know
- *Point in time: 1988 (Australia's bicentenary)*
- *Length: 3,310 miles (5,330km); 6–12 months*
- *Difficulty: Strenuous – rugged; remote; self-reliance required*
- *Best months: May–Nov*
- *Top tip: Triangular markers dot the trail but aren't sufficient to navigate by; a map and guidebook are essential*

It seems fitting to do something big to mark your 200th birthday, which is exactly what Australia did. On the event of its bicentenary in 1988, which commemorated 200 years since the First Fleet of British convict ships arrived in Sydney, the country inaugurated the Bicentennial National Trail (BNT). This goliath of a hiking, biking, and horse-riding route runs parallel to the lengthy eastern seaboard for around 3,310 miles (5,330km). It takes an inland path between the towns of Cooktown, in far north Queensland, and Healesville, in the southern state of Victoria, via snowy mountains, tropical rainforest, and all types of terrain in between. It is a big, beautiful birthday gift of a walk.

The essence of the BNT stretches back far further than 1988. The group that came up with the concept in 1972 dreamed of creating a country-traversing epic that would rival the United States' Appalachian Trail. They also wanted to honour Australia's nineteenth-century drovers. In the early 1800s, these hardy bushmen herded sheep and cattle for vast distances along established stock routes, braving crocodile-infested creeks, dust storms, and drought. The advent of railways and – later – sealed roads diminished the need for these thoroughfares, but not the romance of them. The drovers' pioneering spirit, key to the creation of modern Australia, would live on in the BNT.

The trail also acknowledges Australian Aborigines as the traditional custodians of the land through which it

Map labels:
COOKTOWN
Ngalba Bulal National Park
Mossman
Gunnawarra · Cairns
PACIFIC OCEAN
GREAT DIVIDING RANGE
QUEENSLAND
Brisbane
NORTHERN TABLELANDS · Killarney
Guy Fawkes River National Park
NEW SOUTH WALES
GREAT DIVIDING RANGE
Ebor
Sydney
Snowy Mountains
VICTORIA · Omeo
Melbourne · HEALESVILLE
TASMAN SEA

ABOVE: The Bicentennial National Trail explores the diverse landscapes of eastern Australia.

passes. Where appropriate, trail users are encouraged to explore the Aboriginal heritage around the trail, and to find out more about the Dreaming stories that enrich it. Trail users are also asked to be respectful of sacred sites and places of significance.

The BNT is broken into twelve sections, roughly 250 miles (400km) each, with campsites every 19–25 miles (30–40km). For instance, section one (if you're walking north to south) runs from seaside Cooktown to the cattle station at Gunnawarra. Cooktown is an appropriate embarkation point for a trail that marks the birth of a nation. British explorer Captain James Cook paused here on the 1770 voyage that saw him claim Australia for Britain. From the town, the trail delves into the hinterland of Ngalba Bulal National Park, the wildlife-filled rainforests of Daintree, and through creek-riddled Mossman before veering deeper into the arid interior. The walking is likely to be hot, humid, and damp.

Alternatively, if you walk south to north, your first section covers completely different terrain. Starting in genteel Healesville, just northeast of Melbourne, the trail cuts through a more temperate wilderness. There are cooler forests, trout-filled rivers, subalpine meadows, and the steep undulations of the Great Dividing Range. The section also passes historic gold-mining towns, finishing at Omeo, on the edge of the Snowy Mountains. Here, cattle graze on the high pastures, and the preserved old buildings (log-built jail, 1865 courthouse) provide reminders of the area's past riches.

The remotest part of the BNT is the section that cuts through northern New South Wales. It leads from the nineteenth-century timber town of Killarney (just inside Queensland) to Ebor, lodged at 1,300m (4,300ft) in the Northern Tablelands. There are no facilities en route, but this is true droving territory. The trail runs through the rugged river gorges of Guy Fawkes River National Park and follows an official travelling stock route.

The BNT is not a hike for the faint-hearted. It largely avoids towns (there might be two weeks between supply points). You must have maps and a compass, and know how to use them. You must be utterly self-reliant. In short, you must have the spirit of a true pioneer.

**448
Eldfell Ascent**

*Westman Islands,
Iceland*

Hike to the highest point on Iceland's tiny Heimaey Island, 221m (725ft) high Eldfell. This volcanic cone was created in a fiery eruption on 23 January 1973. The ground still feels hot to the touch.

449

SHANGRI-LA

Yunnan, China

In his 1933 novel *Lost Horizon*, English author James Hilton invented the fictional land of Shangri-La, the ultimate Himalayan utopia. He described it as 'a living essence distilled from the magic of the ages and miraculously preserved against time and death'. The remote, high-plateau town of Zhongdian, China, claims to be the inspiration for Hilton's utopian vision, and renamed itself Shangri-La in 2001. Certainly, the trekking possibilities near here are magical. Drive north to the town of Deqin, the last outpost before Tibet. Then head into the pristine Meili Snow Mountains, where towering, icy summits loom over meadows, waterfalls, green valleys, and the idyllic, isolated village of Yubeng – perhaps a better contender for Shangri-La.

450

ANNAPURNA SANCTUARY

Annapurna Range, Nepal

Nepalese people have always walked among the Himalayas. But it was only after British Army colonel James Roberts – known as 'the father of trekking' – set up Mountain Travel Nepal in 1964 that tourists embraced the idea. Roberts explored the Annapurna Range in the 1950s. What he called the 'Sanctuary of the Gods' is now the location of one of the country's best-loved treks. The classic Annapurna Sanctuary route takes ten to twelve days from the town of Phedi, near the lakeside city of Pokhara. It passes charming villages, rice terraces, forests, and hot springs. It gives close-ups of Machapuchare (Fish Tail) Mountain, and the awesome amphitheatre-like Annapurna Sanctuary. And it tops Poon Hill, where the entire range unfolds in perfect panorama.

CONCORDIA AND K2 BASE CAMP

Eastern Pakistan

{ Get intimate with K2, the world's second-highest and – arguably – most dangerous mountain. }

Need to know
- *Point in time: 1954 (K2 first climbed)*
- *Length: 87 miles (140km); 12–14 days*
- *Difficulty: Strenuous – rugged terrain; remote; high altitudes*
- *Best months: June– Sept*
- *Top tip: Concordia trips take twenty-one days total, including transfers from Islamabad to the trailhead near Skardu*

K2, the world's second-highest summit, is known as the 'Savage Mountain'. This peak, on the Pakistan-China border, is a little shorter than Mount Everest. It is 'only' 8,611m (28,251ft) high, compared with Everest's 8,848m (29,029ft). However, it is a far more treacherous and challenging prospect. It was first summited in 1954 by Italians Lino Lacedelli and Achille Compagnoni, then not again until 1977. Far fewer people have stood on top of K2 than Everest. Chillingly, those who attempt to climb K2 have around a one in four chance of dying on its slopes.

Trekkers can get close to K2 but avoid those kind of deadly odds via a spectacular trek to K2 Base Camp. The trek, which takes two weeks round-trip, begins near the town of Skardu. From here the trail crosses the long Baltoro Glacier. This creaks through an avenue of ever more dramatic mountains to reach the sparkling glacial confluence of Concordia, an icy bowl at 4,500m (14,764ft), engulfed by many of the world's highest summits. These include Gasherbrum IV, Mitre Peak, Broad Peak, Chogolisa, Crystal Peak, and K2 itself. In the 1970s, the American photographer Galen Rowell dubbed Concordia the 'Throne Room of the Mountain Gods' – an apt description.

From Concordia, it's a short walk to K2 Base Camp for breath-snatching close-ups and a visit to the Gilkey Memorial, where plaques remember those who have died on the Savage Mountain's slopes.

RIGHT: The two-week trek to K2 Base Camp is a far less treacherous prospect than a climb to K2's summit.

452

KINDER MASS TRESPASS

Peak District, England, United Kingdom

{ Retrace the route of an act of rebellion that opened up the English countryside for future generations. }

Need to know

- *Point in time: 1932 (Kinder Trespass occurred)*
- *Length: 8 miles (13km); 5–6 hours*
- *Difficulty: Moderate – some steep sections; exposed*
- *Best months: Apr–Oct*
- *Top tip: Buses run to Hayfield; there is a car park at Bowden Bridge*

The Kinder Mass Trespass wasn't originally a walk, it was a rambling revolution. In 1932 around 400 walkers from the British Workers' Sport Federation staged a mass act of civil disobedience. This was a working-class fight for the right to roam, in the face of rich landowners denying them access to large swathes of beautiful countryside. Starting from Bowden Bridge near the Derbyshire village of Hayfield, the hikers set off up 636m (2,087ft) Kinder Scout, on the property of the Duke of Devonshire. Despite a tussle with the duke's gamekeepers, the 400 ramblers pressed on and reached the top of the gritstone plateau, which is the highest point in England's Peak District. Here they celebrated with fellow trespassers who'd hiked up the other side.

After this rebellious ramble, five walkers were imprisoned. However, this served to highlight their cause. Indeed, the Kinder Mass Trespass ultimately precipitated the passage of National Parks legislation in 1949, with the Peak District being the first national park to be designated. It also inspired the Countryside and Rights of Way Act 2000, which secures the 'right of public access on foot to areas of open land'.

Retracing the 8-mile (13km) Kinder Mass Trespass route isn't just about completing a lovely walk, it's about asserting your entitlement to do so. A commemorative plaque marks the start. The route then runs up Snake Path at the foot of William Clough ravine. This is where the ramblers and estate workers scuffled. It then travels via the crashing cascade of Kinder Downfall, continuing with far-reaching views to the game-changing summit.

RIGHT: Enjoy the right to roam through the beautiful Peak District, thanks to the Kinder Mass Trespass.

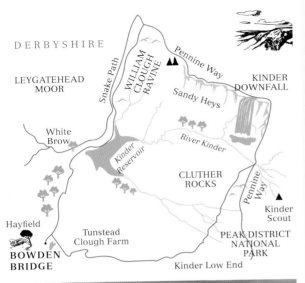

DERBYSHIRE

LEYGATEHEAD
MOOR

Snake Path

WILLIAM
CLOUGH
RAVINE

Pennine Way

KINDER
DOWNFALL

Sandy Heys

White
Brow

Kinder
Reservoir

River Kinder

CLUTHER
ROCKS

Pennine
Way

Kinder
Scout

Hayfield

Tunstead
Clough Farm

BOWDEN
BRIDGE

PEAK DISTRICT
NATIONAL
PARK

Kinder Low End

COAST TO COAST WALK

Northern England, United Kingdom

No one has inspired more people to get out into the British countryside than the fell walker Alfred Wainwright. His much-loved, handwritten, hand-drawn guidebooks to the Lakelands, published between 1952 and 1966, are part practical instruction, part paean. In 1973 Wainwright went on to write *A Coast to Coast Walk*. This describes a 190-mile (305km) hike, from Britain's west coast to its east, from the village of St Bees in Cumbria to Robin Hood's Bay in North Yorkshire. The route has become a true walking classic. It runs through three national parks – the Lake District, Yorkshire Dales, and North York Moors – with each day involving a good hike up and down. The route usually takes about twelve to fourteen days, and it's traditional to dip a foot in the sea at both ends.

454
Heiko's Trail

British Columbia, Canada

This 15-mile (25km) trail along the spine of Canada's Rocky Mountains, near Fernie, is a modern pilgrimage to salute the efforts of volunteer Heiko Socher. He has been restoring the forgotten but magical route since 2000.

455
Balcony Walk

Hajar Mountains, Oman

Make a short hike along a precipitous ridge in the 'Omani Grand Canyon'. The route runs from the hamlet of Khateem to the abandoned village of As Sab. This was evacuated by the modernising government in the early twenty-first century.

456
Shorewalk

New York, United States

Make a full 32-mile (51km) circuit of Manhattan island. Journey around what is arguably the world's most iconic modern metropolis via its green spaces and skyscrapers.

457
Avenida 9 de Julio

Buenos Aires, Argentina

Promenade Buenos Aires's 0.6-mile (1km) thoroughfare, the Avenida 9 de Julio. It was built from the 1930s and is a showy boulevard of Parisian-style edifices, honking traffic, and tree-lined *plazoletas*.

458
MATOBO HILLS

Southern Zimbabwe

British imperialist Cecil Rhodes, whose political maneuverings shaped the fortunes of much of southern Africa, is buried amid Zimbabwe's Matobo Hills. When he died in 1902, the country in which these majestic granite mounds rise was still named Rhodesia, after him. But Rhodes was a latecomer to Matobo. Archaeologists believe that humans have lived here for at least 20,000 years. Stone tools have been found, and many caves conceal ancient rock art. It's also rich in wildlife, such as zebras, cheetahs, leopards, and rhinos. Various hikes are possible. Begin with a walk to World's View, the lofty spot where Rhodes was laid to rest.

MACLEHOSE TRAIL

Hong Kong, China

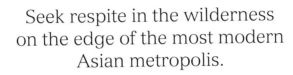

Seek respite in the wilderness on the edge of the most modern Asian metropolis.

Need to know

- *Point in time: 1971–82 (Governor MacLehose in office)*
- *Length: 62 miles (100km); 4–6 days*
- *Difficulty: Easy/ moderate – varied; some steep climbs*
- *Best months: Sept–Feb*
- *Top tip: The trail has ten sections; most trailheads are easily accessible by public transport*

Lord Murray MacLehose was the longest-serving governor of the former British Dependent Territory of Hong Kong. Today, Hong Kong's longest hike is named after him. This seems appropriate. Governor MacLehose (in office from 1971 to 1982) was considered an enlightened, progressive leader. Among many other reforms, he established Hong Kong's network of country parks – areas designated for nature conservation, recreation, and outdoor education. A keen walker, he wanted to ensure that the residents of the burgeoning metropolis (now part of China) could find respite from its relentless roar. He felt it was important that woodlands, meadows, and mountaintops were accessible to everyone.

While high-rise Hong Kong sometimes seems to be an exemplar of the twenty-first-century city, it's actually set amid surprisingly wild terrain. Flanking the skyscrapers and flashing-neon lights are sandy beaches, sweeping bays, vital bird wetlands, rolling hills, rare plants, and mountain peaks rising to over 915m (3,000ft).

The 62-mile (100km) MacLehose Trail is the most comprehensive way to experience this natural richness. Spanning the mainland New Territories area of Hong Kong, the route runs between the town of Tuen Mun in the west and Pak Tam Chung, the easternmost point of the lush Sai Kung Peninsula. The trail is split into ten sections, and most of the trailheads are accessible by public transport. This is another thing for which to thank Murray MacLehose, who initiated the construction of Hong Kong's Mass Transit Railway.

Starting from Pak Tam Chung, the trail skirts a reservoir and curves into Sai Kung Country Park, with views across to Hong Kong's southern islands. It traces the turquoise coast, dipping to beaches aflutter with butterflies, and passing the columnar rhyolite rocks of Long Ke Wan. It then climbs steeply up Sai Wan Shan for fine views over the serrated coast, a squiggle of bays, coves, islets, and headlands. It also passes traditional grave sites, where gold-embossed headstones sit peacefully amid bauhinia trees. From Pak Tam Au, the trail forges into some of Hong Kong's remotest highlands, scattered with the remains of Hakka villages. The Hakka peoples built stone-walled farming terraces here to grow crops such as rice, peanuts, tea, and indigo. Many Hakka have now moved to other areas. The trail then heads into Ma On Shan Country Park, tackling the gully-grooved slopes of 702m (2,303ft) Ma On Shan (Horse Saddle Mountain), via woodland of oak, ash, camellia, and rhododendron.

Next, the trail crosses the Kowloon Peaks, its closest point to the seething urban mass to the south. From Lion Rock, the bustling districts of Kowloon and Hong Kong Island are spread out below. These hills are also dotted with Second World War reminders, including caves excavated by Japanese soldiers and trenches dug by the

British. Dipping down to the Kowloon Reservoir, there are more such relics, such as 'Gin Drinkers Line', part of a string of defences built across the New Territories in the 1930s. There are also rhesus macaques bounding about the trees. From here, the trail crosses Shing Mun Country Park, via Shing Mun Reservoir. Completed in 1936, the reservoir resulted in the relocation of over 700 Hakka people, as eight of their villages were submerged.

After this, the MacLehose climbs Hong Kong's highest mountain, 957m (3,140ft) Tai Mo Shan. As well as affording views that, on a clear day, stretch far into China, the peak is riddled with streams, primordial forest, rare plants, and old tea terraces. At Route Twisk (a steep road) there is a plaque commemorating the opening of the trail by Governor MacLehose on 26 October 1979. The route then bounds into Tai Lam Country Park, with views towards the Pearl River estuary, to finish in the busy city of Tuen Mun.

460
The Peak
Circle Walk

Hong Kong, China

Gaze over the megalopolis of Hong Kong from the 2-mile (3.5km) Peak Circle Walk. It starts along Lugard Road, a narrow cliffside trail built between 1913 and 1914.

BELOW: Explore the varied terrain of Hong Kong's country parks on the MacLehose Trail.

461
PACIFIC CREST TRAIL

Western United States

If you want to 'find yourself' on a walk, this is the walk to choose. The Pacific Crest Trail (PCT) runs from the town of Campo, on the California-Mexico border, to Manning Provincial Park, on the Washington-Canada line. This is a total of 2,650 miles (4,265km), so you will have ample thinking time. This is just what American author Cheryl Strayed did. She headed off on the PCT in 1995. Her book *Wild: From Lost to Found on the Pacific Crest Trail* is about her journey. It became a bestseller and inspired the film *Wild*. Even if you don't 'find yourself', you *will* discover jaw-dropping scenery. This includes the tangled, shrubby chaparral of the Mojave Desert, the glacier-gouged Sierra Nevada, the volcanic peaks of the Cascades, and plenty of wilderness in between.

462
FOOTSTEPS OF AMUNDSEN

South Pole, Antarctica

It requires more than hiking boots and enthusiasm to follow in the ski tracks of Roald Amundsen, leader of the successful 1911 Norwegian expedition to the South Pole. This Antarctic challenge, known as the Footsteps of Amundsen, requires technical mountaineering skills, extremely high levels of strength and fitness, a commitment to pre-trip training, quite a lot of time (it takes thirty-nine days), and rather a lot of money. What an adventure, however. After a ski-plane flight, you climb the mountain-flanked Axel Heiberg Glacier on the Ross Ice Shelf, which Amundsen was the first to discover. Here you access the crevasse-splintered Polar Plateau for the long, cold, exhilarating trudge to the South Pole itself.

463
DYLAN THOMAS BIRTHDAY WALK

Carmarthenshire, South Wales, United Kingdom

Dylan Thomas is the de facto national poet of Wales. However, he's almost as well known for his roisterous drinking as for his verse. He spent his latter days in the Welsh village of Laugharne, on the Taf Estuary. In 1944 he penned 'Poem in October' about a 2-mile (3km) walk taken here on his thirtieth birthday. To follow the route, start at the Boathouse, where Thomas lived (now a museum). Walk past Laugharne's ruined medieval castle and then follow a mossy path up around the estuary, originally built to give cocklers access to the sea. Finish on the shoulder of Sir John's Hill. En route, benches etched with Thomas's words provide places for poetic contemplation.

464
Corfu Trail

Corfu, Greece

Channel the spirit of Gerald Durrell, English naturalist and author of the 1956 classic *My Family and Other Animals*, set in Corfu. This 137-mile (220km) hike visits Corfu's rugged, olive-dotted interior.

465
Picasso Hiking Trail

Catalonia, Spain

Follow in the footsteps of Pablo Picasso – in 1906 he journeyed for 37 miles (59km) from the village of Guardiola to the town of Bellver de Cerdanya. He paused to paint at the village of Gósol, now home to a Picasso museum.

466
Aberdare National Park

Kenya

Many trails lead through the wildlife-rich forest and uplands of Kenya's Aberdare National Park. Treetops Lodge is a good trekking base. Princess Elizabeth was here in 1952, when she received news that her father (King George VI) had died, making her the Queen of the United Kingdom.

467
Titanic Trail

Southampton, England, United Kingdom

The Titanic Trail is a 1-mile (1.6km) stroll through the city of Southampton. Its name refers to the RMS *Titanic,* the doomed liner that left the English port on 10 April 1912. Of the 1,517 people who perished when the ship sank, 549 were from Southampton.

KARISOKE TREK

Volcanoes National Park, Rwanda

{ Hack through Rwanda's misty, tangled jungle to the camp where Dian Fossey carried out pioneering research into Africa's endangered gorillas. }

Need to know
- *Point in time: 1985 (Dian Fossey killed)*
- *Length: 3 miles (5km); 3–4 hours*
- *Difficulty: Moderate – steep; muddy; short*
- *Best months: May–Oct*
- *Top tip: Permits are required for gorilla-tracking hikes*

The locals called the American zoologist Dian Fossey 'Nyiramachabelli'. In Kinyarwanda (the official language of Rwanda), this word translates as 'the old woman who lives alone in the forest without a man'. However, Dian Fossey wasn't really living alone in the tangled jungle of Volcanoes National Park. She had plenty of company. She was living among the mountain gorillas.

Born in San Francisco in 1932, Fossey studied to be a vet, although she ended up switching to occupational therapy. Her love of animals, coupled with a desire to see more of the world, inspired a trip to Africa in 1963. There, she met archaeologist Louis Leakey, who told her of the need for long-term field research into Africa's great apes. She also met zoologist George Schaller, who had carried out a pioneering study of mountain gorillas.

Armed with funding from Leakey – and truckloads of determination – Fossey returned to Africa in 1966. First she set up a research camp in the Congo (then Zaire), but the political situation forced her to leave. Next she went to Rwanda. On 24 September 1967, after weeks of searching Volcanoes National Park for the perfect spot, Fossey established the Karisoke Research Center. It was named after Mount Karisimbi, which loomed over her camp to the south, and Mount Visoke, which reared up to the north. From the Karisoke Research Center, Fossey could see every extinct volcano in the Virunga chain.

ABOVE: Visit Rwanda's Volcanoes National Park to track gorilla groups, as studied by Dian Fossey.

Fossey's 'research centre' was actually two tents, which functioned as bedroom, kitchen, study, bathroom, and everything else. She lived on tinned food and potatoes, and her only human contact was with the few local men hired to help. However, they didn't speak English and she didn't speak Kinyarwanda. It rained relentlessly, turning the forest floor to sludge, and the slopes to death traps. Disease and poachers were ever-present threats. It was a tough existence, but one she loved. In her book *Gorillas in the Mist* (subsequently made into a film), Fossey wrote: 'The sense of exhilaration I felt when viewing the heartland of the Virungas for the first time from those distant heights is as vivid now as though it had occurred only a short time ago. I have made my home among the mountain gorillas'.

Fossey was killed at the Karisoke Research Center in 1985, and buried right next to her favorite gorilla, Digit (he was killed by poachers in 1977). Little remains of her physical

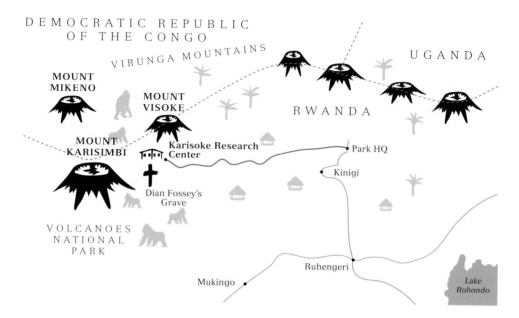

DEMOCRATIC REPUBLIC
OF THE CONGO

VIRUNGA MOUNTAINS

UGANDA

MOUNT
MIKENO

MOUNT
VISOKE

RWANDA

MOUNT
KARISIMBI

Karisoke Research
Center

Park HQ

Dian Fossey's
Grave

Kinigi

VOLCANOES
NATIONAL
PARK

Ruhengeri

Mukingo

Lake
Ruhondo

camp. There are a few stone pillars on which the tents once
sat, the framework of a hut, and an old stove. The area was
abandoned during the horrific Rwandan genocide of the
1990s. However, Fossey's work lives on. She brought the
plight of these endangered primates to the world's attention,
and a fund in her name continues to protect the animals and
their habitats.

Many ecotourists now visit Volcanoes National Park to
track habituated gorilla groups. This might involve a short,
easy hike or a daylong jungle-slashing expedition, depending
on where the animals are. It can be a tough, grimy, sweaty
haul. But all hardship is soon forgotten when you find the
gorillas and have the privilege of observing their strangely
human behaviour, just as Fossey once did.

It's also possible to hike up to Karisoke. It takes about three
hours to climb from Volcanoes National Park headquarters
to the camp, which sits at over 3,000m (9,000ft). The trail,
steep at first and often sucky with mud, leads through stands
of Hagenia–Hypericum forest, meadows pocked with giant
lobelia, and huge stinging nettles. At the camp itself,
bushbuck graze the grasses, and trees drip with mosses and
lichen. You will also find Fossey's grave, with its eternal views
of her beloved misty mountains.

469
Castro's Footsteps

Sierra Maestra, Cuba

Castro's Footsteps is a 2.5-mile (4km) hike from the Alto del Naranjo lookout point into the Sierra Maestra mountain range. It leads to Comandancia de la Plata, where Fidel Castro was based between 1958 and 1959, until the Cuban Revolution was won.

470
Haunted Woods Trail

Prince Edward Island, Canada

Walk through the childhood haunts of Canadian author Lucy Montgomery, which inspired her 1908 book *Anne of Green Gables* . The 0.6-mile (1km) loop passes near Cavendish Cemetery, where Montgomery is buried.

471
Auyán-tepui

Canaima, Venezuela

Trickling down the side of the 2,450m (8,038ft) tabletop mountain Auyán-tepui is Angel Falls, the world's highest waterfall. It was first spotted by American aviator Jimmie Angel in 1933. Summit expeditions take eight days.

472
Fallingwater

Pennsylvania, United States

Frank Lloyd Wright, one of the greatest architects of all time, designed Fallingwater (or the Kaufman Residence) in 1935 as a house at one with its setting. It is built over a waterfall. Trails lead through the grounds.

473
THESIGER'S ARABIAN SANDS

Empty Quarter, Oman

Bedouin nomads have walked across the seemingly endless sands of the Arabian Peninsula's Rub' al Khali (Empty Quarter) for thousands of years. Between 1945 and 1950, British explorer Wilfred Thesiger did the same, enlisting local Arabs to help him traverse the dune-rippled emptiness. His 1959 book *Arabian Sands* recounts his journeys and records the vanishing Bedouin way of life. Trekking in this vast wilderness remains a huge challenge. So do as Thesiger did, and hire a guide. Travel from the city of Salalah, in southern Oman, to the ruins of Shisr (purported to be the legendary 'Lost City' of Ubar). Then head into the desert for a few days, hiking up curvaceous dunes and camping out under the stars.

RUTA DEL CHE

Central Bolivia

{ Relive the final days of Ernesto 'Che' Guevara, one of the world's most recognisable revolutionaries. }

Need to know
- *Point in time: 1967 (Che Guevara executed)*
- *Length: 93 miles (150km); 7 days*
- *Difficulty: Moderate/ strenuous – varied terrain; not waymarked*
- *Best months: May–Oct*
- *Top tip: Buses run from the regional hub of Santa Cruz to Samaipata*

The picture of intense-eyed, beret-toting Ernesto 'Che' Guevara captured by Cuban photographer Alberto Korda in 1960 is one of the world's most recognisable and iconic images. It has become global shorthand for a sense of anti-establishmentarianism. Guevara was born to an upper-class Argentine family in 1928. He was later radicalised by his motorcycle travels among the poor of South America, and played a vital role in the Cuban Revolution. He was a potent revolutionary force during his lifetime but arguably became a more potent symbol after his death.

Guevara was executed in Bolivia in 1967. He had chosen Bolivia – centrally located in South America – as a base from which he hoped to ignite a continent-wide revolt. It didn't work. The 93-mile (150km) Ruta del Che (Che Trail) links some of the sites key to his last rebellious acts. It runs from Samaipata, a town with Inca ruins on the edge of lushly forested Amboró National Park, to the scruffy village of La Higuera, where Guevara was shot in the schoolhouse. In between lie the town of Vallegrande, where Guevara's body was put on display (before being buried in a secret spot), and Quebrada del Churo, the canyon near La Higuera where Guevara fought his last battle.

This is rough, rugged terrain – one reason why it was favoured by Guevara and his *guerrilleros* – and most hikers don't walk the whole route. Instead, four-wheel-drive tours facilitate hiking access to shorter sections, giving an insight into this twentieth-century icon's final days.

AMBORÓ
NATIONAL PARK

Cochambamba

Santa Cruz

SAMAIPATA

Aiquilo

Vallegrande

Rio Grande

LA
HIGUERA

Sucre

Vado del Yeso

Potosi

Lagunillas

BOLIVIA   Muyupampa

Camiri

475
Mary Schäffer Loop

Alberta, Canada

This 2-mile (3km) trail on the shores of Maligne Lake was known only to the Nakoda people until 1908. Pioneering adventuress Mary Schäffer, the first non–First Nations person to see Maligne, walked here in 1908.

476
JFK Assassination Trail

Dallas, United States

Relive the last tragic moments of President John F. Kennedy on a one-hour stroll through Dallas. Kennedy was assassinated in the Dealey Plaza district of Dallas on 22 November 1963.

LEFT: The Ruta del Che links sites key to Che Guevara's last rebellious acts.

EVEREST BASE CAMP

Eastern Nepal

{ Trek to the base camp of Mount Everest, the world's highest mountain, in the boot-prints of its first successful summiteers. }

Need to know
- *Point in time: 1953 (Everest first climbed)*
- *Length: 80 miles (130km); 12–14 days*
- *Difficulty: Moderate/ strenuous – high altitudes*
- *Best months: Oct–Dec; Mar–Apr*
- *Top tip: Simple teahouse accommodation is available along the route*

The Nepalese call Mount Everest 'Sagarmatha', meaning 'Head of the Sky'. The Tibetans call it 'Chomolungma', meaning 'Goddess Mother of the Mountains'. In 1852, when the Great Trigonometrical Survey of India properly measured what had till then been prosaically known as 'Peak XV', it was recognised as the highest mountain in the world.

Such a designation had people itching to climb this 8,848m (29,029ft) Himalayan titan. In 1924 English mountaineers George Mallory and Andrew Irvine got close. They were last seen alive on 8 June, ascending a step around 400m (1,300ft) below the summit. It took another twenty-nine years before Everest was successfully conquered. On 29 May 1953, New Zealander Edmund Hillary and Nepali Sherpa Tenzing Norgay became the first people to stand on its summit.

Unsurprisingly, climbing Everest isn't easy. It's not the most technical climb – it's just so very high. Altitudes above 7,000m (23,000ft) are classed as the 'death zone'. This is where oxygen levels are too low to sustain human life for long, and the body starts to die. Climbing Everest is also expensive. Today, it can cost more than $50,000 a trip.

A more accessible and affordable way to experience Everest is to trek to Everest Base Camp instead. The classic out-and-back route from Lukla takes around fourteen days, and covers about 80 miles (130km). It follows the Dudh Kosi River to the bustling village of Namche Bazaar before heading along the Khumbu Valley to reach the base camp. This sits at 5,340m (17,520ft). The route is the same

RIGHT: The 5,340m (17,520ft) high Everest Base Camp is as far as most people go.

taken to the mountain's foot by Hillary, Norgay, and many
subsequent summiteers. Indeed, set off in April or May
(climbing season) and the trail will be busy with hopeful
expedition parties on their way to the top.

The first challenge facing Everest Base Camp trekkers is
the forty-minute flight from Kathmandu into the 2,800m
(9,383ft) high town of Lukla. The short, steep airstrip here
(built by Hillary's Himalayan Trust in 1964) is considered the
most dangerous airport in the world. It's also the gateway
to a realm of fluttering prayer flags, welcoming teahouses,
and Himalayan adventure.

From Lukla, the trail heads north, passing under a *kani*
(archway with prayer wheels) before going downhill along
the river to the small village of Phakding. It then runs via

pine forest, vertiginous suspension bridges, and steep switchbacks to 3,440m (11,286ft) Namche Bazaar. Tucked between ridges amid the Khumbu Valley's colossal peaks, Namche Bazaar is the main hub of the Sherpa people, and a centuries-old trading settlement. Now, alongside traditional corn and yak wool, stalls also sell Gore-Tex boots and down jackets. On a clear day, Mount Everest might be glimpsed from here.

From Namche Bazaar, the trail heads northeast to Thyangboche, set on a ridge above pine and rhododendron forest. Sunsets here, over a panorama of peaks, are spectacular. John Hunt, leader of the 1953 British Mount Everest expedition, was suitably impressed: 'My senses were intoxicated by the fantastic surroundings,' he wrote. 'Thyangboche must be one of the most beautiful places in the world.'

Busy with burdened yaks, the trail delves deeper into the Khumbu region, the landscapes becoming increasingly raw as it hits the village of Pangboche, crosses the Imja River, and reaches Dingboche. At this village, 8,516m (27,940ft) Mount Lhotse dominates. Everest itself remains elusive despite its proximity, hiding behind other snow-capped giants as the trail passes the terminal moraine of the Khumbu Glacier and then Chukpo Lari, where there are memorials to climbers who have died on the mountain.

The trek proceeds to Gorak Shep, a frozen lakebed covered with sand. Finally, it reaches Everest Base Camp. This is where the 1953 expedition made its final preparations. It is also where many others have spent sleepless nights since, contemplating their own attempts. And you still don't get a good view of the mountain from here – although the Khumbu Icefall, the first obstacle for would-be summiteers, looms large indeed. The best views require a two-hour slog from Base Camp up 5,545m (18,192ft) Kala Pattar. Here – finally – Everest is revealed in all its terrifying glory.

478
Hollywood Walk of Fame

Los Angeles, United States

Walk on top of the stars laid out in the Hollywood Walk of Fame. They honour various show-business legends, from Frank Sinatra to Mickey Mouse; the first star was laid in 1960. The full route is 1.3 miles (2.1km) long.

479
Desolation Peak Trail

Washington, United States

This is a 7-mile (11km) climb in the North Cascades, where American author Jack Kerouac stayed in the summer of 1956, writing in his book *Lonesome Traveler* (1960): 'I needed solitude . . . I just wanted to lie in the grass and look at the clouds.'

HILLARY TRAIL

North Island, New Zealand

> Walk in the pristine coastal wilderness so loved by Sir Edmund Hillary, one of the first men to conquer Everest.

Need to know
- *Point in time: 1919–2008 (life of Sir Edmund Hillary)*
- *Length: 44 miles (70km); 4 days*
- *Difficulty: Moderate – rough terrain; potentially slippery; undulating*
- *Best months: Oct–Mar*
- *Top tip: Arataki Visitor Centre is 15 miles (25km) southwest of central Auckland*

The Waitakere Ranges, not far from downtown Auckland, don't look a lot like the Nepalese Himalayas. However, the two disparate places are bound together by the same man – the mountaineer and explorer Sir Edmund Hillary. He was born in Auckland in 1919, and spent many happy days exploring the wilderness of native bush, black-sand beaches, waterfalls, and wave-smacked headlands to the city's west. In 1953, along with Sherpa Tenzing Norgay, he became the first to summit Mount Everest. After this, the Waitakere Ranges became his place of escape when he wanted a break from the fame of conquering the world's highest mountain.

The 44-mile (70km) Hillary Trail, which opened in 2010 on the second anniversary of Hillary's death, is described as: 'a challenging wilderness adventure designed to introduce families and young people to the joys of multiday tramping'. Encouraging future generations to climb seems a fitting legacy for New Zealand's best-known mountaineer.

The trail starts at Arataki Visitor Centre, runs through the Waitakere Ranges, and continues along the coast to Muriwai Beach. It takes in giant dunes and ancient kauri trees. It passes the six-drop cascade of Kitetkite Falls, the pounding surf and ebony sand at Piha Beach, and the boisterous clifftop gannet colony by Muriwai Beach. It negotiates the Te Henga Walkway, a steep, wild section that traces the precipice between two beaches. Plus, it skips amid the boulders and pristine forest around Anawhata Stream – said to be Hillary's favourite stretch.

RIGHT: Follow the Hillary Trail around the Waitakere Ranges on North Island.

MURIWAI BEACH

Auckland →

N E W
Z E A L A N D

Te Henga Walkway

NORTH ISLAND

Anawhata Stream

Piha Beach

Kitetkite Falls

ARATAKI
VISITOR
CENTRE

WAITAKERE RANGES

TASMAN SEA

481
Royal Trek

Annapurna, Nepal

This three-day hike from Nepal's
lakeside city of Pokhara travels
through the glorious, village-dotted
Annapurna foothills. It was named
after Prince Charles, who walked this
way in the 1980s.

482
Shaoshan

Hunan Province, China

Climb the mountain overlooking
Shaoshan village, birthplace of Mao
Zedong. He went on to found the
People's Republic of China in 1949.
Mao's poetry has been inscribed at
the peak's base.

483
Philosopher's Path

Kyoto, Japan

Stroll the 1.2-mile (2km) canal-side Philosopher's Path in spring, when it is lined with cherry trees in blossom. The philosopher in question is Nishida Kitaro (1870–1945), who used the route to commute to Kyoto University.

484
Laurie Lee Wildlife Way

Gloucestershire, England, United Kingdom

Take the 6-mile (9km) Laurie Lee Way through the Slad Valley. The green, rolling Cotswold countryside inspired the English writer's 1959 classic, *Cider with Rosie*.

485
Tioman Traverse

Malaysia

Make the 4-mile (7km) crossing of the jungly, paradisiacal island of Tioman. It is claimed that Tioman's beaches were depicted as Bali Hai in the 1958 movie *South Pacific*.

486
Tolkien Trail

Lancashire, England, United Kingdom

English author J.R.R. Tolkien wrote much of the *Lord of the Rings* trilogy while staying in Lancashire. This trail is an inspiring 6-mile (9.5km) loop through the county, from the village of Hurst Green.

487
ROYAL HERITAGE TREK

Central Bhutan

The 28-mile (45km) Royal Heritage Trek traces the route first followed by Jigme Wangchuck, second king of Bhutan (1926–52). It was the journey he made from his summer residence, Wangdicholing Palace in Bumthang, to his new winter residence of Kuenga Rabten in Trongsa (built in 1928). It took him and his elaborate entourage three days. Today's hikers take about the same time, but with less fanfare. The route stops at a picnic spot used by the royals, climbs passes over 4,000m (13,125ft), visits traditional palaces, and goes via decorated *lhakhangs* (temples). It is great for spotting birds and wildflowers, and affords views of the Indian lowlands, the Black Mountains, and the Himalayas.

488
JUBILEE WALKWAY

London, England, United Kingdom

{ Amble through the United Kingdom's historic capital, exploring its Roman roots and its regal hangouts. }

Need to know
- *Point in time: 1977 (Queen Elizabeth II's Silver Jubilee)*
- *Length: 15 miles (24km); 1 day*
- *Difficulty: Easy – simple to follow; flat*
- *Best months: Apr–Oct*
- *Top tip: The route is well marked – discs featuring the cross of a crown indicate the route direction; gold discs mark sites of historic events*

Londinium was established by the Romans in the first century AD. Subsequently it flourished, withered, and resurged. It was attacked by Vikings and Normans, and has suffered the Black Death, the Great Fire, Nazi bombs, and terrorist attacks. All of these have helped mould it into the global powerhouse it is today. In short, London is an urban onion, every street multilayered with history.

Queen Elizabeth II didn't preside over all these events, but she's seen more than her fair share. Born in 1926, she ascended to the throne in 1953 and, in September 2015, became the United Kingdom's longest-reigning monarch (breaking Queen Victoria's record of sixty-three years, seven months, and two days). However, it was in the 1970s, on the occasion of Elizabeth II's Silver Jubilee, that the 15-mile (24km) Jubilee Walkway was opened. Its aim was to celebrate Elizabeth's twenty-five years on the throne by creating a central London walk taking in the key sights of her illustrious capital. The queen herself opened the route on 9 June 1977.

The Jubilee Walkway is a continuous loop. A good starting point is bustling Trafalgar Square, dominated by 52m (170ft) Nelson's Column. From the square, the route leads beneath Admiralty Arch and onto the Mall. This is part of the ceremonial route taken by the Queen's state coach to Westminster Abbey for her coronation. Also here is Horse Guards Parade, where the Trooping the Colour is performed every June to mark the Queen's official birthday. The Mall leads to Buckingham Palace, the official London residence of the British monarchy

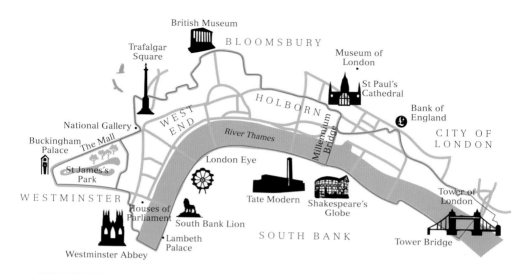

British Museum

BLOOMSBURY

Trafalgar Square

Museum of London

St Paul's Cathedral

National Gallery

WEST END

HOLBORN

Bank of England

CITY OF LONDON

The Mall

River Thames

Millennium Bridge

Buckingham Palace

St James's Park

London Eye

Tower of London

WESTMINSTER

Tate Modern

Shakespeare's Globe

Houses of Parliament

South Bank Lion

Tower Bridge

Lambeth Palace

SOUTH BANK

Westminster Abbey

since 1837. In front of the palace, the Changing of the Guard, a colourful ceremony of pomp and pageantry, occurs most days at 11:30 a.m.

Continuing around St James's Park, the walkway passes Westminster Abbey and the Houses of Parliament. Parliament's oldest part is medieval timber-roofed Westminster Hall, built in 1097. This is where deceased British monarchs lie in state, on public view, before they are buried.

The route next crosses the river Thames, visiting Lambeth Palace, official London base of the archbishop of Canterbury since the thirteenth century. It follows the Thames Path northeastward, via the South Bank Lion (where the Queen opened the walkway in 1977). It also passes the London Eye wheel (an integral part of the skyline since 2000), and a range of arts spaces including the South Bank Centre, Royal Festival Hall, Tate Modern, and Shakespeare's Globe theatre.

The trail crosses back to the north side of the river over the twin-turreted span of Tower Bridge, completed in 1894. This leads to the Tower of London, which has a history of imprisoning criminals (and royals) and safekeeping royal jewels that stretches back 1,000 years. From here the walkway turns west, past the monument to the 1666 Great Fire, and into the City of London. This is the site of the original Roman Londinium, once enclosed within protective walls and now home to the capital's financial district. Roman remains and the Bank of England sit here. Wiggling via the Museum of London, the walk next passes the 111m (365ft) dome of St Paul's Cathedral. Rebuilt after the Great Fire, St Paul's was London's tallest building from 1710 to 1962.

A loop north explores Bloomsbury and Holborn. This is where the influential Bloomsbury Group, which included authors such as Virginia Woolf and E.M. Forster, hung out in the early twentieth century. The British Museum, one of the greatest repositories of world artifacts, is also here. Finally, the route heads into the West End theatre district via the street performers of Covent Garden to finish at the National Gallery back in Trafalgar Square. The whole route is a stroll through 2,000 years of history.

489
Canol Heritage Trail

Northwest Territories, Canada

This 218-mile (350km) tundra-traversing wilderness trail from the town of Norman Wells is one of Canada's most challenging. It follows the Canol Pipeline, completed in 1944, constructed to transport oil during the Second World War.

490
Black Cat Trail

Papua New Guinea

The tough 31-mile (50km) trail from the town of Salamaua to the Black Cat Gold Mine was used by miners from the 1920s. Military relics en route nod to its later use by Australian soldiers during the Second World War.

LEFT: Take a riverside stroll along London's South Bank on the Jubilee Walkway.

PEAKS OF THE BALKANS TRAIL

Albania, Montenegro, and Kosovo

{ Hike through the relatively untouched mountains of the Balkans on a route that has only just opened to trekkers. }

Need to know
- Point in time: 1941–85 (rule of Enver Hoxha)
- Length: 119 miles (192km); 10–13 days
- Difficulty: Moderate – remote; mountainous; varied
- Best months: June–Oct
- Top tip: The trail is waymarked, but hiking in a group or with a guide is recommended

This trail was not possible until the end of the twentieth century. Enver Hoxha, socialist leader of Albania from 1941 until his death in 1985, kept his country isolated from the world for more than forty years. 'Let everyone understand clearly,' he wrote in one of his memoirs, 'the walls of our fortress are of unshakable granite.' Albania was virtually off-limits. Also, in the 1990s, vicious wars raged in the Balkans, resulting in the disintegration of Yugoslavia. Montenegro and Kosovo declared independence in 2006 and 2008, respectively.

Today, a tri-country hike in this once-troubled region is not only feasible but positively tantalising, not least because no one from the outside has been allowed in until recently. The countryside remains culturally rich and wonderfully undeveloped.

The 119-mile (192km) Peaks of the Balkans Trail is a circuit, using shepherd paths to loop via high peaks (up to 7,545ft / 2,300m), verdant valleys, rivers, waterfalls, and traditional villages. Here, *kulas* (old stone houses) provide authentic accommodation, and local people provide delicious home-made bread and cheese.

You can start the trail in Albania, Montenegro, or Kosovo. In Albania, begin in the town of Theth, nestled in the Accursed Mountains. In Montenegro, start in the Ottoman-era town of Plav, which sits by a lake at the foot of the Prokletije range. In Kosovo, access the trail from the tiny city of Pejë, near the Rugova Canyon.

RIGHT: Explore Albania, Montenegro, and Kosovo on the exciting Peaks of the Balkans Trail.

BARIO LOOP

Borneo, Malaysia

Until the early twentieth century, the indigenous people of Borneo's remote Kelabit Highlands in eastern Sarawak (near Indonesian Kalimantan) remained isolated from the outside world. The Kelabit Highlands became more accessible during the Second World War. This was when an airstrip was built by British and Australian forces in the Kelabit Highlands' capital of Bario. Previously, the soldiers (who set up camp here when fighting the Japanese) had to make an inhospitable two-week walk from the nearest large town of Marudi. Today you can take a plane to the start of the 19-mile (31km) Bario Loop. The route passes primary rainforest, cool river valleys, paddy fields, buffalo pastures, and the remains of a British Army outpost. You can stay overnight in friendly Kelabit longhouses en route.

493
POLISH-CZECH FRIENDSHIP TRAIL

Poland and Czech Republic

When the 18.5-mile (30km) Polish-Czech Friendship Trail opened in 1961, it wasn't overly friendly. Border checks were still carried out as hikers traversed the Karkonosze Mountains, hopping between Poland and what was then Czechoslovakia. The trail closed entirely from 1981 to 1984, when the communist government of Poland introduced martial law. However, the two nations joined the Schengen Area in 2007, which did away with border formalities. The walk from the 1,362m (4,469ft) peak of Szrenica to the Okraj Pass is now hassle-free, passing pine forest, sculptural rock formations, glacial cirques, mountain-tucked lakes, and old border posts that are now huts for hikers.

494
MOUNT TRIGLAV

Northwest Slovenia

Mount Triglav is Slovenia's highest summit and its foremost symbol of national identity. During the Second World War, as the Julian Alps around it became a battlefield, Triglav became a rallying beacon for Slovenes flighting the Nazis. Resistance forces even donned three-peaked 'Triglav caps'. When Slovenia became independent from Yugoslavia in 1991, it was only natural that the 2,864m (9,396ft) mountain should feature on the new flag. A classic climb takes one or two days. There are several routes. They all require different amounts of work on *via ferrata* (clipping onto fixed metal lines). They all provide views over a sea of rippling peaks.

495
Nordkalottleden Trail

Norway, Sweden, and Finland

This wilderness epic covers 500 miles (800km) and hops across Nordic borders multiple times. En route it passes the Treriksröset, where the three nations meet. This boundary was first marked in 1901.

496

SCHENGEN WITHOUT BORDERS TRAIL

Luxembourg, France, and Germany

Although this trail measures only a little over 5 miles (8.5km), it encompasses three countries: Luxembourg, France, and Germany. This seems entirely appropriate, as it begins and ends in the town of Schengen. This is where, in 1985, the 'Schengen Agreement' was first conceived. This is a European accord that allows free movement of people between participating countries. The walk starts near the European Museum in Schengen, on the banks of the Moselle River, and runs south through the Stromberg Nature Reserve into France. It climbs up from the village of Contz-les-Bains for sweeping views over the verdant river valley, where Germany beckons, freely accessible, on the other side.

497

NATCHAUG TRAIL AND CCC LOOP

Connecticut, United States

The 1930s were tough for the United States. The stock market crash of 1929 saw the country plummet into the Great Depression, which lasted a decade. At the Great Depression's nadir, 15 million Americans were unemployed. In an attempt to provide work and raise morale, the Civilian Conservation Corps (CCC) was formed, giving unemployed men jobs on nature projects. One such project was the CCC Loop Trail, a 3-mile (5km) hike among the deer-nibbled trees and streams of Connecticut's Natchaug State Forest. The loop also forms part of the 19.5-mile (31km) Natchaug Trail, which runs through the Natchaug State Forest and the James Goodwin Forest, and is one of the state's Blue-Blazed Hiking Trails. Many of these trails were built by CCC hands.

EL CAMINITO DEL REY

Málaga Province, Southern Spain

{ Brave the precipitous ledges of the 'world's most dangerous walk' – now a little safer, thanks to a modern makeover. }

Need to know

- *Point in time: 1905 (El Caminito del Rey first opened)*
- *Length: 5 miles (8km); 3–4 hours*
- *Difficulty: Moderate – vertiginous; tickets required*
- *Best months: Mar–June; Sept–Nov*
- *Top tip: The Caminito is open year-round but is closed on Mondays*

BELOW: Dare your way along El Caminito del Rey's precipitous ledges.

Welcome to the 'world's most dangerous walk' – or what *was* known as the world's most dangerous walk until the Spanish authorities spent around £1.8 million renovating it in 2015. The route, which clings to the sheer limestone walls of the Desfiladero de los Gaitanes gorge between the village of El Chorro and the Guadalhorce Reservoir, was originally completed in 1905 so that engineers could gain access to the newly built hydroelectric plant. It was named the Balconcillos de los Gaitanes on account of the narrow, precipitous ledges on its upper section. In 1921 Spain's King Alfonso XIII paid a visit, which is when the route gained its new moniker: El Caminito del Rey, meaning 'King's Little Pathway'.

However, El Caminito del Rey fell into disuse. Sections tumbled down into the turquoise river, leaving just rusting metal spurs protruding from the dizzying rock walls, some 100m (325ft) up. A few brave people still attempted the trail. Several fell to their deaths.

Thankfully, the recent makeover has made this 5-mile (8km) linear walk much safer. Forest-lined footpaths lead to the main 1.85-mile (3km) white-knuckle section. Here the gorge takes on a cathedralic scale and majesty. Boardwalks, glass floors, safety lines, and steel bolts have been punctured into the vertical cliff face, and hikers must wear helmets. However, through the new wooden slats you can see the remains of the old path crumbling away below.

500
MAMANG TRAIL

Fitzgerald River National Park, Western Australia

When rabbits were released in Australia in the 1850s, no one guessed how destructive these speedy breeders would be. It got so bad that, from 1901, three rabbit-proof fences were built to protect the pastures of Western Australia. In total, these wire divides measured 2,023 miles (3,256km). Fence No. 2 ended at Point Ann, on Western Australia's spectacular south coast. This is now the starting point for the 19-mile (31km) Mamang Trail, which runs northeast to Fitzgerald Inlet. The trail takes in Point Ann's fence history and whale lookouts (southern right whales are known to swim by, between June and October). It then runs via wooded hills, white-sand beaches, valley forest, and native royal hakea shrub, which thankfully the rabbits didn't destroy.

There are several routes up three-peaked Mount Triglav in Slovenia's Julian Alps. All provide spectacular views over a sea of rippling mountaintops. A classic summer climb using *via ferrata* takes one or two days (p. 388).

INDEX

ACKNOWLEDGEMENTS

Sarah would like to thank Paul Bloomfield for his endless support, patience, and coffee-making; her dearly departed Grandma B and Grandad S for instilling a love of travel and nature respectively; Sonya Patel Ellis for her excellent editing, encouragement, and all-around hard work; Tania Gomes for somehow managing to fit so many walks into such a small space; Lynn Hatzius and Paula Lewis for bringing the idea to life – there's nothing as inspiring as a good map; Caroline Elliker for her continued support; and Darci and Gizmo for their therapeutic cuddles.